Lecture Notes in Computer Science   11484

Commenced Publication in 1973
Founding and Former Series Editors:
Gerhard Goos, Juris Hartmanis, and Jan van Leeuwen

More information about this series at http://www.springer.com/series/7407

Rodrigo Miani · Lasaro Camargos ·
Bruno Zarpelão · Erika Rosas ·
Rafael Pasquini (Eds.)

Green, Pervasive, and Cloud Computing

14th International Conference, GPC 2019
Uberlândia, Brazil, May 26–28, 2019
Proceedings

Springer

Editors
Rodrigo Miani 🆔
Federal University of Uberlândia
Uberlândia, Brazil

Lasaro Camargos 🆔
Federal University of Uberlândia
Uberlândia, Brazil

Bruno Zarpelão 🆔
State University of Londrina
Londrina, Brazil

Erika Rosas 🆔
Federico Santa María Technical University
San Joaquin, Chile

Rafael Pasquini 🆔
Federal University of Uberlândia
Uberlândia, Brazil

ISSN 0302-9743   ISSN 1611-3349 (electronic)
Lecture Notes in Computer Science
ISBN 978-3-030-19222-8   ISBN 978-3-030-19223-5 (eBook)
https://doi.org/10.1007/978-3-030-19223-5

LNCS Sublibrary: SL1 – Theoretical Computer Science and General Issues

This Springer imprint is published by the registered company Springer Nature Switzerland AG
The registered company address is: Gewerbestrasse 11, 6330 Cham, Switzerland

Preface

On behalf of the Organizing Committee, we are pleased to present the proceedings of the International Conference on Green, Pervasive and Cloud Computing (GPC 2019), held in Uberlândia, Brazil, during May 26–28.

The goal of the International Conference on Green, Pervasive and Cloud Computing is to establish a high-standard world forum for researchers and practitioners alike to share their novel ideas and experiences in the areas of green computing and communications, pervasive computing, and cloud computing. Previous editions were organized all over the world: Taichung, Taiwan (2006), Paris, France (2007), Kunming, China (2008), Geneva, Switzerland (2009), Hualien, Taiwan (2010), Oulu, Finland (2011), Hong Kong (2012), Seoul, Korea (2013), Wuhan, China (2014), Plantation Island, Fiji (2015), Xian, China (2016), Cetara, Amalfi Coast, Italy (2017), and Hangzhou, China (2018).

The GPC 2019 edition was marked by high-quality paper submissions and a rigorous review process implemented by a Technical Program Committee of 43 members, plus four additional reviewers. Each of the 38 submissions received at least three reviews and 17 of them were selected for presentation at the conference, yielding an acceptance rate of 44%. The conference also featured invited talks by leading personalities in industry.

GPC 2019 was successful thanks to the help and support of many people. First and foremost, the authors who submitted and presented their contributions. Second, the Program Committee members and reviewers who dedicated their time to the advancement of knowledge. Third, all the chairs and members of the Steering Committee, for without their hard work and guidance, the conference simply would not have happened. Last, but not least, the attendees, who besides attending the talks, also briefly experienced life in the heart of Brazil.

We hope you enjoy the conference proceedings.

May 2019

Rodrigo Miani
Lasaro Camargos
Bruno Zarpelão
Erika Rosas
Rafael Pasquini

Organization

Honorary Chair

Pedro Frosi Rosa   Federal University of Uberlândia, Brazil

General Chairs

Rafael Pasquini   Federal University of Uberlândia, Brazil
Erika Rosas   University Santa Maria, Chile

Program Committee Chairs

Lásaro Camargos   Federal University of Uberlândia, Brazil
Rodrigo Sanches Miani   Federal University of Uberlândia, Brazil

International Advisory Committee

Sandra L. Céspedes   University of Chile, Chile
Soudeh Ghorbani   Johns Hopkins University, USA
Luciana Arantes   Inria, France
Fatma Omara   Cairo University, Egypt

Local Organization Chairs

Flávio de Oliveira Silva   Federal University of Uberlândia, Brazil
João H. S. Pereira   Federal University of Uberlândia, Brazil

Publications Chairs

Lásaro Camargos   Federal University of Uberlândia, Brazil
Rodrigo Sanches Miani   Federal University of Uberlândia, Brazil
Bruno B. Zarpelão   State University of Londrina, Brazil

Steering Committee

Hai Jin   Huazhong University of Science and Technology,
           China
Nabil Abdennadher   University of Applied Sciences, West Switzerland
Christophe Cerin   University of Paris XIII, France
Sajal K. Das   Missouri University of Science and Technology, USA
Jean-Luc Gaudiot   University of California - Irvine, USA
Kuan-Ching Li   Providence University, Taiwan, China

Cho-Li Wang	The University of Hong Kong, SAR China
Chao-Tung Yang	Tunghai University, Taiwan, China
Laurence T. Yang	St. Francis Xavier University, Canada

Program Committee

Daniele Manini	Università di Torino, Italy
Sylvio Barbon	State University of Londrina, Brazil
Bruno B. Zarpelão	State University of Londrina, Brazil
Javier Rubio Loyola	CINVESTAV, Mexico
Flavio Silva	Universidade Federal de Uberlândia, Brazil
Xiapu Luo	The Hong Kong Polytechnic University, SAR China
Ah Lian Kor	Leeds Beckett University, UK
Sophia Petridou	Aristotle University of Thessaloniki, Greece
Florin Pop	University Politehnica of Bucharest, Romania
Andrea F. Abate	University of Salerno, Italy
Alfredo Navarra	Università degli Studi di Perugia, Italy
Silvio Barra	University of Salerno, Italy
Gustavo B. Figueiredo	Federal University of Bahia, Brazil
Billy Pinheiro	Federal University of Pará, Brazil
Xiaowen Chu	Hong Kong Baptist University, SAR China
Roopak Sinha	Auckland University of Technology, New Zealand
Andrea De Salve	University of Pisa, Italy
Hermes Senger	Federal University of São Carlos, Brazil
Javier Baliosian	Universidad de la República
David Moura	State University of Campinas, Brazil
Alexandre Amaral	Federal Institute of Santa Catarina, Brazil
Jean-Philippe Georges	University of Lorraine, France
Dan Grigoras	University College Cork, Ireland
Paulo Ditarso Maciel Jr.	Federal Institute of Paraíba, Brazil
Jorge G. Barbosa	University of Porto, Portugal
Kuo-Chan Huang	National Taichung University of Education, Taiwan
Yanmin Zhu	Shanghai Jiao Tong University, China
Raphaël Couturier	University of Bourgogne Franche-Comté, France
Changyu Dong	Newcastle University, UK
Alessio Merlo	University of Genoa, Italy
Ling Chen	Zhejiang University, China
Mario Donato Marino	Leeds Beckett University/University of Sao Paulo, UK/Brazil
Xiaofeng Chen	Xidian University, China
Carlos Kamienski	Federal University of ABC, Brazil
Tommi Mikkonen	University of Helsinki, Finland
Marco A. Amaral H.	State University of Campinas, Brazil
Alex Vieira	Universidade Federal de Juiz de Fora, Brazil
Erisa Karafili	Imperial College London, UK

Zeyar Aung   Khalifa University of Science and Technology, United
                             Arab Emirates
Marek Ogiela   AGH University of Science and Technology, Poland
Fu-Hau Hsu   National Central University, Taiwan
Maycon Leone   Federal University of Bahia, Brazil

Additional Reviewers

Marco Favorito
Lauren Stacey Ferro
Pedro Damaso
Ana Costa

Contents

Cloud and Related Technologies

Machine Learning

Evaluating the Four-Way Performance Trade-Off for Stream Classification

Victor G. Turrisi da Costa[✉], Everton Jose Santana, Jessica F. Lopes, and Sylvio Barbon Jr.

Computer Science Department, Londrina State University, Londrina, Brazil
{victorturrisi,evertonsantana,jessicafernandes,barbon}@uel.br

Abstract. Machine Learning (ML) solutions need to deal efficiently with a huge amount of data available, addressing scalability concerns without sacrificing predictive performance. Moreover, this data comes in the form of a continuous and evolving stream imposing new constraints, e.g., limited memory and energy resources. In the same way, energy-aware ML algorithms are gaining relevance due to the power constraints of hardware platforms in several real-life applications, as the Internet of Things (IoT). Many algorithms have been proposed to cope with the mutable nature of data streams, with the Very Fast Decision Tree (VFDT) being one of the most widely used. An adaptation of the VFDT, called Strict VFDT (SVFDT), can significantly reduce memory usage without putting aside the predictive performance and time efficiency. However, the analysis of energy consumption regarding data stream processing of the VFDT and SVFDT is overlooked. In this work, we compare the four-way relationship between predictive performance, memory costs, time efficiency and energy consumption, tuning the hyperparameters of the algorithms to optimise the resources devoted to it. Experiments over 23 benchmark datasets revealed that the SVFDT-I is the most energy-friendly algorithm and greatly reduced memory consumption, being statistically superior to the VFDT.

Keywords: Machine Learning · Data stream mining · Energy efficiency

1 Introduction

Across the years, different tasks from multiple domains have been tackled with Machine Learning (ML), e.g., performing anomaly detection for network security, filtering spam, weather forecasting, medical diagnosis, image classification, and driving autonomous vehicles. Recently, a growing demand for ML-based solutions capable of dealing very large volumes of data emerged. This type of data usually comes in the form of a continuous and evolving stream, imposing a series of constraints. Memory is finite and it is impossible to store all data available. Likewise, ML solutions need to be continuously updated since data streams have a mutable nature. This can lead to the occurrence of concept drifts (CD) which

© Springer Nature Switzerland AG 2019
R. Miani et al. (Eds.): GPC 2019, LNCS 11484, pp. 3–17, 2019.
https://doi.org/10.1007/978-3-030-19223-5_1

are characterised as the change of data distribution over time [19,32]. Solutions need to address memory and time limitations, be incremental and handle changes in the data stream [10,13,19].

Many ML algorithms have been proposed for data stream classification [4, 7,13,25,29]. Among them, the Very Fast Decision Tree (VFDT) [7] is one of the most used. It induces a decision tree in an online fashion using a statistical property called the Hoeffding Bound (HB). Although vastly experimented in multiple datasets [4,7,13,19,25,29,30], to the best of our knowledge, the energy consumption of this algorithm has only been evaluated in Garcia-Martin et al. [11]. Since scalability is a challenging issue for traditional ML, these costs should also not be overlooked.

It is known that software optimisation to decrease energy consumption is part of green computing [17]. The Information and Communications Technology has been pointed out as responsible for significant power demand, which generates carbon and other pollutant emissions during its production [11,31]. Besides, the Internet of Things (IoT) applications and mobile devices, two common domains for data stream mining, usually rely on batteries. This increases the relevance of algorithms with low power consumption because using them reduce the need of substituting, recharging or disposing of those batteries [2,27]. Also, the greater the energy consumption, the greater the heat produced, which affects the durability and reliability of hardware components [2] and demands higher expenses with cooling systems [15]. In this sense, when evaluating the usability of an algorithm in the real world, the importance of energy costs should be considered concomitantly to predictive performance, memory or time costs.

A modification of the VFDT, called Strict VFDT (SVFDT) [29], was proposed to control tree growth while maintaining predictive performance and processing time. Although this was achieved, energy consumption was not explored, and depending on the application, low energy consumption is preferable to the detriment of high accuracy. Here, we empirically evaluated the four most important aspects (predictive performance, memory costs, time costs, and energy consumption) of the SVFDTs and compared them with the VFDT. We chose to compare only these techniques since the VFDT is widely used and the SVFDTs reduced time costs [29], which are directly linked to energy consumption. Hyperparameters were varied to analyse their relationship with the four performance metrics.

We summarise the main contributions of this work as follows:

1. Investigated the energy consumption of the VFDT and SVFDTs in order to reduce energy footprint.
2. Analysed the four-way relationship of predictive performance, memory costs, time costs and energy consumption while varying multiple hyperparameters.
3. Evaluated and statistically compared the three algorithms in multiple benchmark datasets.

The remainder of this work is organised as follows: Sect. 2 details the VFDT algorithm. The SVFDT algorithm is described in Sect. 3. Section 4 presents an overview of energy consumption and details the PowerAPI. In Sect. 5 we present the experimental setup. Results and Discussions are contained in Sect. 6. Section 7 presents conclusions and future work.

2 Very Fast Decision Tree

The VFDT [7] is a tree-based ML algorithm for data streams based on the Hoeffding Bound (HB) theorem. Consider a continuous variable v, whose values are bounded by the interval $[v_{min}, v_{max}]$, with a range of values $R = v_{max} - v_{min}$, that is independently observed n times and, according to these observations, has a mean of $\bar{v}$. Then, the HB theorem states that the mean of this variable when $n \to \infty$ is $\bar{v}_{n \to \infty}$ is bounded by the interval $[\bar{v} - \epsilon, \bar{v} + \epsilon]$ with statistical probability $1 - \delta$, where

$$\epsilon = \sqrt{\frac{R^2 \, ln(\frac{1}{\delta})}{2\,n}}. \tag{1}$$

When growing a tree, the VFDT employs the HB to perform splits. After evaluating the candidate features at a split attempt with a heuristic measure $G(.)$ (e.g., Information Gain (IG) or Gini Index (GI)), VFDT uses the HB theorem to check whether the best split candidate would remain the best if the tree received additional instances. This is done by computing ϵ and checking if $G(best) - G(second\_best) = \Delta G < \epsilon$, where $G(best)$ and $G(second\_best)$ are the $G(.)$ values of the best split candidate feature and second best candidate.

VFDT keeps and updates the instances class distribution in a vector at each leaf to count the number of instances from each class. Likewise, counting procedures and numerical estimators are also employed to maintain the relationship between the feature values and class distributions. By doing so, VFDT can induce a model from a single instance at a time using limited computational memory resources. Additionally, under realistic assumptions, it has the same asymptotic performance as the induction of a decision tree by a standard batch algorithm [10].

Lastly, the VFDT has a hyperparameter τ to allow growth when features have similar $G(.)$ values; uses an Adaptive Naive Bayes (ANB) [9] at leaves to increase predictive performance; and uses a GP hyperparameter that defines the amount of instances needed by each leaf between split attempts.

Now, we present a more detailed discussion about the hyperparameters and their effects:

1. GP: the amount of instances between each split attempt. A high value will result in fewer split attempts and a smaller tree. On the other hand, a low GP allows for a faster adaptation, resulting in a larger tree.
2. τ: allows splits when a high amount of instances were observed regardless of whether the HB was satisfied or not. When increasing it, fewer instances will be needed to ignore the HB. An extremely high value coupled with a low GP results in an overfitted and low-performance tree. Contrarily, very low τ values may retain tree growth, resulting in a small and low-performance tree.

3. δ: used to compute the HB. Considering higher values, ϵ will be smaller, which has a similar effect as increasing τ, whereas a small δ results in a larger ϵ and produces the same effect as decreasing τ.

Although the GP and τ hyperparameters influence in predictive performance, memory and time costs have already been evaluated [7,11,16,29,30,33], energy consumption have, to the best of our knowledge, only been considered in [11]. Additionally, the work only explored four different datasets. A more in-depth analysis of the relationship of the hyperparameters and usage of these resources is needed.

3   Strict Very Fast Decision Tree

The Strict Very Fast Decision Tree algorithm is a modification of the VFDT proposed by Turrisi da Costa et al. [29] which creates smaller decision trees than the VFDT with very similar predictive performance. Two versions were proposed, the SVFDT-I and SVFDT-II, both using the following assumptions:

1. A leaf node should only split when there is a minimum uncertainty of class assumption (e.g. high entropy (H)) associated with the instances, according to previous and current statistics.
2. A similar amount of instances should be observed across all leaf nodes.
3. The feature used for splitting should significantly decrease uncertainty (e.g. a high IG) according to previous statistics.

The SVFDT-II employs additional skipping mechanisms to speed-up growth when class uncertainty is too high or this uncertainty is largely reduced.

In a more concrete way, the SVFDT applies additional rules to block tree growth using the following φ function:

$$\varphi(x, X) = \begin{cases} \text{True,} & \text{if } x \geq \overline{X} - \sigma(X) \\ \text{False,} & \text{otherwise} \end{cases} \tag{2}$$

where X is a set of observed values, $\overline{X}$ is their mean, $\sigma(X)$ is their standard deviation, and x is a new observation.

First, consider that each time a leaf satisfy the conditions imposed by the VFDT the statistics computed at that moment are marked with a *satisfiedVFDT*. The SVFDT splits a leaf l when it satisfies all the conditions imposed by the VFDT and the following:

1. $\varphi(Imp_l, \{Imp_{l_0}, Imp_{l_1}, ..., Imp_{l_L}\})$,
2. $\varphi(Imp_l, \{Imp_{satisfiedVFDT_0}, Imp_{satisfiedVFDT_1}, ..., Imp_{satisfiedVFDT_S}\})$,
3. $\varphi(G_l, \{G_{satisfiedVFDT_0}, G_{satisfiedVFDT_1}, ..., G_{satisfiedVFDT_S}\})$,
4. $n_l \geq \overline{\{n_{satisfiedVFDT_0}, n_{satisfiedVFDT_1}, ..., n_{satisfiedVFDT_S}\}}$,

where Imp is the impurity measure used (e.g. entropy), G is the $G(.)$ value of the candidate feature, L is the total number of leaves at that moment and S is the total number of split attempts that satisfied the VFDT conditions and n is the number of elements seen at a given leaf.

The SVFDT-II uses additional ϖ functions to skip the φ functions in some specific cases. The ϖ function is described as:

$$\varpi(x, X) = \begin{cases} \text{True,} & \text{if } x \geq \overline{X} + \sigma(X) \\ \text{False,} & \text{otherwise} \end{cases} \tag{3}$$

At a split attempt, if:

1. $\varpi(Imp_l, \{Imp_{satisfiedVFDT_0}, ..., Imp_{satisfiedVFDT_S}\})$ or
2. $\varpi(G_l, \{G_{satisfiedVFDT_0}, ..., G_{satisfiedVFDT_S}\})$

hold true, then all the other φ constraints are ignored.

The SVFDT, as evaluated in [29,30], reduces memory consumption without compromising predictive performance and achieves some time speedups. Although the computations added by the SVFDT may be insignificant when considering the mentioned performance metrics, energy consumption can be affected, positively or negatively.

4 Energy Consumption and the PowerAPI

In computing systems, energy - the capacity of producing work - is delivered as electricity [15]. To address the task of measuring this physical quantity, some consumption monitors were developed without the need for additional hardware components [22,26].

In this work, we adopted the PowerAPI, an application programming interface (API) that monitors the power usage of running processes based on information collected from hardware devices of the operating system [22]. When compared with a powermeter, the Power API margin of error is between 0.5% to 3% [23], motivating its choice in this work.

Based on the computational costs (P_{comp}) calculated by this software approach, it is possible to compute the total energy consumption (E) of a process by:

$$E[J] = \sum_{i=1}^{N} P_{comp,i}[W] \times d[s], \tag{4}$$

where N represents the number of samples and d, the period of the sampling intervals.

Physically, energy-efficiency is the ratio between the work done and the total energy spent to accomplish this work, but as expressed in [24], it is a generic term and can be understood as the ratio between the useful output of a process and the energy input into a process. In this sense, when comparing the energy-efficiency of two or more algorithms, the most efficient is the one that uses the least energy to produce the same amount of useful output.

5 Experimental Setup

In order to compare the VFDT and the SVFDTs energetic efficiency, predictive performance and memory and time costs, we used 23 benchmark datasets. Table 1 summarises the main aspects of each dataset.

Table 1. Summary of the datasets used in the experiment.

Dataset	# Instances	# Features			# Classes	% Majority class
		Numeric	Binary	Categorical		
agrawal [1]	1,000,000	6	0	3	2	0.672
airlines [5]	539,383	3	0	4	2	0.555
covType [5,13]	581,012	10	44	0	7	0.488
ctu_1 [12]	2,824,636	9	0	2	2	0.985
ctu_2 [12]	1,808,122					0.988
ctu_3 [12]	4,710,638					0.994
ctu_4 [12]	1,121,076					0.997
ctu_5 [12]	129,832					0.993
ctu_6 [12]	558,919					0.991
ctu_7 [12]	114,077					0.999
ctu_8 [12]	2,954,230					0.998
ctu_9 [12]	2,753,884					0.911
ctu_10 [12]	1,309,791					0.919
ctu_11 [12]	107,251					0.924
ctu_12 [12]	325,471					0.993
ctu_13 [12]	1,925,149					0.979
elec [5]	45,312	6	0	1	2	0.575
hyper [5]	250,000	10	0	0	2	0.500
led [5]	1,000,000	0	24	0	10	0.100
poker [5]	829,200	5	0	5	10	0.501
rbf_1kk [13,14]	1,000,000	10	0	0	2	0.536
sea [28]	60,000	3	0	0	2	0.627
usenet [18]	5930	0	658	0	2	0.504

For each dataset, the prequential learning method [10] was performed ten times to compute the mean energy consumption, accuracy, Kappa M [3], processing time and memory consumption (in MB) of the VFDT, SVFDT-I and SVFDT-II. Kappa M [3] measures how a classifier performs in comparison with a majority class predictor. We also compared the relative performance metrics of energy consumption, accuracy, memory and training time. This is calculated by dividing the value obtained by one of the SVFDTs for the value obtained by the VFDT. When considering accuracy, values greater than 1 represent that one of the SVFDTs outperformed the VFDT, whereas values smaller than 1 represent the opposite. For the other measures, values smaller than 1 mean that the SVFDTs reduced the consumption of a given resource.

The statistical significance of the results was evaluated with the Friedman statistical test [8] ($\alpha = 0.05$). If the null hypothesis is rejected, the Nemenyi post-hoc [21] test can be applied [6]. In the diagram representation, algorithms which are connected by a critical distance (CD) are not significantly different (at α).

The base learners settings are presented in Table 2. Additionally, we used H and IG as impurity and gain metrics.

Table 2. Hyperparameters for the base learners used in the experiment.

GP	τ	δ	Numeric estimator	Leaf predictor
(100, 200, 400, 800, 1000)	(0.01, 0.05, 0.10, 0.15, 0.20)	10^{-5}	Gaussian - 100 bins	ANB

The algorithms were implemented in Python and Cython and the code is publicly available at[1]. The experiments were performed on Intel® Xeon Gold 6128 Processor 3.40 GHz with thermal design power (TDP) 115 W on Intel® AI DevCloud[2] in default configuration. The PowerAPI was configured to capture the mean power of the intervals, using the *procfs* module [20] with a sampling period of 1 ms.

6 Results and Discussions

6.1 General Results

Figure 1 shows the boxplots for energy usage, accuracy, memory consumption and time of the three algorithms. They were constructed using the mean metrics computed across all datasets with all possible hyperparameters setup.

First, considering energy usage, it is possible that the SVFDT-I presented a lower median value than the VFDT. The SVFDT-II presented a slightly higher median value than the VFDT with also a lower normal bound. When considering accuracy, the SVFDT-I obtained a lower median value than the VFDT. Nonetheless, this difference is less than 0.01. The three algorithms do not present high variation. In memory consumption, the VFDT varies between from around 1 MB to almost 25 MB in size, with a median value of approximated 6 MB. Both SVFDTs greatly reduce this, with median values of 2 MB and 4 MB for the SVFDT-I and SVFDT-II. Additionally, the whole SVFDT-I box and its outliers are less than the median value of the VFDT. Lastly, although the SVFDT-II has higher values than the SVFDT-I, its box is limited by a maximum of 10 MB. Finally, when considering training time, a similar pattern as in energy usage appears. The SVFDT-I presents a lower median value than the VFDT, whereas the SVFDT-II has a higher value. Nonetheless, both SVFDTs have lower bounds than the VFDT.

---

[1] https://github.com/vturrisi/pystream.
[2] https://software.intel.com/ai-academy/tools/devcloud.

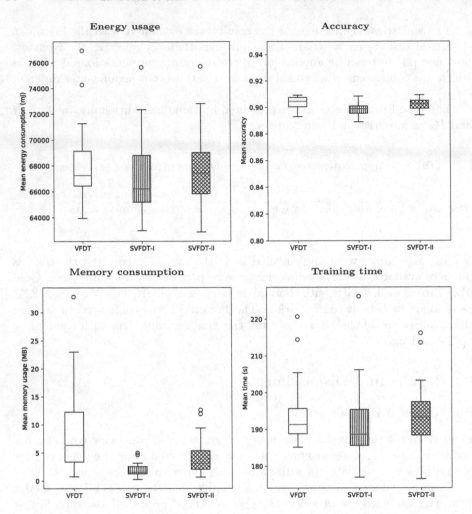

Fig. 1. Boxplots of energy usage, accuracy, memory consumption and time of the VFDT, SVFDT-I and SVFDT-II.

6.2 Statistical Comparison of the Algorithms

We also employed the Friedman statistical test [8] to compare the performance of the three algorithms employing the same values as in the previous subsection. Then, we used the Nemenyi post-hoc test [21] with confidence 0.05 to create the critical distance (CD) diagrams in Fig. 2(a), (b), (c) and (d), for energy, time, memory and accuracy respectively.

Considering energy costs (Fig. 2(a)), the SVFDT-I and SVFDT-II had the best performances, with no statistical difference at $\alpha = 0.05$ between them. For accuracy (Fig. 2(b)), the three classifiers were statistically different, with the VFDT being the best, followed by the SVFDT-II and SVFDT-I. Although there exists statistical difference, the real difference in accuracy is minimal. Regarding memory (Fig. 2(c)), all the algorithms also were significantly different. SVFDT-I was the most conservative, followed by SVFDT-II. It is important to highlight that the differences in rank are very noticeable. Focusing on time (Fig. 2(d)), SVFDT-I was the first in the rank while the SVFDT-II and VFDT were tied in rank and were statistically equivalent. Although the VFDT outperformed the SVFDTs when considering accuracy, Table 3 and Fig. 1 shows, the differences in accuracy were minimal. Moreover, for energy, memory and time, SVFDT-I and SVFDT-II presented better results than VFDT.

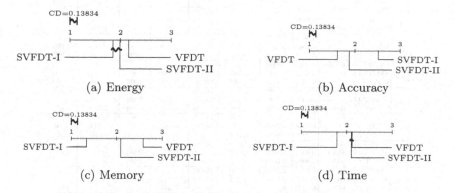

(a) Energy

(b) Accuracy

(c) Memory

(d) Time

Fig. 2. Critical distance diagram for Nemenyi test.

6.3 Exploring the Impacts of the Hyperparameters

Table 3 shows the mean values for energy consumption, accuracy, Kappa M, memory size and training time for each combination of algorithm and hyperparameter.

First, it is possible to observe an inverse correlation between τ and energy consumption. As τ grows, energy consumption is reduced because larger τ values result in more splits, which makes the tree perform less split attempts. To better understand why this happens, consider the following situation. Considering the $GP = 100$ with a stream of 1000 instances, if no splits are made, there would be ten split attempts. On the other hand, if, at 100 instances, a split is made, the remaining 900 instances will fall into different leaves. This can result, for example, in 590 instances falling into one leaf, and the remaining 310 into the other. In this case, five split attempts would have been made in the first leaf, and three on the second. While ten split attempts were performed in the first scenario, nine were performed in the second. With many more instances, larger trees will likely result in fewer split attempts in general, decreasing computations. The same inverse correlation can be perceived between the GP and energy consumption. In this way, as the GP gets larger, less split attempts are made, resulting in fewer computations. The SVFDT-I reduced energy consumption in 20 out of the 25 scenarios, while the SVFDT-II reduced in 17 scenarios.

Table 3. Mean values for energy consumption, accuracy, memory size and training time for each combination of algorithm and hyperparameter. The bold values correspond to the five best results in the corresponding column.

τ	GP	Algorithm	Energy (J)	ACC	Kappa M	Mem. (MB)	Time (s)	RP Energy	RP ACC	RP Memory	RP Time
0.01	100	VFDT	76.96	0.8962	0.6027	1.265	220.70	-	-	-	-
		SVFDT-I	75.65	0.8908	0.4536	**0.529**	226.16	0.983	0.994	0.418	1.025
		SVFDT-II	75.72	0.8960	0.6008	1.119	216.20	0.984	1.000	0.885	0.980
	200	VFDT	74.27	0.8949	0.5875	1.068	214.47	-	-	-	-
		SVFDT-I	72.34	0.8891	0.4492	**0.464**	206.20	0.974	0.994	0.434	0.961
		SVFDT-II	72.82	0.8944	0.5826	0.959	213.60	0.980	1.000	0.898	0.996
	400	VFDT	71.26	0.8944	0.5900	0.870	205.46	-	-	-	-
		SVFDT-I	70.06	0.8897	0.4476	**0.376**	201.22	0.983	0.995	0.433	0.979
		SVFDT-II	71.22	0.8945	0.5798	0.822	203.04	0.999	1.000	0.945	0.988
	800	VFDT	69.13	0.8930	0.5742	0.747	193.78	-	-	-	-
		SVFDT-I	66.06	0.8889	0.4214	**0.388**	189.35	0.956	0.995	0.519	0.977
		SVFDT-II	69.27	0.8941	0.5686	0.681	194.11	1.002	1.001	0.911	1.002
	1000	VFDT	70.90	0.8949	0.5729	0.755	194.63	-	-	-	-
		SVFDT-I	69.59	0.8892	0.4321	**0.287**	192.14	0.982	0.994	0.381	0.987
		SVFDT-II	69.29	0.8949	0.5676	0.675	193.40	0.977	1.000	0.895	0.994
0.05	100	VFDT	71.23	0.9012	0.6547	4.101	200.35	-	-	-	-
		SVFDT-I	71.11	0.8963	0.5273	2.061	202.09	0.998	0.995	0.503	1.009
		SVFDT-II	69.00	0.9004	0.6429	3.282	203.31	0.969	0.999	0.800	1.015
	200	VFDT	69.26	0.9014	0.6484	3.978	193.24	-	-	-	-
		SVFDT-I	68.79	0.8954	0.5216	1.599	193.25	0.993	0.993	0.402	1.000
		SVFDT-II	68.19	0.8991	0.6328	2.889	193.26	0.984	0.997	0.726	1.000
	400	VFDT	67.61	0.9005	0.6363	3.626	189.30	-	-	-	-
		SVFDT-I	65.96	0.8955	0.5185	1.477	187.38	0.976	0.994	0.407	0.990
		SVFDT-II	68.97	0.8991	0.6209	2.606	197.48	1.020	0.999	0.719	1.043
	800	VFDT	66.72	0.8991	0.6246	3.400	186.37	-	-	-	-
		SVFDT-I	65.39	0.8946	0.4862	1.271	185.60	0.980	0.995	0.374	0.996
		SVFDT-II	64.96	0.8990	0.6198	2.063	188.49	0.974	1.000	0.607	1.011
	1000	VFDT	66.45	0.9015	0.6237	3.234	188.80	-	-	-	-
		SVFDT-I	65.76	0.8967	0.4973	0.922	189.06	0.990	0.995	0.285	1.001
		SVFDT-II	65.16	0.8995	0.6173	1.846	190.10	0.980	0.998	0.571	1.007
0.1	100	VFDT	68.99	0.9045	0.6969	12.501	194.37	-	-	-	-
		SVFDT-I	69.93	0.8995	0.5007	2.925	194.60	1.014	0.994	0.234	1.001
		SVFDT-II	66.74	0.9033	0.6893	7.767	194.43	0.967	0.999	0.621	1.000
	200	VFDT	67.77	0.9037	0.6789	11.880	197.02	-	-	-	-
		SVFDT-I	67.06	0.8989	0.5310	2.563	195.45	0.990	0.995	0.216	0.992
		SVFDT-II	67.54	0.9028	0.6638	5.911	196.25	0.997	0.999	0.498	0.996
	400	VFDT	66.81	0.9044	0.6720	9.632	188.91	-	-	-	-
		SVFDT-I	65.83	0.8988	0.5282	1.661	185.73	0.985	0.994	0.172	0.983
		SVFDT-II	66.89	0.9031	0.6503	4.562	187.48	1.001	0.999	0.474	0.992
	800	VFDT	**63.95**	0.9049	0.6576	6.355	185.15	-	-	-	-
		SVFDT-I	64.99	0.8986	0.5073	1.326	**182.96**	1.016	0.993	0.209	0.988
		SVFDT-II	**63.02**	0.9022	0.6398	3.127	**176.54**	0.985	0.997	0.492	0.953
	1000	VFDT	65.85	0.9064	0.6494	5.473	186.54	-	-	-	-
		SVFDT-I	64.51	0.9000	0.5160	1.290	184.67	0.980	0.993	0.236	0.990
		SVFDT-II	65.81	0.9031	0.6220	2.419	187.28	0.999	0.996	0.442	1.004
0.15	100	VFDT	68.48	**0.9092**	0.7051	23.020	195.70	-	-	-	-
		SVFDT-I	68.58	0.9058	0.5496	4.651	197.59	1.001	0.996	0.202	1.010
		SVFDT-II	68.39	**0.9093**	0.6925	11.952	201.41	0.999	1.000	0.519	1.029
	200	VFDT	67.26	**0.9091**	0.7153	18.943	188.95	-	-	-	-
		SVFDT-I	66.20	0.9056	0.4892	2.740	183.45	0.984	0.996	0.145	0.971
		SVFDT-II	67.21	**0.9090**	0.7011	8.839	188.86	0.999	1.000	0.467	1.000
	400	VFDT	**64.44**	0.9074	0.6852	12.294	192.72	-	-	-	-
		SVFDT-I	64.91	0.9009	0.5110	2.456	186.81	1.007	0.993	0.200	0.969
		SVFDT-II	66.12	0.9054	0.6630	4.929	191.40	1.026	0.998	0.401	0.993
	800	VFDT	66.38	0.9073	0.6623	7.133	186.55	-	-	-	-
		SVFDT-I	65.19	0.8991	0.5083	1.412	**183.39**	0.982	0.991	0.198	0.983
		SVFDT-II	64.89	0.9035	0.6422	3.384	183.59	0.977	0.996	0.474	0.984
	1000	VFDT	65.92	0.9059	0.6482	6.199	188.92	-	-	-	-
		SVFDT-I	66.58	0.8985	0.5129	1.544	188.62	1.010	0.992	0.249	0.998
		SVFDT-II	**62.88**	0.9026	0.6210	2.676	185.54	0.954	0.996	0.432	0.982
0.2	100	VFDT	68.13	0.9075	0.7198	32.796	197.14	-	-	-	-
		SVFDT-I	67.72	**0.9083**	0.5557	4.984	195.36	0.994	1.001	0.152	0.991
		SVFDT-II	70.10	0.9070	0.6969	12.634	201.39	1.029	0.999	0.385	1.022
	200	VFDT	66.81	0.9082	0.7152	22.214	189.97	-	-	-	-
		SVFDT-I	65.09	0.9053	0.4876	3.164	**183.15**	0.974	0.997	0.142	0.964
		SVFDT-II	67.50	0.9081	0.7000	9.425	193.40	1.010	1.000	0.424	1.018
	400	VFDT	66.09	0.9078	0.6859	13.361	191.35	-	-	-	-
		SVFDT-I	64.44	0.9013	0.5118	2.815	185.63	0.975	0.993	0.211	0.970
		SVFDT-II	67.41	0.9051	0.6622	5.364	192.82	1.020	0.997	0.401	1.008
	800	VFDT	66.78	0.9079	0.6633	8.071	186.28	-	-	-	-
		SVFDT-I	**62.99**	0.9015	0.5131	1.768	**176.97**	0.943	0.993	0.219	0.950
		SVFDT-II	65.83	0.9053	0.6458	3.694	183.72	0.986	0.997	0.458	0.986
	1000	VFDT	66.67	0.9075	0.6513	7.072	188.39	-	-	-	-
		SVFDT-I	66.29	0.8994	0.5147	1.556	187.14	0.994	0.991	0.220	0.993
		SVFDT-II	67.08	0.9023	0.6203	2.813	188.37	1.006	0.994	0.398	1.000

Accuracy has a direct correlation with τ and an inverse correlation with the GP. This is due to the fact that increasing τ or decreasing the GP result in smaller decision trees. Likewise, decreasing τ or increasing the GP result in larger trees. The SVFDT-I decreased relative accuracy by 1% in the worst case ($\tau = 0.15$ and $GP = 800$) and increased it by 0.09% in the best case ($\tau = 0.20$ and $GP = 100$). The SVFDT-II presented a decrease of 0.5% in relative accuracy for the worst case ($\tau = 0.15$ and $GP = 800$) and an increase of 0.12% for the best case ($\tau = 0.01$ and $GP = 800$). Lastly, Kappa M is directly linked to accuracy and guide to whether or not an algorithm is performing better than a majority class predictor.

Memory is also linked to τ and GP. In the worst case ($\tau = 0.01$ and $GP = 800$) the SVFDT-I reduced memory consumption by 48.1% and the SVFDT-II reduced by 8.9%. However, in the best case ($\tau = 0.20$ and $GP = 200$ for the SVFDT-I and $\tau = 0.20$ and $GP = 100$ for the SVFDT-II) memory consumption decreased by 84.8% for the SVFDT-I and 61.4% for the SVFDT-II. Both SVFDTs can reduce memory consumption across different scenarios without significant predictive performance impacts. The SVFDT-I is a better choice since it trades only 1% of relative accuracy for 48.1% less memory usage considering the individual worst cases for both metrics.

We can observe that training time decreases when τ or GP increases. This is due to the fact that less $G(.)$ computations occur, which are one of the most costly processes employed by the VFDT (and the SVFDTs consequently). For the SVFDT-I, it only trained 2.4% slower in the worst case ($\tau = 0.01$ and $GP = 100$) and 5% faster in the best case ($\tau = 0.20$ and $GP = 800$). The SVFDT-II present similar results, training 2.9% slower in the worst case ($\tau = 0.15$ and $GP = 100$) and 4.7% faster in the best case ($\tau = 0.10$ and $GP = 800$).

For energy and time, the top five values were distributed for τ with values 0.1, 0.15 and 0.2. Considering energy, the VFDT had two out of the five best values, while the SVFDT-I also had two and the SVFDT-II one. For time, VFDT-I had four of the five smallest values and SVFDT-II one. For accuracy, VFDT and SVFDT-II presented two of the highest values, whereas SVFDT-I obtained one, all concentrated in the smallest GPs 100 and 200 and τ 0.15 and 0.20. From the 20 best values (denoted in bold), 11 were obtained by SVFDT- I, 5 by SVFDT-II and 4 by VFDT. None of these values was obtained for $\tau = 0.05$, and for $\tau = 0.01$, the five smallest memory values occurred for SVFDT-I.

Figure 3 presents heatmaps for energy consumption, accuracy, memory usage and time costs for each algorithm while varying the GP value in the x-axis and the τ value in the y-axis. For energy, memory and time, each value is computed by dividing the smallest value obtained by all algorithms by the value obtained for a given algorithm and GP and τ settings. This makes smaller values better. For accuracy, we divided the accuracy of each algorithm by the highest accuracy obtained, making the values a percentage of the best accuracy obtained.

First, consider considering energy efficiency, for the VFDT, although there is no simple relation, such as, the higher the GP and τ the more energy efficient the algorithm, it is possible to see that increasing both hyperparameters to a certain

Scaled energy efficiency according to GP and τ

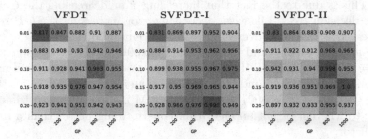

Scaled accuracy performance according to GP and τ

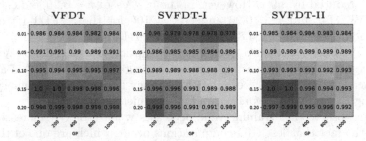

Scaled memory efficiency according to GP and τ

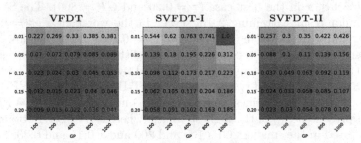

Scaled time efficiency according to GP and τ

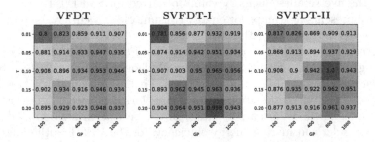

Fig. 3. Heatmaps of each algorithm for each possible GP and τ configuration. Rows correspond to different metrics. Red colours represent better performance (lower energy, memory and time consumption or higher accuracy), while blue colours the opposite. (Color figure online)

extend yield better energy efficiency, which was maximised for $GP = 400$ and $\tau = 0.15$ and $GP = 800$ and $\tau = 0.10$. Similarly, for both SVFDTs, a similar relation seems to occur. For the SVFDT-I, energy efficiency was maximised for $GP = 800$ and $\tau = 0.20$, but, unlike the VFDT, an energy efficient hyperparameter area seems to be more spread. Lastly, the SVFDT-II for $GP = 1000$ and $\tau = 0.15$ and $GP = 800$ and $\tau = 0.10$ were the less energy consuming configuration across all algorithms.

Considering accuracy, there is a clear pattern of higher predictive performance around $\tau = 0.15$ and $\tau = 0.20$ since both hyperparameters produce larger trees. Likewise, lower GP values are also preferred, when considering accuracy alone, since this will result in the trees adapting faster when needed. The highest scaled accuracy was obtained by the SVFDT-II ($\tau = 0.15$ and $GP = 100$ and $\tau = 0.15$ and $GP = 200$) but the SVFDT-I also presented a high value in $\tau = 0.20$ and $GP = 100$. Although the VFDT presented more red zones, both SVFDT-II had very similar performances to it.

For memory efficiency, the worst case for the SVFDT-I consumed less memory than 15 out of 25 possible configurations for the VFDT. This shows the SVFDT-I high capabilities of reducing memory consumption. Furthermore, a similar pattern occurs for the SVFDT-II. Although it consumes more memory than the SVFDT-I, its worst settings also outperforms the VFDT in 5 out of 25 possible settings. Lastly, when considering each setting, the SVFDT-I is always the lightest, followed by the SVFDT-II and the VFDT.

For time efficiency, first, it is possible to see that increasing GP will result in faster trees. This happens due to the fact that less split attempts are made. Additionally, in some cases, increasing τ also has a similar effect. For most configurations, the SVFDT-I is the fastest, although fewer speed variations seem to be present in the VFDT. Likewise, the SVFDT-II presents the fastest configuration.

7   Conclusion and Future Work

In this work, we investigated energy consumption, predictive performance and memory and time costs of two different algorithms for data stream classification. Energy and memory consumption are specifically important for green computing and application domains such as IoT, which rely on devices with few computational resources and batteries. Additionally, considering that fast algorithms with high predictive performance are desired, a four-way trade-off among the four resources consumption exist. The experiments were carried out comparing the VFDT, SVFDT-I and SVFDT-II in 23 datasets with multiple hyperparameter settings. Our results show that the relationship between GP and τ through some optimal hyperparameter settings led to reducing resource usage. We applied the Friedman statistical test and post-hoc Nemenyi analysis and observed a statistical difference in energy consumption of the SVFDTs and the VFDT, with the SVFDT-I consuming less energy. Likewise, the SVFDT-I was also statistically better in memory and time costs than the VFDT, and the SVFDT-II was better in memory. Although the VFDT surpassed the SVFDT-I when considering accuracy, the difference was minimal. As future work, we will deploy the SVFDTs in lightweight hardware to compare their performance with the VFDT.

Acknowledgement. This study was financed in part by the Coordenação de Aperfeiçoamento de Pessoal de Nível Superior - Brasil (CAPES) - Finance Code 001 and the National Council for Scientific and Technological Development - Brazil (CNPq) - Grant of Project 420562/2018-4.

References

1. Agrawal, R., Swami, A., Imielinski, T.: Database mining: a performance perspective. IEEE Trans. Knowl. Data Eng. **5**(6), 914–925 (1993)
2. Albers, S.: Energy-efficient algorithms. Commun. ACM **53**(5), 86–96 (2010)
3. Bifet, A., de Francisci Morales, G., Read, J., Holmes, G., Pfahringer, B.: Efficient online evaluation of big data stream classifiers. In: Proceedings of the XXI ACM SIGKDD International Conference on Knowledge Discovery and Data Mining, KDD 2015, pp. 59–68. ACM, New York (2015)
4. Bifet, A., Gavaldà, R.: Adaptive learning from evolving data streams. In: Adams, N.M., Robardet, C., Siebes, A., Boulicaut, J.-F. (eds.) IDA 2009. LNCS, vol. 5772, pp. 249–260. Springer, Heidelberg (2009). https://doi.org/10.1007/978-3-642-03915-7_22
5. Bifet, A., Holmes, G., Kirkby, R., Pfahringer, B.: MOA: massive online analysis. J. Mach. Learn. Res. **11**, 1601–1604 (2010)
6. Demšar, J.: Statistical comparisons of classifiers over multiple data sets. J. Mach. Learn. Res. **7**, 1–30 (2006)
7. Domingos, P., Hulten, G.: Mining high-speed data streams, pp. 71–80 (2000)
8. Friedman, M.: The use of ranks to avoid the assumption of normality implicit in the analysis of variance. J. Am. Stat. Assoc. **32**(200), 675–701 (1937)
9. Gama, J., Rocha, R., Medas, P.: Accurate decision trees for mining high-speed data streams. In: Proceedings of the IX ACM SIGKDD International Conference on Knowledge Discovery and Data Mining, KDD 2003, pp. 523–528. ACM, New York (2003)
10. Gama, J.: Knowledge Discovery from Data Streams, 1st edn. Chapman & Hall/CRC, Edinburgh/Boca Raton (2010)
11. Garcia-Martin, E., Lavesson, N., Grahn, H.: Energy efficiency analysis of the very fast decision tree algorithm. In: Missaoui, R., Abdessalem, T., Latapy, M. (eds.) Trends in Social Network Analysis. LNSN, pp. 229–252. Springer, Cham (2017). https://doi.org/10.1007/978-3-319-53420-6_10
12. García, S., Grill, M., Stiborek, J., Zunino, A.: An empirical comparison of botnet detection methods. Comput. Secur. **45**(Supplement C), 100–123 (2014)
13. Gomes, H.M., et al.: Adaptive random forests for evolving data stream classification. Mach. Learn. **106**(9), 1469–1495 (2017)
14. Hall, M., Frank, E., Holmes, G., Pfahringer, B., Reutemann, P., Witten, I.H.: The weka data mining software: an update. SIGKDD Explor. Newsl. **11**(1), 10–18 (2009)
15. Harizopoulos, S., Shah, M., Meza, J., Ranganathan, P.: Energy efficiency: the new holy grail of data management systems research. arXiv preprint arXiv:0909.1784 (2009)

16. Holmes, G., Richard, K., Pfahringer, B.: Tie-breaking in Hoeffding trees (2005)
17. Hooper, A.: Green computing. Commun. ACM **51**(10), 11–13 (2008)
18. Katakis, I., Tsoumakas, G., Vlahavas, I.: Tracking recurring contexts using ensemble classifiers: an application to email filtering. Knowl. Inf. Syst. **22**(3), 371–391 (2010)
19. Krawczyk, B., Minku, L., Gama, J., Stefanowski, J.: Ensemble learning for data stream analysis: a survey. Inf. Fusion **37**, 1–86 (2017)
20. Mouw, E.: Linux kernel procfs guide (2001). http://lib.hpu.edu.vn/handle/123456789/21423
21. Nemenyi, P.: Distribution-free Multiple Comparisons. Ph.D. thesis, Princeton University (1963)
22. Noureddine, A., Bourdon, A., Rouvoy, R., Seinturier, L.: A preliminary study of the impact of software engineering on GreenIT. In: 2012 First International Workshop on Green and Sustainable Software (GREENS), pp. 21–27. IEEE (2012)
23. Noureddine, A., Rouvoy, R., Seinturier, L.: A review of energy measurement approaches. ACM SIGOPS Oper. Syst. Rev. **47**(3), 42–49 (2013)
24. Patterson, M.G.: What is energy efficiency?: Concepts, indicators and methodological issues. Energy Policy **24**(5), 377–390 (1996)
25. Pfahringer, B., Holmes, G., Kirkby, R.: New options for hoeffding trees. In: Orgun, M.A., Thornton, J. (eds.) AI 2007. LNCS (LNAI), vol. 4830, pp. 90–99. Springer, Heidelberg (2007). https://doi.org/10.1007/978-3-540-76928-6_11
26. PowerTop. https://01.org/powertop. Accessed 01 Jan 2019
27. Singh, S., Sharma, P.K., Moon, S.Y., Park, J.H.: Advanced lightweight encryption algorithms for IoT devices: survey, challenges and solutions. J. Ambient Intell. Humaniz. Comput. 1–18 (2017)
28. Street, W.N., Kim, Y.: A streaming ensemble algorithm (SEA) for large-scale classification. In: Proceedings of the Seventh ACM SIGKDD International Conference on Knowledge Discovery and Data Mining - KDD 2001, vol. 4, pp. 377–382 (2001)
29. Turrisi da Costa, V.G., de Carvalho, A.C.P.L.F., Barbon, S.: Strict very fast decision tree: a memory conservative algorithm for data stream mining. Pattern Recognit. Lett. **116**, 22–28 (2018)
30. Turrisi da Costa, V.G., Mastelini, S.M., de Carvalho, A.C.P.L.F., Barbon, S.: Making data stream classification tree-based ensembles lighter. In: 2018 7th Brazilian Conference on Intelligent Systems (BRACIS), pp. 480–485, October 2018
31. Vereecken, W., Van Heddeghem, W., Colle, D., Pickavet, M., Demeester, P.: Overall ICT footprint and green communication technologies. In: 2010 4th International Symposium on Communications, Control and Signal Processing (ISCCSP), pp. 1–6. IEEE (2010)
32. Webb, G.I., Hyde, R., Cao, H., Nguyen, H.L., Petitjean, F.: Characterizing concept drift. Data Min. Knowl. Discov. **30**(4), 964–994 (2016)
33. Yang, H., Fong, S.: Incremental optimization mechanism for constructing a decision tree in data stream mining. In: Mathematical Problems in Engineering (2013)

Integration of Data Mining Classification Techniques and Ensemble Learning for Predicting the Type of Breast Cancer Recurrence

Jesús Silva[1(✉)], Omar Bonerge Pineda Lezama[2], Noel Varela[3],
and Luz Adriana Borrero[3]

[1] Universidad Peruana de Ciencias Aplicadas, Lima, Peru
jesussilvaUPC@gmail.com
[2] Universidad Tecnológica Centroamericana (UNITEC),
San Pedro Sula, Honduras
omarpineda@unitec.edu
[3] Universidad de la Costa, St. 58 #66, Barranquilla, Atlántico, Colombia
{nvarela2,lborrero2}@cuc.edu.co

Abstract. Conservative surgery plus radiotherapy is an alternative to radical mastectomy in the early stages of breast cancer, presenting equivalent survival rates. Data mining facilitates to manage the data and provide the useful medical progression and treatment of cancerous conditions as these methods can help to reduce the number of false positive and false negative decisions. Various machine learning techniques can be used to support the doctors in effective and accurate decision making. In this paper, various classifiers have been tested for the prediction of type of breast cancer recurrence and the results show that neural networks outperform others.

Keywords: Breast cancer · Recurrence events · Nonrecurrence events · K-means clustering

1 Introduction

Worldwide, breast cancer is the most common neoplasm among women; During 2016, more than two million new cases were registered and 810 712 deaths due to this disease. In the United States of America, during the same year, 409,995 new cases were identified, of which almost 83,000 women died. In Mexico, the incidence of breast cancer is lower, however, reported 21 064 cases and 8310 deaths [1].

Due to its detection in earlier stages as well as advances in adjuvant chemotherapy, it has been possible to reduce recurrence and mortality [2]. Micrometastatic disease is the cause of recurrence and suggests the use of adjuvant therapy. The calculation of the risk of recurrence in early breast cancer is established through the analysis of various characteristics of the patient and the tumor; the age at diagnosis, tumor size, state of the axillary ganglia, degree of differentiation and the presence or absence of vascular or lymphatic invasion, have been some widely validated prognostic factors [3].

© Springer Nature Switzerland AG 2019
R. Miani et al. (Eds.): GPC 2019, LNCS 11484, pp. 18–30, 2019.
https://doi.org/10.1007/978-3-030-19223-5_2

The status of hormone receptors (estrogen and progesterone receptors) and over-expression of the protein or amplification of the HER2 oncogene have been shown to be useful in establishing the prognosis and predicting the response to specific treatment modalities [4]. Distant Metastasis is diagnosed after minimum of three months from primary tumor and this accounts for 60% to 70% of the patients [5]. However, using Machine Learning (ML) tools it is possible to extract key factors that help to predict the recurrence of the disease.

Machine learning has been practiced for some years, and with good results, in the social sciences, marketing, finance and applied sciences. In medicine it has barely been used, partly for cultural and philosophical reasons that assume that a computer will never be as capable as a human doctor; and by the refusal of some doctors to feel questioned, supervised or advised by a machine or by an engineer [6, 7].

Thus, even in the biological sciences and genomic medicine, advanced computational methods are already used; while clinicians have to deal with increasingly large and complex databases using traditional statistical methods [8–10].

Due to its characteristics of complexity and uncertainty, medicine is one of the fields of knowledge that can benefit most from an interaction with disciplines such as computing and machine learning to strengthen processes such as clinical diagnosis and perform predictive analyzes about patients and their prognosis, resulting in a more efficient health system and better use of resources [11].

The objective of this paper is the Integration of Data Mining Classification Techniques and Ensemble Learning for Predicting the Type of Breast Cancer Recurrence. Various data mining algorithms such as Support Vector Machine (SVM), Decision Tree (DT), Naïve Bayes (NB) and Neural Networks which includes the Generalized Regression Neural Network (GRNN) can be used for the prediction of type of breast cancer recurrence.

2 Bibliographic Review

Traditional statistics are not enough to handle large amounts of variables, as they are found in many current databases. Machine learning is knowledge gained by computationally processing training data contained in those databases [12]. The recognition of statistical patterns is an approach to explore a set of data and discover previously unsuspected relationships, without the need for a hypothesis. The problems that arise and the strategies to solve them can be divided into: clustering, reduction of dimensions (dimensionality reduction) and classification [13].

In recent years lot of study has been done for breast cancer prognosis using machine learning techniques. Also these algorithms have been applied for predicting the key factors in breast cancer recurrence. Table 1 provides the details of literature survey done for the same.

Table 1. Different data mining techniques for breast cancer prognosis

Title of the paper	Techniques used	Results
Predicting Breast Cancer Recurrence Using Data Mining Techniques [14], 2010	DT, ANN are used to predict the breast cancer recurrence	DT accuracy: 71.17% ANN Accuracy: 65.75
Clustering-based approach for detecting breast cancer recurrence [15], 2010	Clustering algorithms (cluster network, Self Organizing Map and k-means	SOM: 72% k-means: 62% Cluster network 83%
Classification of Neural Network Structures For Breast Cancer Diagnosis [16], 2012	Radial Basis Function (RBF), GRNN, Probabilistic Neural Network (PNN), Multi layer Perceptron model and Back propagation Neural Network (BPNN)	Back Propagation Neural Network gave good diagnostic performance of 99.28%
Three artificial intelligence techniques for finding the key factors in breast cancer [17], 2013	DT, SVM, and Logistic Regression for predicting the survival and death rates of patients	DT best Accuracy: 94.9% Sensitivity: 95.7% Specificity: 94.3%
Robust predictive model for evaluating breast cancer survivability. Engineering Applications of Artificial Intelligence [18], 2013	SVM, ANN, SSL(Semi Supervised Learning) are used for prognosis of breast cancer survivability	SSL best results with accuracy of 0.71, Sensitivity = 0.76, Specificity = 0.65
Predicting Breast Cancer Recurrence using effective Classification and Feature Selection technique. [19], 2016	SVM, Naïve Bayes, Decision Tree are used for predicting breast cancer recurrence	Accuracy for SVM: 75.75%, Naïve Bayes: 67.17%, DT: 73.73%
Using Machine Learning Algorithms for Breast Cancer Risk Prediction and Diagnosis[20], 2016	SVM, Decision Tree, Naïve Bayes, k-NN are compare to predict the risk of breast cancer	SVM accuracy (97.13%)
Prediction Models for Estimation of Survival Rate and Relapse for Breast Cancer Patients [21]	Naïve Bayes, DT, SVM, Logistic Regression, K-Nearest Neighbor, ANN are used for prediction models for estimation of survival rate and relapse for Breast Cancer Patients	ANN best accuracy: 83.60%
A Study on Prediction of Breast Cancer Recurrence using Data Mining Techniques [22], 2017	Classification Algorithm: SVM, C5.0, Naïve Bayes, KNN Clustering Algorithm: EM, PAM, Fuzzy c-means are used to predict breast cancer recurrence	Classification Accuracy for SVM, C5.0: 81% Best Clustering Accuracy for EM: 68%

3   Data and Methods

3.1   Determination of the Data Set to Intervene

The UCI (University of California, Irvine) Machine Learning Repository is a collection of databases, domain theories, and data generators that are used by the machine learning community for the empirical analysis of machine learning algorithms. The archive was created as an ftp archive in 1987 by David Aha and fellow graduate students at UC Irvine. Since that time, it has been widely used by students, educators, and researchers all over the world as a primary source of machine learning data sets. As an indication of the impact of the archive, it has been cited over 1000 times, making it one of the top 100 most cited "papers" in all of computer science. The current version of the web site was designed in 2007 by Arthur Asuncion and David Newman, and this project is in collaboration with Rexa.info at the University of Massachusetts Amherst. Funding support from the National Science Foundation is gratefully acknowledged [23].

Table 2.   UCI breast cancer dataset

Attributes	Details	Values
Age	It determines the age when the primary tumor was detected	10–19, 20–29, 30–39, 40–49, 50–59, 60–69, 70–79, 80–89, 90–99
Menopause	The age when the menstruation cycle stops in women. Here the menopause status of the patient at the time of diagnosis is considered	lt40, ge40, premeno
Tumor-size	It describes the size of the lump that is formed. The tumor size is measured in millimeter (mm)	0–4, 5–9, 10–14, 15–19, 20–24, 25–29, 30–34, 35–39, 40–44,45–49, 50–54, 55–59
Inv-nodes	It tells the number of axillary nodes that carry symptoms of breast cancer when the histological examination is done	0–2, 3–5, 6–8, 9–11, 12–14, 15–17, 18–20, 21–23, 24–26, 27–29, 30–32, 33–35, 36–39
Node-caps	It tells if the tumor has diffused into the node capsule or not	Yes, no
Deg-malig	Range 1–3 the histological grade of the tumor i.e. the resemblance of tumor cells with normal cells	1, 2, 3
Breast	Breast cancer may occur in either breast	Left, right
Breast-quad	Breast can be divided into four quadrants considering nipple as the central point	Left-up, left-low, right-up, right-low, central
Irradiation	Radiation therapy is a treatment that uses high-energy x-rays to destroy cancer cells	Yes, no
Class	Output class depending upon reappearing symptoms of breast cancer in the patients after treatment	No-recurrence-events, recurrence-events

The breast cancer recurrence Dataset has been taken from UCI Machine Learning Repository available online [23]. It is provided by the University Medical Centre, Institute of Oncology, Ljubljana, Yugoslavia. It consists of 286 instances and 10 attributes (explained in Table 2) which includes a Class attribute that decides the outcome of the breast cancer being recurrence and non-recurrence. The italicized terms in the Table 2 are the standard terms used in UCI Machine Learning Repository.

3.2 Data Cleansing and Data Pre-processing

The large quantities of information contained in the database require an efficient presentation, not only to reduce the dimensionality, but also to preserve the information relevant for an efficient classification, for which the fields were checked to eliminate the ones which did not contain relevant information for the forecasting process [24].

3.3 Reduction of Variables

In the process of reduction of the variables it is important to identify the type of information they transmit. Such information can be of three types: (i) Redundant: repetitive or predictable information; (ii) Irrelevant: Information that is not relevant for the information discovery process; and (iii) Basic: the relevant that constitutes an important part in a process of prediction or discovery of information [25]. The importance of the reduction of data lies in the improvement of the input data for the algorithms to efficiently classified the relationship between variables.

3.4 Attribute Filters

WEKA [16–26] allows manipulations on the data by applying filters. They can be applied in two levels, attributes and instances. It was decided to apply a refinement to the model in order to get a slightly higher probability of success. Filtering operations have the option to apply "cascading", so that each filter takes the data set resulting from a previous filter as an input. In the model, the method of exhaustive search was used, which can be expressed as a tuple [27], p. 3:

$$(X_1, X_2, ...X_n) \tag{1}$$

Satisfying some restrictions.

$$P(X_1, X_2, ...X_n) \tag{2}$$

Optimizing a certain objective function. In each moment, the algorithm will be found in a certain k level, with a partial solution.

$$(X_1, ...X_k) \tag{3}$$

Each set of possible values of the tuple represents a node of the tree of solutions. The process continues until the partial solution is a complete solution of the problem, or until there are no more possibilities to try.

3.5 Evaluation of Data Mining Techniques

For the development of this research, the classification and prediction techniques were used in the construction of models from the data to determine the recurrence of breast cancer. The Bayesian classifier (Naive Bayes) was used as the initial classifier and, in the second instance, decision trees C4.5 (J48), later Support Vector Machine (SVM) and Generalized Regression Neural Network (GRNN). The data mining tool called WEKA was used to classify data, and the predicted class was compared with the current class of the instances to measure the effectiveness of the classification algorithm. There are several ways to carry out the assessment. In this case, "use training set" was applied to use the same sample to train and test. [28] Among the algorithms provided by WEKA, the following were analyzed:

Naive Bayes Algorithm
A Bayesian classifier is a probabilistic classifier based on the Bayes theorem and some additional simplifying hypotheses [29]. The Bayes classifier combines this model with a decision rule. The first rule in common is to collect the hypothesis of the more likely one, also known as the maximum a posteriori or MAP. The Bayer classifier (the function Classify) [30], p. 6 is defined as:

$$p(X_1 = x_1, \ldots, X_n = x_n/C = c) = \prod_{i=1}^{n} p(X_i = x_i/C = c) \qquad (4)$$

Where: In the case of n predictor variables X_1, ..., X_n are continuous, the Naive Bayes paradigm is converted to find the value of the variable C, which is denoted by c, which maximizes the a posteriori probability of the variable C, given the evidence expressed as an instantiation of the variables X_1, ..., X_n, this is, $X = (X_1, \ldots, X_n)$." Therefore, in the Naïve Bayes paradigm, the search for the most probable diagnosis, c*, once known the symptoms $(X_1, \ldots, X_n)$ of a particular patient, is reduced to:

$$c^* = arg_c Max \, \rho(C = c|X_1 = x_1, \ldots, X_n = x_n) \qquad (5)$$

$$= arg_c Max \, p(C = c) \prod_{i=1}^{n} p(X_i = x_i/C = c) \qquad (6)$$

Algorithm C4.5 (J48)
The algorithm C4.5 builds decision trees of a data system of training in the same way that the ID3 algorithm, which uses the concept of information entropy. The data of the training are a system S = s1, S2, ... of samples already classified. Each example s_i = {x_1, x_2, ...} is a vector where x_1, x_2, ... represent the attributes or characteristics of the example. The training data are augmented with a vector C = {c_1, c_2, ...} where c_1, c_2, ... represent the class to which it belongs in each sample. C4.5 is an extension of the ID3 algorithm developed earlier by Quinlan. Decision Trees

generated by C4.5 can be used for classification, and for this reason, C4.5 is almost always referred to as a statistical classifier [31].

Support Vector Machine (SVM)
SVM is a useful technique for data classification. Even though it's considered that Neural Networks are easier to use than this, however, sometimes unsatisfactory results are obtained. A classification task usually involves with training and testing data which consist of some data instances [32]. Each instance in the training set contains one target values and several attributes. The goal of SVM is to produce a model which predicts target value of data instances in the testing set which are given only the attributes [33].

Classification in SVM is an example of Supervised Learning. Known labels help indicate whether the system is performing in a right way or not. This information points to a desired response, validating the accuracy of the system, or be used to help the system learn to act correctly. A step in SVM classification involves identification as which are intimately connected to the known classes. This is called feature selection or feature extraction. Feature selection and SVM classification together have a use even when prediction of unknown samples is not necessary. They can be used to identify key sets which are involved in whatever processes distinguish the classes [33].

Generalized Regression Neural Network (GRNN)
Artificial Intelligence (AI) has a significant impact on the current research trends due its numerous applications in different aspects of the life. Artificial Neural Networks (ANNs) are one of the major parts of AI. ANNs have different applications including regression and approximation, forecasting and prediction, classification, pattern recognition and more. ANNs are useful since they can learn from the data and they have global approximation abilities. A feed-forward neural network with at least single hidden layer and sufficient number of hidden neurons can approximate any arbitrary continuous function under certain conditions [34]. ANNs have two main types: the Feed Forward ANNs (FFANNs) in which the input will only flow to the output layer in the forward direction and the Recurrent ANNs (RANNs) in which data flow can be in any direction. Generalized Regression Neural Networks (GRNN) [35] are single-pass associative memory feed-forward type Artificial Neural Networks (ANNs) and uses normalized Gaussian kernels in the hidden layer as activation functions.

GRNN advantages include its quick training approach and its accuracy. On the other hand, one of the disadvantage of GRNN is the growth of the hidden layer size. However, this issue can be solved by implementing a special algorithm which reduces the growth of the hidden layer by storing only the most relevant patterns [36].

3.6   Definition of the Data Mining Technique

The evaluation of data obtained from the application of the methods is carried out by using the following variables as a comparison: Correct instances, absolute error, confusion matrix and ease for the interpretation of the data [24].

4 Results

4.1 Data Pre-processing

The number of instances in the data set presented in Table 3. It also includes few duplicate rows which are eliminated and the count of the recurrence and non-recurrence instances is presented in the table.

Table 3. No. of instances in breast cancer dataset used in the study. Based on the UCI public database.

Total no. of instances	Recurrence events (R)	Non-recurrence events (NR)
286 (original)	85	201
272 (after removing duplicity)	81	191

The dataset so obtained after cleaning is nominal in nature [37]. So it is converted into numeric form to be used for further processing (see Table 4).

Table 4. Breast cancer dataset after normalization

Attributes	Description	Values
Age	The age intervals are taken as the values of the lower limit	10, 20, 30, 40, 50, 60, 70, 80, 90
Menopause	Numeric values assigned to each of the variables	premeno = 1, ge40 = 2, lt40 = 3
Tumor-size	All the tumor intervals are written as values with lower limit	0, 5, 10, 15, 20, 25, 30, 35, 40, 45, 50, 55
Inv-nodes	The values of the variables are written as the values of the lower limits	0, 3, 6, 9, 12, 15, 18, 21, 24, 27, 30, 33, 36
Node-caps	Numeric values assigned to each of the variables	Yes = 1, no = 0
Deg-malig	It is kept unchanged as it is already numeric in nature	1, 2, 3
Breast	Numeric values assigned to each of the variables	Left = 0, right = 1
Breast-quad	Numeric values assigned to each of the variables	Left-up = 0, left-low = 1, right-low = 2, right-up = 3, central = 4
Irradiation	Numeric values assigned to each of the variables	Yes = 1, no = 0

4.2 Evaluation of Data Mining Techniques

Comparison between the results of the Naive Bayes algorithm, C4.5 (J48), Support Vector Machine (SVM) and GRNN, are shown in Table 5.

Table 5. Comparison between classification algorithms

% Training	% Validation	% Classification J48	% Naive Bayes Classification	% Support Vector Machine (SVM)	GRNN
10	90	89	89	89	89
20	80	91	90	90	91
40	60	92	90	90	92
50	50	92	90	90	92
70	30	92	90	90	92
80	20	92	90	90	92
	Simple average	91	89	89	91

With respect to the training data with 10% of the data, all the algorithms present 89% correct classification, the difference lies in the fact that the greater number of training dates, the better the J48 and GRNNN algorithm classifies, with a 91% efficiency compared to 89% of the Naive Bayes and SVM algorithm.

• Comparison of arrays of confusion

One of the benefits of the confusion matrices is that they allow to see if the system is confusing two classes [38]. Below the matrices of confusion generated by each of the algorithms applied to the same data set are shown. Table 6 shows that the values of the diagonal are the right findings and the rest are the errors. According to the Naive Bayes Algorithm, out the 260 users with profile b, 240 were well classified and 20 presented errors; in the profile c, 149 were well classified and 131 presented error; in the profile d, 120 were well classified and 40 presented error; and in profile e, 280 were well classified.

Table 6. Confusion matrix - adapted from: bayes classifiers.weka.NaiveBayes

Confusion matrix					
a	b	c	d	e	← Classified as
100	0	0	0	0	a = sR
0	240	20	0	0	b = Low
0	80	149	51	0	c = Medium
0	0	0	120	40	d = High
0	0	0	0	280	e = VHigh

For the Algorithm J48 in Table 7, out of the 260 users with profile a, 240 were well classified and 20 presented errors, and for the 160 users with profile d, 120 were well classified and 40 presented errors.

Table 7. Confusion matrix - adapted from: weka.classifiers.trees.J48 -C 0.25 -M2

Confusion matrix					
a	b	c	d	e	← Classified as
100	0	0	0	0	a = sR
0	240	20	0	0	b = Low
0	0	280	0	0	c = Medium
0	0	0	120	40	d = High
0	0	0	0	280	e = VHigh

SVM is applied on the nominal form of data with 79% split to get the classification accuracy of 63.48%. In the Table 8 are show the values of confusion.

Table 8. Confusion matrix - SVM

Confusion matrix					
a	b	c	d	e	← Classified as
100	0	0	0	0	a = sR
0	225	35	0	0	b = Low
0	0	280	0	0	c = Medium
0	0	0	115	45	d = High
0	0	0	0	280	e = VHigh

The numeric form of data is used here and this GRNN is used for classification in MATLAB with training and testing data ratio as 70% and 30% respectively. The data is randomly selected for training and testing and value of $\sigma = 1$ [23] (Table 9).

Table 9. Confusion matrix - GRNN

Confusion matrix					
a	b	c	d	e	← Classified as
100	0	0	0	0	a = sR
0	250	10	0	0	b = Low
0	0	280	0	0	c = Medium
0	0	0	140	20	d = High
0	0	0	0	280	e = VHigh

The accuracy measures such as Sensitivity, Specificity, Precision and Recall [39] for all the classifiers are presented in Table 10.

Table 10. Accuracy measures of different classifiers

Classifier	Sensitivity	Specificity	Precision	Recall
SVM	1.000	0.891	0.6348	1.000
Decision Tree J48	0.9442	0.9214	0.8214	0.9548
Naive Bayes	0.936	0.921	0.7789	0.956
GRNN	0.9452	0.9387	0.8849	0.958

5   Conclusions

In this paper, several types of classification algorithms have been used here and can have that neural network classifiers have performed better than other learning classifiers. In the future, the accuracy can be increased by adding more features or by increasing the instances of the dataset. Also, the combination of existing classification techniques can be used to enhance the efficiency. Besides this a discussion with medical professional can be done to verify the features for the type of recurrence.

References

1. McPherson, K., Steel, C.M., Dixon, J.M.: ABC of breast diseases: breast cancer-epidemiology, risk factors, and genetics. BMJ **321**(7261), 624–628 (2000)
2. López-Ríos, O., Lazcano-Ponce, E.C., Tovar-Guzman, V., Hernández-Avila, M.: Epidemiology of cancer of the breast in Mexico. Consequences of demography transition. Salud Publica Mex. **39**(4), 259–265 (1997)
3. Romieu, I., Lazcano-Ponce, E., Sanchez-Zamorano, L.M., Willett, W., Hernández-Avila, M.: Carbohydrates and the risk of breast cancer among Mexican women. Cancer Epidemiol. Prev. Biomark. **13**(8), 1283–1289 (2004)
4. Rivera-Dommarco, J., Shamah-Levy, T., Villalpando-Hernandez, S., Gonzalez-de Cossio, T., Hernández-Prado, B., Sepulveda, I.: Encuesta Nacional de nutrición 1999. Estado nutricional de niños y mujeres en México. Instituto Nacional de Salud Pública, Cuernavaca (2001)
5. Simpson, J.F., Page, D.L.: Status of breast cancer prognostication based on histopathologic data. Am. J. Clin. Pathol. **102**(4 Suppl. 1), S3–S8 (1994)
6. Pereira, H., Pinder, S.E., Sibbering, D.M., Galea, M.H., Elston, C.W., Blamey, R.W., et al.: Pathological prognostic factors in breast cancer. IV: Should you be a typer or a grader? A comparative study of two histological prognostic features in operable breast carcinoma. Histopathology **27**(3), 219–226 (1995)
7. Ellis, I.O., Galea, M., Broughton, N., Locker, A., Blamey, R.W., Elston, C.W.: Pathological prognostic factors in breast cancer. II. Histological type. Relationship with survival in a large study with long-term follow-up. Histopathology **20**(6), 479–489 (1992)
8. Elston, C.W., Ellis, I.O.: Pathological prognostic factors in breast cancer. I. The value of histological grade in breast cancer: experience from a large study with long-term follow-up. Histopathology **19**(5), 403–410 (1991)
9. NIH Consensus Conference: Treatment of early-stage breast cancer. JAMA **265**(3), 391–395 (1991)

10. Dabbs, D.J., Silverman, J.F.: Prognostic factors from the fine-needle aspirate: breast carcinoma nuclear grade. Diagn. Cytopathol. **10**(3), 203–208 (1994)
11. Masood, S.: Prognostic factors in breast cancer: use of cytologic preparations. Diagn. Cytopathol. **13**(5), 388–395 (1995)
12. Fisher, E.R., Redmond, C., Fisher, B., Bass, G.: Pathologic findings from the National Surgical Adjuvant Breast and Bowel Projects (NSABP). Prognostic discriminants for 8-year survival for node-negative invasive breast cancer patients. Cancer **65**(9 Suppl.), 2121–2128 (1990)
13. Hortobagyi, G.N., Ames, F.C., Buzdar, A.U., Kau, S.W., McNeese, M.D., Paulus, D., et al.: Management of stage III primary breast cancer with primary chemotherapy, surgery, and radiation therapy. Cancer **62**(12), 2507–2516 (1988)
14. Fan, Q.: Predicting breast cancer recurrence using data mining techniques, pp. 310–311 (2010)
15. Belciug, S., Gorunescu, F., Salem, A.B., Gorunescu, M.: Clustering-based approach for detecting breast cancer recurrence. In: 2010 10th International Conference on Intelligent Systems Design and Applications (ISDA), pp. 533–538 (2010). https://doi.org/10.1109/ISDA.2010.5687211
16. Swathi, S., Rizwana, S., Babu, G.A.: Classification of neural network structures for breast cancer diagnosis. Int. J. Comput. Sci. Commun. **3**(1), 227–231 (2012)
17. Chao, C., Kuo, Y., Cheng, B.: Three artificial intelligence techniques for finding the key factors in breast cancer. J. Stat. Manag. 37–41 (2014). https://doi.org/10.1080/09720510.2012.10701632
18. Park, K., Ali, A., Kim, D., An, Y., Kim, M., Shin, H.: Robust predictive model for evaluating breast cancer survivability. Eng. Appl. Artif. Intell. **26**(9), 2194–2205 (2013). https://doi.org/10.1016/j.engappai.2013.06.013
19. Pritom, A.I., Munshi, M.A.R., Sabab, S.A., Shihab, S.: Predicting breast cancer recurrence using effective classification and feature selection technique (n.d.)
20. Asri, H., Mousannif, H., Al Moatassime, H., Noel, T.: Using machine learning algorithms for breast cancer risk prediction and diagnosis. Procedia Comput. Sci. **83**(Fams), 1064–1069 (2016)
21. Paper, C., Ninkovic, S., Centar, K.: Prediction models for estimation of survival rate and relapse for breast cancer patients (2015/2016)
22. Prghov, F., Prghov, F., Errvwlqj, D.: 527–530 (2017)
23. The UCI (University of California, Irvine): Machine Learning Repository (2019). https://archive.ics.uci.edu/ml/datasets/breast+cancer
24. Viloria, A., Bucci, N., Luna, M.: Comparative analysis between psychosocial risk assessment models. J. Eng. Appl. Sci. **12**(11), 2901–2903 (2017). ISSN 1816-949X
25. Caamaño, A.J., Echeverría, M.M., Retamal, V.O., Navarro, C.T., y Espinosa, F.T.: Modelo predictivo de fuga de clientes utilizando minería de datos para una empresa de telecomunicaciones en chile. Universidad Ciencia y Tecnología **18**(72), 100–109 (2015)
26. Mark Hall y otros 5 autores: The WEKA data mining software: an update. SIGKDD Explor. **11**(1) (2009)
27. Anon, D.: Búsqueda exhaustiva. Universidad de Murcia, España (2016). http://dis.um.es/~domingo/apuntes/AlgBio/exhaustiva.pdf
28. Hepner, G.F.: Artificial neural network classification using a minimal training set. Comparison to conventional supervised classification. Photogramm. Eng. Remote Sens. **56**(4), 469–473 (1990)

29. Agarwal, B., Mittal, N.: Text classification using machine learning methods - a survey. In: Babu, B.V., et al. (eds.) Proceedings of the Second International Conference on Soft Computing for Problem Solving (SocProS 2012), December 28-30, 2012. AISC, vol. 236, pp. 701–709. Springer, New Delhi (2014). https://doi.org/10.1007/978-81-322-1602-5_75

30. Larrañaga, P., Inza, I., y Moujahid, A.: Tema 6. Clasificadores Bayesianos. Departamento de Ciencias de la Computación e Inteligencia Artificial (En línea: http://www.sc.ehu.es/ccwbayes/docencia/mmcc/docs/t6bayesianos.pdf. acceso: 9 de enero de 2016), Universidad del País Vasco-Euskal Herriko Unibertsitatea, España (1997)

31. Quinlan, J.R.: C4. 5: Programs for Machine Learning. Elsevier, Burlington (1993)

32. Kumar, G., Malik, H.: Generalized regression neural network based wind speed prediction model for western region of India. Procedia Comput. Sci. **93**(September), 26–32 (2016). https://doi.org/10.1016/j.procs.07.177

33. Sun, G., Hoff, S., Zelle, B., Nelson, M.: Development and comparison of backpropagation and generalized regression neural network models to predict diurnal and seasonal gas and PM 10 concentrations and emissions from swine buildings, vol. 0300, no. 08 (2008)

34. Cigizoglu, H.K.: Generalized regression neural network in monthly flow forecasting. Civ. Eng. Environ. Syst. **22**(2), 71–84 (2005). https://doi.org/10.1080/10286600500126256

35. Kişi, Ö.: Generalized regression neural networks for evapotranspiration modelling generalized regression neural networks for evapotranspiration modelling, 6667 (2010)

36. Kartal, S., Oral, M.: New pattern reduction method for generalized regression neural network. Int. J. Adv. Res. **7**(2), 122–129 (2017). https://doi.org/10.23956/ijarcsse/V7I2/01213

37. Cross, A.J., Rohrer, G.A., Brown-Brandl, T.M., Cassady, J.P., Keel, B.N.: Feed-forward and generalised regression neural networks in modelling feeding behavior of pigs in the grow-finish phase. Biosyst. Eng. 1–10 (2018). https://doi.org/10.1016/j.biosystemseng.2018.02.005

38. Corso, C.L.: Alternativa de herramienta libre para implementación de aprendizaje automático. http://www.investigacion.frc.utn.edu.ar/labsis/Publicaciones/congresos_labsis/cynthia/Alternativa_de_herramienta_para_Mineria_Datos_CNEISI_2009.pdf. acceso: 10 de agosto de 2015), Argentina (2009)

39. Manickam, R.: Back propagation neural network for prediction of some shell moulding parameters. Period. Polytech. Mech. Eng. **60**(4), 203–208 (2016). https://doi.org/10.3311/PPme.8684

RETRACTED CHAPTER: U-Control Chart Based Differential Evolution Clustering for Determining the Number of Cluster in k-Means

Jesús Silva[1(✉)], Omar Bonerge Pineda Lezama[2], Noel Varela[3],
Jesús García Guiliany[4], Ernesto Steffens Sanabria[5],
Madelin Sánchez Otero[6], and Vladimir Álvarez Rojas[7]

[1] Universidad Peruana de Ciencias Aplicadas, Lima, Peru
jesussilvaUPC@gmail.com
[2] Universidad Tecnológica Centroamericana (UNITEC),
San Pedro Sula, Honduras
omarpineda@unitec.edu
[3] Universidad de la Costa, Barranquilla, Colombia
nvarela2@cuc.edu.co
[4] Universidad Simón Bolívar, Barranquilla, Colombia
jesus.garcia@unisimonbolivar.edu.co
[5] Corporación Universitaria Latinoamericana, Barranquilla, Colombia
steffensse@ul.edu.c
[6] Corporación Universitaria Rafael Núñez, Cartagena, Colombia
madelin.sanchez@curnvirtual.edu.co
[7] Corporación Universitaria Minuto de Dios - UNIMINUTO,
Bello, Antioquia, Colombia
vladimir.alvarez@uniminuto.edu

Abstract. The automatic clustering differential evolution (ACDE) is one of the clustering methods that are able to determine the cluster number automatically. However, ACDE still makes use of the manual strategy to determine k activation threshold thereby affecting its performance. In this study, the ACDE problem will be ameliorated using the u-control chart (UCC) then the cluster number generated from ACDE will be fed to k-means. The performance of the proposed method was tested using six public datasets from the UCI repository about academic efficiency (AE) and evaluated with Davies Bouldin Index (DBI) and Cosine Similarity (CS) measure. The results show that the proposed method yields excellent performance compared to prior researches.

Keywords: K-means · Automatic clustering · Differential evolution · K activation threshold · U control chart · Academic efficiency (AE)

1 Introduction

The aim of this study is to apply the u-chart control (UCC) method to determine the k-activation threshold on Automatic Clustering Differential Evolution (ACDE) in order to identify behavior patterns and relations between the different attributes, enabling to

The original version of this chapter was retracted: The retraction note to this chapter is available at https://doi.org/10.1007/978-3-030-19223-5_18

identify and predict the likelihood of student desertion by foreseeing the factors influencing their permanence, generating knowledge for timely decisions, and offering competitive advantage to the institution where ACDE is used to determine the number of clusters in k-means automatically and improving the performance of k-means.

The k-means method is one of the hard partition methods in cluster analysis of the data mining field. The k-means has advantages, i.e. it is easy to implement grouping a large dataset, and with stable performance over different problems (Salem et al. [1]; Chakraborty and Das [2]). However, the clustering results of k-means depends on a certain number of clusters as inputs. If the estimated number of clusters does not tally with the final solution, the chances of clustering are very low (Masud et al. [3]; Rahman et al. [4]; Rahman and Islam [5]; Ramadas et al. [6]). Meanwhile, getting the number of k as an input on k-means is still not an easy task because the user requires a prior specification number of the cluster (Yaqian et al. [7]). This condition is termed a local optimum problem (Tîrnăucă et al. [8]). In practice, the local optimum problem is overcome by applying the method several times with a different number of k, then choosing the best results. Determining the number of clusters is significant for the k-means method (Xiang et al. [9]). Automatic clustering methods are a solution that helps the user determine the optimal number of clusters (Garcia and Flores [10]). Therefore, the automatic clustering method is an effective solution to this problem.

Researches on the determination of the number of clusters used automatic clustering methods which are based on the Evolutional Computation (EC) technique. K-means method has done a lot and has been published with different methods, namely Automatic Clustering using Differential Evolution (ACDE) (Das et al. [11]), combining methods between PSO and k-means on Dynamic Clustering with Particle Swarm Optimization (DCPSO) (Omran et al. [12]), and Genetic Clustering for unknown k clustering (GCUK) (Bandyopadhyay and Maulik [13]).

Automatic clustering methods have been used to determine the number of clusters in the k- means but are yet to achieve an accurate cluster result. Therefore, it is necessary to improve the performance of automated grouping methods used for determining the number of clusters. The ACDE method is the most popular EC technique which has effectively improved the performance of automatic clustering methods proposed by previous researchers (Das et al. [11]). ACDE predicated on the differential evolution (DE) method is one of the strongest, fastest, and most efficient global search heuristics methods in the world that is very easy to use with high-dimensional data. It can be employed using polynomial functions and other functions because it is easy to change the values of control variables such as NP, F, and CR to obtain good search results (Ramadas et al. [6]). However, ACDE has a weakness in determining the k activation threshold that is still dependent on user judgment (Tam et al. [14]).

The ACDE was then developed by (Kuo et al. [15]) and the combination of ACDE and k-means methods was termed the automatic clustering approach based on the differential evolution method combined with k-means for crisp clustering method aimed at improving clustering performance in the k-means method (ACDE-k-means). The ACDE method can find the number of clusters automatically and is able to balance the evolutionary process of DE methods to achieve better partitions than the classic DE. However, the classic DE method still depends on user's considerations to determine the k activation threshold thereby affecting the performance of the DE method (Piotrowski [16]).

The U-Control Chart (UCC) method is employed to determine the k activation threshold that is used for the initial step to get the value of the variables sought before initialization of the variable vector. The UUC is a method from statistical process control (SPC) which has proved to be effective in solving the problem of management control attributes (Kaya [17]). Other methods such us P-Control Chart and C-Control Chart are valid methods, but not used. This research focuses just on UCC. The UCC method used to average the data to be measured is then reduced and added to find upper and lower bound values on the number of attributes for the searched variables. A product is said to have a good quality if the average value is at a threshold or the average value is between the upper and lower bound. Based on the above assumption, the data is good if it is within the threshold of the U-Control Chart.

2 Theoretical Review

Several studies have been carried out to find the number of clusters of k-means on automatic clustering evolutionary methods. The most used clustering methods, that is, the main methods, combined with evolutionary computation methods, are DCPSO (Omran et al. [12]), GCUK (Bandyopadhyay and Maulik [13]), ACDE-k-means (Kuo et al. [15]) and are often used for improving automatic clustering k-means results. So far, the clustering performance method to achieve optimal cluster number results is still a subject of further research because the best performance from all evaluations has not been completely achieved.

In [10], they proposed the Genetic Clustering for Unknown k (GCUK) method to find the number of automatic clusters k-means. This method begins by encoding several clusters premise on the prototype don't-care. Chromosome compatibility is determined by objective function using the DBI to guide evolutionary search (Bandyopadhyay and Maulik [13]). The value of the valid partition result is the smallest value of the objective function (Das et al. [11]). It employs public datasets from the UCI machine learning repositories such as cancer, synthetic, spot image, and iris data. The result indicated that this method can automatically find few land-cover varieties even when the size of the data set is considerably large.

Omran et al. [12] proposed a combination of PSO and k-means for finding the number of clusters in an unlabeled data named Dynamic Clustering PSO (DCPSO). PSO is implemented to find the number of clusters in a data and k-means is implemented to do repair grouping. However, they are still limited to testing the original image data and some of the synthetic image data (Dobbie et al. [18]). The authors employ two different dataset types: natural images and synthetic image data (10 datasets) (Lenna, Mandrill, Jet, Peppers, MRI, and Tahoe) from UCI machine learning repository where each DBI average of sample natural images and this method can achieve a decrease in the performance of k-means.

A new method called ACDE-k-means proposed by Kuo et al. [15] is developed from a combination of ACDE and k-means method for crisp clustering. In this case, ACDE uses the basic DE method that has weaknesses as described earlier and differential evolution clustering is considered as automatic. The aim of this method is to find the optimal number of clusters in k-means without knowing the information from the data a priori. Also, the differential evolution clustering automatic efficiency for the high-dimensional dataset outperforms other related studies such as GCUK and DCPSO [10]. The two indexes of evaluation used are DBI and CS, then, dataset tested is from UCI repository: Breast Cancer, Iris, Vowel end Glass, and Wine. Finally, the decreasing average value of DBI was determined and CS measure of each dataset of k-means.

3 Materials and Methods

3.1 Database

The UCI Machine Learning Repository is a collection of databases, domain theories, and data generators that are used by the machine learning community for the empirical analysis of machine learning algorithms. The archive was created as an ftp archive in 1987 by David Aha and fellow graduate students at UC Irvine. Since that time, it has been widely used by students, educators, and researchers all over the world as a primary source of machine learning data sets. As an indication of the impact of the archive, it has been cited over 1000 times, making it one of the top 100 most cited "papers" in all of computer science. The current version of the web site was designed in 2007 by Arthur Asuncion and David Newman, and this project is in collaboration with Rexa.info at the University of Massachusetts Amherst. Funding support from the National Science Foundation is gratefully acknowledged [19]. The proposed method was tested using two different datasets, namely artificial and real datasets. Each dataset can be seen in Table 1.

Table 1. Description of the UCI database tables

Databases	Type of dataset	Number of records	No. attributes	Class (k)
Synthetic	Artificial	458	69	4
Wine quality	Artificial	215	10	4
Abalone	Artificial	750	4	7
Poker hand	Real	278	4	4
Glass	Real	1520	8	20
Iris	Real	576	27	5

3.2 Methods

The Objective function is a simulated search on a dataset to guide towards an optimal global solution. In the case of the clustering problems, the objective function usually uses the cluster validity index [10]. In this case, Davies Building index (DBI) and cosine similarity measure (CS) are used as objective function based on the finding of Das et al. [11] as follows Eqs. (1) and (2).

$$f1 = \frac{1}{CS_i(K) + eps} \tag{1}$$

The eps is a small bias term equal to $2 * 10^{-6}$ near zero. $2 * 10^{-6}$ is a cluster k for k with set number of clusters as initialization to cluster of the datasets.

$$f2 = \frac{1}{DBI_i(K) + eps} \tag{2}$$

Where DBIi is the DB index, evaluated on the partitions yielded by the i-th vector and eps is the same as before.

In this research, a combination of the U-Control Chart (UCC) and Automatic Clustering using Differential Evolution method is proposed to determine the number of clusters on k-means. The aim of the UCC method is to control k activation threshold of the Automatic Clustering using the Differential Evolution method. The latter will automatically search the optimal number of clusters in the data as required by k-means. The representation of chromosome used is based on [12], because the Automatic Clustering using Differential Evolution method produce a premature cluster, the k-means is implemented to repair the premature cluster. As shown in Fig. 1, the steps for the complete proposed method are given here.

Step 1. Prepare datasets.

Step 2. Initialize each chromosome containing a selected number of k randomly selected clusters and specify the k activation threshold using the UCC method defined with a stage as follows Eqs. (3), (4) and (5). In Eq. (3), the average value is given by the average of all attributes. After that Eq. (4), the upper bound (ub) is calculated. Next Eq. (5) the lower bound (lb) is calculated.

$$\bar{u} = \sum x_i \tag{3}$$

$$ub = \bar{u} + K\sqrt{\frac{\bar{u}}{n_i}} \tag{4}$$

$$lb = \bar{u} - K\sqrt{\frac{\bar{u}}{n_i}} \tag{5}$$

Step 3. Generate initial population randomly based on predetermined k activation threshold values.

Step 4. Find the active cluster center, which is defined as shown in the following.

IF $V_{i,k}T_k > 0.5$ THEN cluster center $V_{i,k}m_k$ is ACTIVE

ELSE $V_{i,k}m_k$ is INACTIVE.

Where the center of the $V_{i,k}$ cluster on the chromosome will be active or selected if $V_{i,k}T_k > 0.5$. Conversely, if $V_{i,k}T_k > 0.5$ the center of the cluster $V_{i,k}$ is not active in the i-th chromosome. $V_{i,k}T_k$ is the cost population of the data generation, while the best solution, cost or $V_{i,k}m_k$ is the best solution for each iteration.

Step 5. For iteration is the best solution for each iteration
- Find the distance of each data vector from all active centroids of the i-th chromosome,
- Allocate each data vector to a cluster with the shortest distance,
- Change member(s) of the population (based on DE method) using the objective function to make the selected population better.
- Apply k-means method. The active cluster number is used as input k-means to adjust i-th active chromosome.

Step 6. The minimum objective is the output of the global best chromosome.

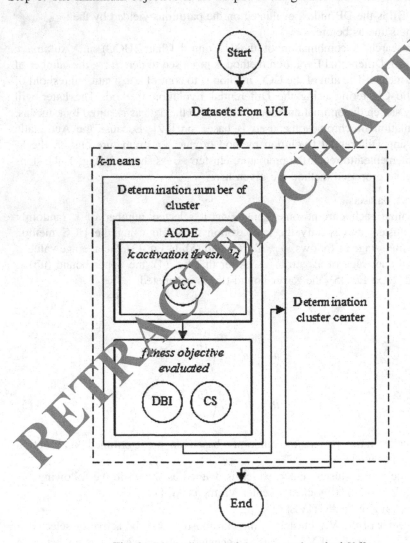

Fig. 1. Block diagram of the proposed method [16].

4 Results

The experiments were conducted using a computing platform with Intel Celeron 2.16 GHz CPU, 8 GB RAM and Microsoft Windows 10 Home 64-bit used as the operating system, and MATLAB version R2016a used as the data analytics tool. MATLAB would produce a model performance as the calculation output, such as the average value best cluster DBI and CS measure.

4.1 Data Transformation Stage

In the transformation stage, useful features are observed to represent the data depending on the goal of the data mining process. Methods are used for reducing dimensions or reducing the effective number of variables under consideration or to find invariant representations of the data [3].

At this stage, the UCI dataset was built, integrating the attributes of the different tables of the database (see Table 1). Items with missing data were suppressed, new attributes were built (see Table 2) and the continuous attributes were discretized the numerical values were transformed into discrete or nominal attributes. Some of the discretized attributes are shown in Tables 3, 4 and 5.

On the other hand, the UCI dataset was adapted to the ARFF format (Attribute, Relation, File, Format).

The structure of the ARFF format [12] is the following:

- Header: defines the name of the relationship and its format is as follows:
- @Relation <name-of-the-relationship>
- Statements by the attributes. In this section, the attributes that will compose the ARFF file with its type are declared. The syntax is as follows:
- @Attribute <attribute name> <type>
- Data section. The data that make up the relationship between commas separating the attributes and with lines break in relationships are declared.

Table 2. Resume of new attributes in the data set UCI

Databases	Type of dataset	Number of records	No. attributes	Class (k)
Synthetic	Artificial	351	48	4
Wine quality	Artificial	178	10	4
Abalone	Artificial	651	3	7
Poker hand	Real	206	3	4
Glass	Real	1315	5	20
Iris	Real	508	19	5

Finally, the data set with 26 UCI.ARFF was obtained with 26 attributes and 20.329 records, ready to apply the data mining techniques, using the described methodology to obtain the patterns of low academic performance and/or desertion of students from the Colombian universities.

Table 3. Discretization of the attributes of Wine Quality

Wine Quality	Value	No. records
Color	A	15
Aroma	B	20
Flavor	C	18
Ripening period	D	62

Table 4. Discretization of the attributes of Glass

Glass	Value	No. records
Color	A	21
Air	B	40
Sulfur quality	C	30
Silicon quality	D	17

Table 5. Discretization of the attributes of Iris

Iris	Value	No. records
Color	A	42
Age	B	10
Sex	C	12
Class	D	80

The proposed method was applied to the six databases listed in Table 1. The Parameter setting for proposed method based on the recommendation of Das et al. [13] is as follows: maxiter = 300, pop-size = 10 * dim, CRmax = 1.0 and CRmin = 0.45. Max iteration indicates the amount of iteration, pop-size is the size of the population, cross-over probability is used to initialize the position of a particle or chromosome.

The best model automatic clustering on each dataset is highlighted with boldfaced print and the best optimal cluster result is marked with (1) and (2) squared on each dataset. As shown in Table 6, the second experiment UCC+ACDE-k-means is outperforming in almost all datasets with respect to DBI (5 of 6 datasets) and the optimal search k results of both methods are extremely good except for the vowel dataset. Results comparison ACDE-k-means only vs UCC+ACDE-k-means.

Table 6. Results comparison ACDE-k-means only vs UCC+ACDE-k-means.

Datasets	Class optimal (k)	Mean validity index and number cluster optimal							
		DBI		k		CS		k	
		(1)	(2)	(1)	(2)	(1)	(2)	(1)	(2)
Synthetic	3	0.5345	0.5012	3*	3*	0.7854	0.5781	3*	3*
Wine Q	3	0.0457	0.5013	3*	3*	0.0354	0.2997	3*	3*
Abalone	5	0.6987	0.4897	3#	7#	0.0506	0.0458	5*	5*
Poker H	3	0.4015	0.2233	3*	3*	0.0089	0.2850	3*	3*
Glass	5	1.2877	1.0478	5*	4#	0.7785	0.8961	2#	3#
Iris	3	0.11123	0.0589	4*	4*	2.5475	1.4520	3*	3*

[1]ACDE-k-means only; [2]UCC-ACDE-k-means; *Number cluster optimal, #not optimal

Meanwhile, the first experiment (ACDE-k-means only) only outperforms in Wine Quality. Concerning CS, the first and the second experiment on each dataset produced excellent three different datasets. Meanwhile, regarding the determination of the number of k optimal, both methods are extremely good except in the Glass. However, based on this study, the overall second experiment outperformed and is better than the first experiment since the main evaluation method used in finding the number of the optimal cluster such as all six datasets used is DBI.

Finally, the proposed method was compared with prior researches such as Omran et al. [12] method, MAcQueen (1967) method, Kuo et al. [15] method as well as Bandyopadhyay and Maulik [13] method. Table 7 shows the comparison of prior research and proposed method with all datasets.

Table 7. Comparison to prior search based on DBI and CS as objective function for all datasets.

Dataset	Objective function	Methods			
		GCUK	DCPSO	ACDE-k-means	Proposed method
Synthetic	DBI	0.5213 (2)	0.6402 (2)	0.5742 (3)	**0.4951 (3)**
	CS	0.8254 (8)	0.8754 (4)	0.6952 (3)	**0.5496 (3)**
Wine Q	DBI	0.0218 (4)	0.0495 (6)	**0.03899 (3)**	0.5078 (3)
	CS	0.0332 (3)	0.0654 (3)	**0.04165 (3)**	0.3090 (3)
Abalone	DBI	1.4998 (4)	0.6001 (6)	0.7318 (3)	**0.4999 (6)**
	CS	0.0720 (3)	0.3399 (6)	0.0495 (6)	**0.0362 (6)**
Poker H	DBI	0.5487 (3)	0.4784 (7)	0.3899 (3)	**0.2078 (3)**
	CS	1.3347 (3)	0.5921 (9)	**0.0070 (3)**	0.2254 (3)
Glass	DBI	1.101 (13)	**0.9567 (8)**	1.2834 (5)	1.0478 (4)
	CS	1.1479 (13)	0.9317 (6)	**0.7820 (2)**	0.9314 (3)
Iris	DBI	0.1099 (4)	0.1687 (3)	0.1011 (4)	**0.0998 (4)**
	CS	2.7777 (4)	2.8412 (3)	2.5013 (4)	**1.3783 (4)**

The proposed method shows the best lowest clustering results and outperforms in a few prior researches [20, 21] and [22]. As indicated in Table 7, all existing methods have their complexity using evolutionary strategy automatic clustering methods for determining the number of clusters automatically in k-means, while the proposed method uses technical-statistical control for problem-solving of ACDE as an automatic clustering strategy for finding the optimal number of clusters in k-means method.

5   Conclusions

In this study, the proposed method is employed to find out the number of clusters in the k- means method. The tests were carried out using six datasets of UCI repository. Then, there is a comparison of the proposed method with previous related studies of k-Means, ACDE-k-means, GCUK, and DCPSO. The five methods are measured by DBI and CS evaluations. The method with the smallest evaluation value of the two evaluations that approaches zero is the best method. The experimental result reveals that the proposed method has the lowest value both in DBI and CS measure for all datasets compared with prior researches. These results showed that the proposed method achieves an excellent and promising performance. The use of U-Control Chart (UCC) method with automatic clustering differential evolution (ACDE) to determine the number of clusters in k-means has been proven to increase the performance of ACDE. Hence, it can be concluded that the U-Control Chart method can enhance ACDE-k-means performance in determining the number of clusters in k-means.

References

1. Salem, S.B., Naouali, S., Chtourou, Z.: A fast and effective partitional clustering algorithm for large categorical datasets using a k-means based approach. Comput. Electr. Eng. **68**, 463–483 (2018). https://doi.org/10.1016/j.compeleceng.2018.04.023
2. Chakraborty, S., Das, S.: Simultaneous variable weighting and determining the number of clusters—a weighted Gaussian means algorithm. Stat. Probab. Lett. **137**, 148–156 (2018). https://doi.org/10.1016/j.spl.2018.01.015
3. Masud, M., Huang, J.Z., Wei, C., Wang, J., Khan, I., Zhong, M.: I-nice: a new approach for identifying the number of clusters and initial cluster centres. Inf. Sci. (NY) (2018). https://doi.org/10.1016/j.ins.2018.07.034
4. Rahman, M.A., Islam, M.Z., Bossomaier, T.: ModEx and seed-detective: two novel techniques for high quality clustering by using good initial seeds in k-means. J. King Saud Univ. – Comput. Inf. Sci. **27**, 113–128 (2015). https://doi.org/10.1016/j.jksuci.2014.04.002
5. Rahman, M.A., Islam, M.Z.: A hybrid clustering technique combining a novel genetic algorithm with k-means. Knowl.-Based Syst. **71**, 345–365 (2014). https://doi.org/10.1016/j.knosys.2014.08.011
6. Ramadas, M., Abraham, A., Kumar, S.: FSDE-forced strategy differential evolution used for data clustering. J. King Saud Univ. - Comput. Inf. Sci. (2016). https://doi.org/10.1016/j.jksuci.2016.12.005
7. Yaqian, Z., Chai, Q.H., Boon, G.W.: Curvature-based method for determining the number of clusters. Inf. Sci. (NY) (2017). https://doi.org/10.1016/j.ins.2017.05.024

8. Tîrnăucă, C., Gómez-Pérez, D., Balcázar, J.L., Montaña, J.L.: Global optimality in k-means clustering. Inf. Sci. (NY) **439–440**, 79–94 (2018). https://doi.org/10.1016/j.ins.2018.02.001

9. Xiang, W., Zhu, N., Ma, S., Meng, X., An, M.: A dynamic shuffled differential evolution algorithm for data clustering. Neurocomputing (2015). https://doi.org/10.1016/j.neucom.2015.01.058

10. Garcia, A.J., Flores, W.G.: Automatic clustering using nature-inspired metaheuristics: a survey. Appl. Soft Comput. (2016). https://doi.org/10.1016/j.asoc.2015.12.001

11. Das, S., Abraham, A., Konar, A.: Automatic clustering using an improved differential evolution algorithm. IEEE Trans. Syst. Man Cybern. - Part A Syst. Hum. **38**, 218–237 (2008). https://doi.org/10.1109/TSMCA.2007.909595

12. Omran, M.G.H., Engelbrecht, A.P., Salman, A.: Dynamic clustering using particle swarm optimization with application in image segmentation. Pattern Anal. Appl. 332–344 (2006). https://doi.org/10.1007/s10044-005-0015-5

13. Bandyopadhyay, S., Maulik, U.: Genetic clustering for automatic evolution of clusters and application to image classification. Pattern Recogn. **35**, 1197–1208 (2002)

14. Tam, H., Ng, S., Lui, A.K., Leung, M.: Improved activation scheme of automatic clustering using differential evolution algorithm. In: IEEE Congress on Evolutionary Computation (CEC), pp. 1749–1756 (2017). https://doi.org/10.1109/CEC.2017.7969513

15. Kuo, R., Suryani, E., Yasid, A.: Automatic clustering combining differential evolution algorithm and k-means algorithm. In: Proceedings of the Institute of Industrial Engineers Asian Conference 2013, pp. 1207–1215 (2013). https://doi.org/10.1007/978-981-4451-98-7

16. Piotrowski, A.P.: Review of differential evolution population size. Swarm Evol. Comput. **32**, 1–24 (2017). https://doi.org/10.1016/j.swevo.2016.05.003

17. Kaya, I.: A genetic algorithm approach to determine the sample size for attribute control charts. Inf. Sci. (NY) **179**, 1552–1566 (2009). https://doi.org/10.1016/j.ins.2008.09.024

18. Dobbie, G., Sing, Y., Riddle, P., Ur, S.: Research on particle swarm optimization based clustering: a systematic review of literature and techniques. Swarm Evol. Comput. **17**, 1–13 (2014). https://doi.org/10.1016/j.swevo.2014.02.001

19. Departamento Administrativo Nacional de Estadística: Página principal. Recuperado de: DANE (2018). http://www.dane.gov.co/

20. Torres-Samuel, M., Vásquez, C.L., Viloria, A., Varela, N., Hernández-Fernandez, L., Portillo-Medina, R.: Analysis of patterns in the university world rankings webometrics, Shanghai, QS and SIR-SCimago: case Latin America. In: Tan, Y., Shi, Y., Tang, Q. (eds.) DMBD 2018. LNCS, vol. 10943, pp. 188–199. Springer, Cham (2018). https://doi.org/10.1007/978-3-319-93803-5_18

21. Vásquez, C., Torres, M., Viloria, A.: Public policies in science and technology in Latin American countries with universities in the top 100 of web ranking. J. Eng. Appl. Sci. **12**(11), 2963–2965 (2017)

22. Torres-Samuel, M., et al.: Efficiency analysis of the visibility of Latin American universities and their impact on the ranking web. In: Tan, Y., Shi, Y., Tang, Q. (eds.) DMBD 2018. LNCS, vol. 10943, pp. 235–243. Springer, Cham (2018). https://doi.org/10.1007/978-3-319-93803-5_22

A Distributed Algorithm for Scalable Fuzzy Time Series

Petrônio Cândido de Lima e Silva[1,3][(✉)] (iD), Patrícia de Oliveira e Lucas[2,3] (iD), and Frederico Gadelha Guimarães[3,4] (iD)

[1] Instituto Federal do Norte de Minas Gerais - Campus Januária, Januária, Brazil
petronio.candido@ifnmg.edu.br
[2] Instituto Federal do Norte de Minas Gerais - Campus Salinas, Salinas, Brazil
[3] Machine Intelligence and Data Science Lab (MINDS UFMG), Belo Horizonte, Brazil
[4] Department of Electrical Engineering, Universidade Federal de Minas Gerais, UFMG, Belo Horizonte, Brazil
http://www.minds.eng.ufmg.br/

Abstract. Time series forecasting, an essential task in management of Smart Cities and Smart Grids, becomes challenging when it needs to deal with big data. The development of highly accurate machine learning models is yet harder when considering the optimization of hyper-parameters, an expensive computational task. To tame these challenges this work proposes the Weighted Multivariate Fuzzy Time Series method, a simple and non-parametric forecasting method with high scalability and accuracy. A stack of methods is presented, which comprises a sequential training and forecasting procedure and a Map/Reduce extension for distributed processing. The stack of proposed methods was evaluated using a cluster with commodity hardware and a big data of solar energy time series, achieving good performance in feasible processing time.

Keywords: Fuzzy Time Series · Cluster computing · Big data

1 Introduction

Distributed computing has been determinant to enable the processing of data-intensive and computationally expensive tasks. Such kind of tasks are spread over several areas in science and engineering, and specially in smart environments, such as smart grids and cities, where there are networks of smart sensors continuously monitoring all system components and streaming historical data with high volume and velocity [10]. In these smart environments, there is increasing demand for evolving and optimized management methods, which encompass description, diagnostic, prediction/forecasting and prognostic tasks.

In recent years the search for renewable energy sources has grown and, as most of them are not perennial power sources, its integration on smart environments will require ability to predict their output generation.

© Springer Nature Switzerland AG 2019
R. Miani et al. (Eds.): GPC 2019, LNCS 11484, pp. 42–56, 2019.
https://doi.org/10.1007/978-3-030-19223-5_4

But traditional forecasting methods, and even some new ones, were not designed to deal with such high volume of data. The most critical issues are the high dimensionality (dozens of hundreds of attributes) and volume (hundreds of millions or billions of samples) [16]. Such data volume cannot be grounded on a single machine memory and demands a distributed architecture of storage and processing. New technologies are emerging to tackle these issues, for instance the Map Reduce based frameworks [11], a divide-and-conquer approach which is the basis of Hadoop clusters [30], where the processing units also act as storage units of the data subsets.

On the other hand, some forecasting methods are black-boxes and find legal barriers or resistance due to its lack of transparency and auditability. The exposed scenario brings the opportunity to exploit the Fuzzy Time Series (FTS) methods [28], which have been drawing more attention and relevance in recent years due to many studies reporting its good accuracy compared with other models [27]. FTS forecasting methods produce data driven and non-parametric models, and have become attractive due to their simplicity, versatility, forecasting accuracy and computational performance, and it also produces human readable representations of the time series patterns, making its knowledge transferable, auditable, easily reusable and updatable. Examples of successful applications are shown in energy load forecasting [19–22], stock index prices prediction [18,23,29], seasonal time series [13,25] among others.

There are many enhancements possible (and necessary) to adapt the current FTS methods for big data scalability. This work proposes a stack of methods named Weighted Multivariate FTS (WMVFTS), which includes methods for sequential and distributed model training and forecasting, implemented with open source Map Reduce frameworks and commodity hardware.

The remainder of this work is organized as follows: in Sect. 2, the main concepts of Fuzzy Time Series are introduced, in Sect. 3, the WMVFTS sequential procedures for training and forecasting are presented and in Sect. 4 the distributed extensions of these procedures are discussed. In Sect. 5 computational experiments are performed to asses the effectiveness of the model, using a large environmental time series. Finally, in Sect. 6, the main findings of the research are synthesized.

2   Preliminaries

Fuzzy Time Series (FTS) were introduced in [28] to deal with vague and imprecise knowledge in time series data. Given a univariate time series $Y \in \mathbb{R}^1$, and its individual values $y(t) \in Y$, for $t = 0, 1, \ldots, T$, the Universe of Discourse (UoD) U is delimited by the known bounds of Y, such that $U = [\min(Y), \max(Y)]$. A linguistic variable $\tilde{A}$ is defined upon U, where the linguistic terms are fuzzy sets A_i, for $i = 1 \ldots k$, each one with its own membership function (MF) μ_{A_i}. This step is called UoD partitioning and depends on three hyperparameters: the number of partitions k, the partitioning method and the membership function μ. Commonly the membership functions are triangular, trapezoidal, sigmoid or

Gaussian functions. The k parameter is one of the most important parameters of the FTS methods because it directly impacts on the model bias/variance.

The partitioning method partitions U on k fuzzy sets with membership function μ, and these fuzzy sets will make up the linguistic variable $\tilde{A}$. Many partitioning methods are present in the FTS literature, such as the simplest Grid method [28] (all partitions have the same length), heuristic methods [4,6,14], meta-heuristic methods [3,15], entropy based [9] and clustering based. Each method has its own features and the best choice depends on the nature of the data and the associated context.

There are several categories of FTS methods, varying mainly by their *order* and time-variance. The order is the number of time-delays (lags) that are used in modeling the time series. Given the time series data F, First Order models need $F(t-1)$ data to predict $F(t)$, while Higher Order models require $F(t-1),\dots,F(t-p)$ data to predict $F(t)$.

After [28], Conventional FTS (CFTS) was proposed in [5] in order to simplify the training and forecasting procedures, also generating more readable rules. The Weighted FTS (WFTS), proposed in [31], adds weights in the rules to prioritize the recent ones. The more recent, the greater the weight of the rule. Trend Weighted FTS (TWFTS) [8] applies three different weights based on a trend component which can be ascending, descending or linear. Exponentially Weighted FTS (EWFTS) [17] is very similar to the WFTS, but uses exponential relation of weights.

The multivariate time series are matrices $Y \in \mathbb{R}^n$ where $n = |\mathcal{V}|$ and $\mathcal{V}$ is the set of attributes of Y. Each vector $y(t) \in Y$ contains all attributes $\mathcal{V}_i \in \mathcal{V}$ and there is a temporal dependence between these datapoints such that their temporal ordering - given by the time index $t \in T$ - must be respected. There are, on FTS literature, some methods for multivariate time series as [2] and [7].

There are on literature several FTS extensions embracing other aspects of time series forecasting. In [4] the α-cut parameter is discussed as a noise reduction and regularization parameter. An approach for dealing with non-stationarity is proposed in [1]. A interval forecasting approach were proposed in [23] (IFTS) and a probabilistic forecasting approach, based on ensemble methods, were proposed in [25].

Apply Big Data to machine learning algorithms is a trending topic in recent years [33]. But the literature of taming big time series did not board FTS methods directly, although exists approaches involving other fuzzy approaches [26].

Usually the FTS training and forecasting methods are not computationally expensive tasks, but one of the most notable drawbacks of above methods is the lack of scalability if the input data is very large. To fix this drawback this works proposes the Multivariate Weighted FTS method, a simple FTS method with focus on scalability that will be discussed on the next section.

3   The Multivariate Weighted Fuzzy Time Series Method

The Weighted Multivariate Fuzzy Time Series (WMVFTS) method was designed to allow several models to be trained individually with subsets of a greater dataset and later to be merged into a single model, feature that enhances the performance of model creation by enabling its distribution.

For each chosen variable $\mathcal{V}_i \in \mathcal{V}$ on Y, WMVFTS also incorporates several features present in the literature, represented by the hyperparameters on Table 1, giving versatility and flexibility to the model. The method is composed of two procedures: the training procedure and the forecasting procedure.

Table 1. WMVFTS hyperparameters for each variable $\mathcal{V}_i \in \mathcal{V}$

Alias	Parameter	Type	Description
k_i	Number of partitions	$\mathbb{N}^+$	The number of fuzzy sets that will be created in the linguistic variable $\widetilde{\mathcal{V}}_i$
μ	Membership function	$\mu : U \to [0,1]$	A function that measure the membership of a value $y \in U$ to a fuzzy set
α	α-cut	$[0,1]$	The minimal membership grade to take account on fuzzyfication process

The WMVFTS is a first order point forecaster of type Multiple Input/Single Output (MISO), then for the set of variables $\mathcal{V}$ one of them is chosen as the target (or endogenous) variable and the others are referred as the explanatory (or exogenous) variables. From now on, the target variable will be distinguished from the others by an asterisk, as $*\mathcal{V}$.

The training procedure, explained in Subsect. 3.1 and illustrated in Fig. 1, is a three stage process responsible to create a multivariate weighted FTS model $\mathcal{M}$. The final WMVFTS model $\mathcal{M}$ consists of a set of variables $\mathcal{V}$, a fuzzy linguistic variable $\widetilde{\mathcal{V}}_i$ for each $\mathcal{V}_i \in \mathcal{V}$ and a set of weighted fuzzy rules over the linguistic variables $\widetilde{\mathcal{V}}_i$. The inputs of the training procedure are the crisp time series training data Y and the set of hyperparameters for each $\mathcal{V}_i \in \mathcal{V}$.

The forecasting procedure, explained in Subsect. 3.2, aims to produce a point estimate $\widehat{y}(t+1)$ for the target variable $*\mathcal{V}$, given an input sample Y, using the linguistic variables $\widetilde{\mathcal{V}}_i$ and the induced fuzzy rules on model $\mathcal{M}$.

3.1 Training Procedure

Stage 1 *Partitioning*:

(a) *Defining $U_{\mathcal{V}_i}$*: The Universe of Discourse $U_{\mathcal{V}_i}$ defines the sample space, i.e., the known bounds of the variable $\mathcal{V}_i$, such that $U_{\mathcal{V}_i} = [\min(Y^{\mathcal{V}_i}) - D_1, \max(Y^{\mathcal{V}_i}) + D_2]$, where $D_1 = \min(Y^{\mathcal{V}_i}) \times 0.2$ and $D_2 = \max(Y^{\mathcal{V}_i}) \times 0.2$ are used to extrapolate the known bounds as a security margin, $\forall \mathcal{V}_i \in \mathcal{V}$.

(b) *$U_{\mathcal{V}_i}$ Partitioning*: Split $U_{\mathcal{V}_i}$ in k_i intervals U_j with midpoints c_j, for $j = 0..k_i$, where all the intervals have the same length;

(c) *Define the linguistic variable $\widetilde{\mathcal{V}}_i$*: For each interval $U_j \in U_{\mathcal{V}_i}$ create an overlapping fuzzy set $A_j^{\mathcal{V}_i}$, with the membership function $\mu_{A_j^{\mathcal{V}_i}}$. The midpoint

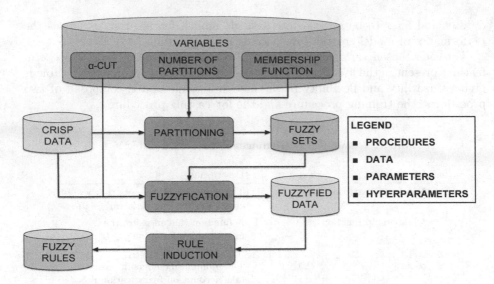

Fig. 1. WMVFTS sequential training process

of the fuzzy set $A_j^{\mathcal{V}_i}$ will be c_j, the lower bound $l_j = c_{j-1}$ and the upper
bound $u_j = c_{j+1} \; \forall \; j > 0$ and $j < k_i$, and $l_0 = \min U_{\mathcal{V}_i}$, $l_k = \max U_{\mathcal{V}_i}$.
Each fuzzy set $A_j^{\mathcal{V}_i}$ is a linguistic term of the linguistic variable $\widetilde{\mathcal{V}}_i$;

Stage 2 *Fuzzyfication*:

Transform the original numeric time series Y into a fuzzy time series
F, where each data point $f(t) \in F$ is an $n \times k$ array with the fuzzyfied
values of $y(t) \in Y$ with respect to the linguistic terms $A_j^{\mathcal{V}_i} \in \widetilde{\mathcal{V}}_i$, where
the fuzzy membership is greater than the predefined α-cut, i.e., $f(t) = \{A_j^{\mathcal{V}_i} \mid \mu_{A_j^{\mathcal{V}_i}}(y(t)^{\mathcal{V}_i}) \geq \alpha_i \; \forall A_j^{\mathcal{V}_i} \in \widetilde{\mathcal{V}}_i\}$;

Stage 3 *Rule Induction*:

(a) *Generate the temporal patterns*: The fuzzy temporal patterns associate
the fuzzyfied values $\mathcal{V}$ to a set of possible values of the target variable
$*\mathcal{V}$, such that $\mathcal{V} \to *\mathcal{V}$, with the format $A_j^{\mathcal{V}_0}, ..., A_j^{\mathcal{V}_n} \to A_j^{*\mathcal{V}}$, where the
precedent, or left hand side (LHS), is $f(t-1) = A_j^{\mathcal{V}_i}, \forall \mathcal{V}_i \in \mathcal{V}$, and the
consequent, or right hand side (RHS), is $f(t+1) = A_j^{*\mathcal{V}}$, $A_j^{*\mathcal{V}} \in \widetilde{*\mathcal{V}}$.

(b) *Generate the rule base*: Select all temporal patterns with the same precedent and group their consequent sets creating a rule with the format
$\mathcal{V} \to w_k \cdot A_k^{*\mathcal{V}}, w_j \cdot A_j^{*\mathcal{V}}, ...$, where the LHS is $f(t-1) = A_j^{\mathcal{V}_i}, \forall \mathcal{V}_i \in \mathcal{V}$ and
the RHS is $f(t+1) \in \{A_k^{*\mathcal{V}}, A_j^{*\mathcal{V}}, ...\}$ and the weights $w_j, w_k, ...$ are the
normalized frequencies of each temporal pattern such that:

$$w_i = \frac{\#A_j^{*\mathcal{V}}}{\#RHS} \quad \forall A_j^{*\mathcal{V}} \in RHS \tag{1}$$

where $\#A_i$ is the number of occurrences of A_i on temporal patterns with
the same precedent *LHS* and $\#RHS$ is the total number of temporal

patterns with the same precedent LHS. Each rule can be understood as the weighted set of possibilities which may happen on time $t + 1$ (the consequent) when a certain precedent $A_{i0}, ..., A_{i\Omega}$ is identified on previous lag (the precedent).

3.2 Forecasting Procedure

Step 1 *Fuzzyfication*: Compute the membership grade μ_{ji} for $y(t-1) \in Y$ such that $\mu_{ji} = \mu_{A_j^{\mathcal{V}_i}}(y(t-1))$, for each $A_j^{\mathcal{V}_i} \in \tilde{\mathcal{V}}_i$, for each $\mathcal{V}_i \in \mathcal{V}$;

Step 2 *Rule matching*: Select the K rules where all fuzzy sets $A_j^{\mathcal{V}_i}$ on the LHS, for each $\mathcal{V}_i \in \mathcal{V}$, have $\mu_{ji} > \alpha_i$; The rule fuzzy membership grade is shown below, using the minimum function as T-norm.

$$\mu_q = \bigcap_{j \in \tilde{\mathcal{V}}_i \; ; \; i \in \mathcal{V}} \mu_{ji} \tag{2}$$

Step 3 *Rule mean points*: For each selected rule q, compute the mean point mp_q of the target variable $*\mathcal{V}$ as below, where c_j is the c parameter of the μ function from fuzzy set $A_j^{*\mathcal{V}}$:

$$mp_q = \sum_{j \in *\tilde{\mathcal{V}}_i} w_j \cdot c_j \tag{3}$$

Step 4 *Defuzzyfication*: Compute the forecast as the weighted sum of the rule mid-points mp_q by their membership grades μ_q for each selected rule j:

$$\hat{y}(t+1) = \sum_{q \in K} \mu_q \cdot mp_q \tag{4}$$

3.3 Discussion

The selection of the hyperparameters k_i and α_i impact directly on the model accuracy and parsimony. The number of partitions of each variable affects the number of model rules directly, given that the maximum number of rules is a cartesian product between the fuzzy sets $A_j^{\mathcal{V}_i} \in \tilde{\mathcal{V}}_i$, for each $\mathcal{V}_i \in \mathcal{V}$.

There is a non-linear relationship between the number of rules and the model accuracy, a bias-variance trade off. Too few fuzzy sets makes the model underfit and too much makes the model overfit. The optimal number of k_i must be optimized for each problem, balancing the accuracy and the number of rules. The model parsimony affects the computational performance due the rule matching on forecasting procedure.

The α_i-cut, in the other hand, controls the variable sensibility by eliminating, on the rule induction stage, values with lower membership grades. It reduces the number of rules by preventing the capture of spurious patterns, generated by insignificant memberships or noise. The α_i-cut also enhances the forecasting process by eliminating lower related rules on rule search.

As cited before, the number of rules on the model may turn its matching computationally expensive. The implementation of the model used a KD-Tree indexed with the midpoints of each fuzzy set on the LHS of each rule, optimizing the search for applicable rules on rule matching step of the forecasting procedure.

Both procedures were designed to work *ad hoc*, i.e., sequentially. In the next section these methods will be embodied in a high level procedure that is able to distribute the training and forecasting to computational clusters.

4   Distributed Execution

Several stages of the training process defined on Sect. 3.1 can be executed in parallel, on a Single Instruction/Multiple Data (SIMD) approach, since the data splits preserve the inherent time ordering. This characteristic allows the procedure's distribution to enhance their scalability and enable it to handle big time series.

The Map/Reduce [11] was chosen as distribution paradigm due to its high adoption on Big Data literature. In such paradigm the computational cluster contains a master node, which centralizes the management of the tasks, and several slave nodes responsible for working tasks. The distributed execution is divided into two main phases, the map (scattering) and reduce (gathering). The Map phase splits the original dataset into smaller subsets and distributes them to the slave nodes. Each individual slave node will perform the same predefined set of computations on data and send the results back to the master node. The Reduce phase collects the results from the slave nodes and performs final aggregations of results.

The popularity of the Map/Reduce paradigm to tame Big Data problems became more visible after the first open source infrastructure frameworks became available, for instance Apache Hadoop[1]. More recently some infrastructure was developed to allow in-memory processing, turning the processing yet more efficient. In the next sections, the distribution strategies for the sequential methods are discussed using the Map/Reduce paradigm.

4.1   Distributed Training Procedure

The adaption of the sequential procedure defined on Sect. 3.1 to the distributed one requires just few interventions. The Stage 1 deeply depends on finding the universe of discourse of each variable $V_i \in V$. The general procedure splits the dataset over the working nodes where the U_{V_i} universes of discourse are computed. In the final step a general linguistic variable $\tilde{V}_i, \forall V_i \in V$ is computed by merging the locals U_{V_i} as $U = \bigcup U_{V_i}$ where $\bigcup$ is the merge step.

On the other hand, the design of WMVFTS allows the complete execution of stages 2 and 3 of training process without changes, as shown in Fig. 2. In this way, each computational node will produce its own complete model $\mathcal{M}_i$ using

---

[1] https://hadoop.apache.org/.

its subset of the data, and on the final step a unique model $\mathcal{M}$ is generated by merging the local models $\mathcal{M}_i$ as $\mathcal{M} = \bigcup \mathcal{M}_i$, where $\bigcup$ is the merge step. The complete distributed training procedure is listed below and illustrated in Fig. 2:

1. **Partitioning**:
   (a) **Share**: The hyperparameters k_i and μ_i for each $\mathcal{V}_i \in \mathcal{V}$ are shared across the cluster;
   (b) **Map**: Distribute the Y dataset over the slave nodes and, for each $\mathcal{V}_i \in \mathcal{V}$, find $U_{\mathcal{V}_i}^p$ returning it back to the master node;
   (c) **Reduce**: Collect the $U_{\mathcal{V}_i}^p$ from the slave nodes, mixing it on a unique interval as $U_{\mathcal{V}_i} = \bigcup U_{\mathcal{V}_i}^p$, where the $\bigcup$ will select the smallest lower bound and the greatest upper bound of each given interval;
   (d) **Create**: Once the universe of discourses $U_{\mathcal{V}_i}$ were defined, the partitioning of each linguistic variable $\widetilde{\mathcal{V}}_i$ is performed as the steps 2 and 3 of Stage 1 of the sequential procedure, creating the linguistic variables $\widetilde{\mathcal{V}}_i$.
2. **Fuzzyfication & Rule Induction**:
   (a) **Share**: The linguistic variables $\widetilde{\mathcal{V}}_i$, the target variable $*\mathcal{V}$ and the α_i hyper-parameter for each $\mathcal{V}_i \in \mathcal{V}$ are shared across the cluster;
   (b) **Map**: Distribute the Y dataset over the slave nodes and perform the fuzzyfication and rule induction for each subset, generating a local WMVFTS model $\mathcal{M}_p$ which is returned to the master;
   (c) **Reduce**: Collect all $\mathcal{M}_p$ models;
   (d) **Merge**: Create an empty WMVFTS model $\mathcal{M}$. For each rule $LHS \rightarrow RHS$ in all collected models $\mathcal{M}_p$:
      i. If $\mathcal{M}$ does not contain the LHS, then append the entire rule on $\mathcal{M}$;
      ii. If $\mathcal{M}$ contains the LHS, then for each $w_j \cdot A_j^{*\mathcal{V}} \in RHS$:
         A. If the RHS on $\mathcal{M}$ does not contain $A_j^{*\mathcal{V}}$, then append $w_j \cdot A_j^{*\mathcal{V}}$ on RHS and add w_j on $\#RHS$
         B. If the RHS on $\mathcal{M}$ contains $A_j^{*\mathcal{V}}$, then add w_j on existing weight and add w_j on $\#RHS$

4.2 Distributed Forecasting Procedure

The computational cost of the forecasting procedure, when compared with the training procedure, is low. The forecasting procedure bottlenecks are the fuzzyfi-cation and rule matching steps, and both of them can be optimized using spatial indexes, as proposed in Sect. 3.3, which are more efficient when executed locally. Also, as on every distributed procedure, the communication overhead makes this procedure inefficient for data with low volume.

However, there are occasions where the model needs to be used for forecasting in batch, where the input has high volume and one step ahead forecasting will be performed for each data point. These scenario is common in model testing, simulation and hyper-parameter optimization. In these cases it is profitable to share the parameters of the model $\mathcal{M}$ across several slave nodes and perform the forecasting on data splits, keeping its time ordering. The steps of the distributed forecasting procedure are listed below:

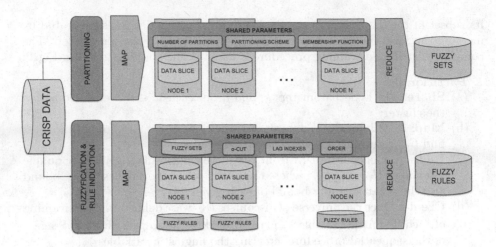

Fig. 2. Distributed training process with Map/Reduce

1. **Share**: The linguistic variables $\widetilde{\mathcal{V}}_i \in \mathcal{V}$ and the rules $\mathcal{M}$ are shared across the cluster;
2. **Map**: Distribute the Y dataset over the slave nodes, such that each split is labelled with its time ordering;
3. **Forecast** Each slave node receives a data split Y_p and executes the sequential process of Sect. 3.2, generating the estimates $\hat{Y}_p$, sending it back to the master node with the same time label received with Y_p;
4. **Reduce**: Collect the $\hat{Y}_p$ estimates from the slave nodes;
5. **Merge**: Sort the $\hat{Y}_p$ estimates by their time label and concatenate them on a unique dataset $\hat{Y}$.

5   Computational Experiments

The objective of this section is to evaluate empirically the performance of the proposed method stack using a large environmental time series focused on solar renewable energy.

The dataset used in this research came from SONDA - Sistema de Organização Nacional de Dados Ambientais (Brazilian National System of Environmental Data Organization)[2], a governmental project which groups environmental data (solar radiance, wind speed, precipitation, etc.) from INPE - Instituto Nacional de Pesquisas Espaciais (Brazilian Institute of Space Research). The chosen time series was the global solar horizontal radiation from the Brasilia telemetry station[3], recorded between 2012 and 2015, by minute, summing 2 million instances, where 70% were used on training and validation inside the hyperparameter grid search and the remaining data only for testing the generated

---

[2] http://sonda.ccst.inpe.br/.
[3] Code: BRB. Coordinates: 15°36' 03" S 47°42'47" O. Alt.: 1023m.

model. This time series has a long memory, multi-seasonality and several sources of noise, characteristics that the WMVFTS is expected to deal with.

To find the best hyper-parameters for the model and asses the performance of the distributed methods for several configurations, a Grid Search was performed. The search spaces for each hyper-parameter were presented on Table 2. The proposed methods were implemented using Python language using pyFTS library [24] infrastructure. The distributed procedure adopts the Apache Spark[4] implementation. The grid search involved experiments on a unique machine (with one core) and on computational clusters with 3, 5, 7 and 9 nodes.

Table 2. Hyper-parameters search spaces for each variable

Parameter	Search space
k	$[10, 100]$
μ	Triangular, trapezoidal, gaussian
α	$\{0, .05, .15, .2, .25, .3, .35, .4, .45, .5\}$

Table 3 and Figs. 3 and 4 show the performance of the sequential and distributed methods on above cited clusters, in terms of execution time (in seconds) and the speed up from the sequential, such that $S_p = \frac{T_1}{T_p}$, where S_p is the speed up for p nodes, T_1 is the time of the sequential execution and T_p is the time of the distributed execution with p nodes.

The experiments show that the trade-off between the distribution overhead and the benefit of the distributed computations starts to be profitable above the third node on the cluster. Up to 3 nodes the network overhead for the length of data makes the distributed algorithm not interesting. However, it can be seen that an average speed up of 1.6x was achieved on the training procedure, showing that the performance tends to increase on more robust computational clusters.

Table 3. Speed ups provided by the distributed method

Cores	Training		Forecasting	
	Time	Speed Up	Time	Speed Up
1	693.41 ± 11.05	-	232.24 ± 7.42	-
3	746.15 ± 29.30	0.92 ± 0.03	246.25 ± 10.82	0.94 ± 0.04
5	508.75 ± 12.21	1.35 ± 0.03	200.50 ± 6.34	1.15 ± 0.03
7	455.25 ± 7.98	1.51 ± 0.02	181.75 ± 5.06	1.27 ± 0.03
9	414.25 ± 8.16	1.66 ± 0.03	176.00 ± 3.93	1.31 ± 0.02

---

[4] https://spark.apache.org/.

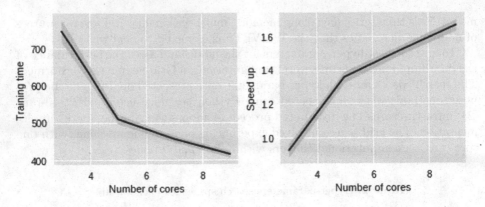

Fig. 3. Training times and speed ups

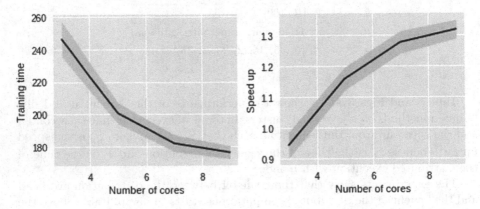

Fig. 4. Forecasting times and speed ups

The best WMVFTS hyper-parameters found on Grid Search are presented on Table 4, which generate the partitioning shown in Fig. 5. A sample of the generated model performance is shown in Fig. 6. This best generated model achieved an average RMSE of 58.8 ± 10.5 with 3,157 rules (the total possible number of rules, found by combining all linguistic variables, is 10,080).

Finally, the experiments generated an accurate forecasting model for the proposed time series, whose training procedure could be executed in feasible time thanks to the scalability provided by the distributed Map/Reduce implementation. The horizontal distribution increased the training and forecasting performances of the proposed method, enabling it to deal with high volume time series using cheap and easily affordable hardware.

Table 4. Best hyper-parameters found on Grid Search

Parameter	Month	Hour	Radiation
k	12	24	35
μ	Triangular	Triangular	Triangular
α	0.15	0.15	0.25

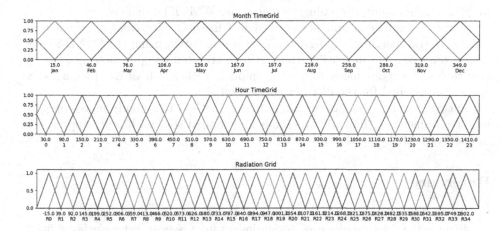

Fig. 5. Linguistic variables generated

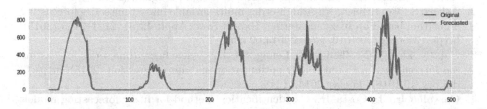

Fig. 6. Sample performance of best model generated

6 Conclusion

Fuzzy Time Series are data driven/non parametric forecasting methods with model readability, simplicity and accuracy. But even such methods suffer to handle big time series data, which *a priori* demand expensive computational resources.

The optimization of machine learning models for big time series is a challenging task to execute with sequential procedures or even parallel ones executed on a single machine. Thanks to the distributed computation frameworks, these methods are now enabled to work with massive datasets using cheap and available hardware infrastructure.

This work proposed the Weighted Multivariate Fuzzy Time Series method (WMVFTS) family which encompass sequential and distributed procedures for model training and forecasting. The distributed approaches were implemented using the Map/Reduce paradigm over an Hadoop/Spark cluster infrastructure.

This work also applied the proposed methods in the modelling and forecasting of a renewable energy source, the solar radiation on SONDA dataset - a big environmental multivariate time series with 2 million records supported by the brazilian government, obtaining very accurate WMVFTS models.

Computational experiments showed the method effectiveness, which performed a grid search for hyper-parameter optimization using the SONDA time series, only possible in feasible time with distributed computation, generating accurate and parsimonious forecasting models with low RMSE error and 1.6x speed up provided for the distributed method.

Future research will extend the proposed method to embody more complex hyper-parameter optimization methods and comparisons with other approaches in the literature.

References

1. Alves, M.A., Silva, P.C.D.L., Severiano, C.A.J., Vieira, G.L., Guimaraes, F.G., Sadaei, H.J.: An extension of nonstationary fuzzy sets to heteroskedastic fuzzy time series. In: 26th European Symposium on Artificial Neural Networks, Computational Intelligence and Machine Learning, Bruges, Belgium (2018)
2. Askari, S., Montazerin, N.: A high-order multi-variable fuzzy time series forecasting algorithm based on fuzzy clustering. Expert Syst. Appl. **42**(4), 2121–2135 (2015). https://doi.org/10.1016/j.eswa.2014.09.036
3. Cai, Q., Zhang, D., Zheng, W., Leung, S.C.H.: A new fuzzy time series forecasting model combined with ant colony optimization and auto-regression (2015). https://doi.org/10.1016/j.knosys.2014.11.003
4. Carvalho Jr., J., Costa Jr., C.: Identification method for fuzzy forecasting models of time series. Appl. Soft Comput. **50**, 166–182 (2017). https://doi.org/10.1016/j.asoc.2016.11.003
5. Chen, S.M.: Forecasting enrollments based on fuzzy time series. Fuzzy Sets Syst. **81**(3), 311–319 (1996). https://doi.org/10.1016/0165-0114(95)00220-0
6. Chen, S.M., Phuong, B.D.H.: Fuzzy time series forecasting based on optimal partitions of intervals and optimal weighting vectors. Knowl.-Based Syst. (2017). https://doi.org/10.1016/j.knosys.2016.11.019
7. Chen, S.M., Tanuwijaya, K.: Multivariate fuzzy forecasting based on fuzzy time series and automatic clustering techniques. Expert Syst. Appl. **38** (2011). https://doi.org/10.1016/j.eswa.2011.02.098
8. Cheng, C.H., Chen, T.L., Teoh, H.J., Chiang, C.H.: Fuzzy time-series based on adaptive expectation model for TAIEX forecasting. Expert Syst. Appl. **34**, 1126–1132 (2008). https://doi.org/10.1016/j.eswa.2006.12.021
9. Cheng, C.H.H., Chang, J.R.R., Yeh, C.A.A.: Entropy-based and trapezoid fuzzification-based fuzzy time series approaches for forecasting IT project cost. Technol. Forecasting Soc. Change **73**(5), 524–542 (2006). https://doi.org/10.1016/j.techfore.2005.07.004

10. Coelho, V.N., et al.: A self-adaptive evolutionary fuzzy model for load forecasting problems on smart grid environment. Appl. Energy **169**, 567–584 (2016). https://doi.org/10.1016/j.apenergy.2016.02.045
11. Dean, J., Ghemawat, S.: MapReduce: simplified data processing on large clusters. Commun. ACM **51**(1), 107–113 (2008)
12. Dincer, N.G., Akkuş, Ä.: A new fuzzy time series model based on robust clustering for forecasting of air pollution. Ecol. Inform. **43**, 157–164 (2018). https://doi.org/10.1016/J.ECOINF.2017.12.001
13. Guney, H., Bakir, M.A., Aladag, C.H.: A novel stochastic seasonal fuzzy time series forecasting model. Int. J. Fuzzy Syst. (2018). https://doi.org/10.1007/s40815-017-0385-z
14. Huarng, K.: Effective lengths of intervals to improve forecasting in fuzzy time series. Fuzzy Sets Syst. **123**(3), 387–394 (2001). https://doi.org/10.1016/S0165-0114(00)00057-9
15. Pal, S.S., Kar, S.: Fuzzy time series model for unequal interval length using genetic algorithm. In: Chandra, P., Giri, D., Li, F., Kar, S., Jana, D.K. (eds.) Information Technology and Applied Mathematics. AISC, vol. 699, pp. 205–216. Springer, Singapore (2019). https://doi.org/10.1007/978-981-10-7590-2_15
16. Qiu, J., Wu, Q., Ding, G., Xu, Y., Feng, S.: A survey of machine learning for big data processing. EURASIP J. Adv. Sig. Process. **67** (2016). https://doi.org/10.1186/s13634-016-0355-x
17. Sadaei, H.J., Enayatifar, R., Abdullah, A.H., Gani, A.: Short-term load forecasting using a hybrid model with a refined exponentially weighted fuzzy time series and an improved harmony search. Int. J. Electr. Power Energy Syst. **62**(from 2005), 118–129 (2014). https://doi.org/10.1016/j.ijepes.2014.04.026
18. Sadaei, H.J., Enayatifar, R., Lee, M.H., Mahmud, M.: A hybrid model based on differential fuzzy logic relationships and imperialist competitive algorithm for stock market forecasting. Appl. Soft Comput. J. **40**, 132–149 (2016). https://doi.org/10.1016/j.asoc.2015.11.026
19. Sadaei, H.J., Guimarães, F.G., Silva, C.J.D., Lee, M.H., Eslami, T.: Short-term load forecasting method based on fuzzy time series, seasonality and long memory process. Int. J. Approximate Reason. **83**, 196–217 (2017). https://doi.org/10.1016/j.ijar.2017.01.006
20. Severiano, C.A.C., Silva, P.P.C.L., Sadaei, H.J.H., Guimarães, F.F.G.: Very short-term solar forecasting using fuzzy time series. In: 2017 IEEE International Conference on Fuzzy Systems, Naples, Italy (2017). https://doi.org/10.1109/FUZZ-IEEE.2017.8015732
21. Silva, G.C., et al.: Fuzzy time series applications and extensions: analysis of a short term load forecasting challenge. In: International Conference on Time Series and Forecasting (ITISE 2018), vol. 770, Granada, Spain (2018). https://www.researchgate.net/publication/327756074
22. Silva, G.C., Silva, J.L.R., Lisboa, A.C., Vieira, D.A.G., Saldanha, R.R.: Advanced fuzzy time series applied to short term load forecasting. In: 4th IEEE Latin American Conference on Computational Intelligence. IEE, Guadalajara (2017)
23. Silva, P., Sadaei, H.J., Guimarães, F.: Interval forecasting with fuzzy time series. In: IEEE Symposium Series on Computational Intelligence (IEEE SSCI 2016), Athens, Greece (2016). https://doi.org/10.1109/SSCI.2016.7850010
24. de Lima e Silva, P.C.: pyFTS: Fuzzy Time Series for Python (2018). https://doi.org/10.5281/zenodo.597359

25. de Lima e Silva, P.C., Severiano Jr., C.A., Vieira, G.L., Guimarães, F.G., Sadaei, H.J.: Probabilistic forecasting with seasonal ensemble fuzzy time-series. In: XIII Brazilian Congress on Computational Intelligence, Rio de Janeiro (2017)
26. Singh, P.: Big Data Time Series Forecasting Model: A Fuzzy-Neuro Hybridize Approach (2015). https://doi.org/10.1007/978-3-319-16598-1_2
27. Singh, P.: A brief review of modeling approaches based on fuzzy time series. J. Mach. Learn. Cybern. **8**(2), 397–420 (2017).https://doi.org/10.1007/s13042-015-0332-y
28. Song, Q., Chissom, B.S.: Fuzzy time series and its models. Fuzzy Sets Syst. **54**(3), 269–277 (1993). https://doi.org/10.1016/0165-0114(93)90372-O
29. Talarposhti, F.M., Sadaei, H.J., Enayatifar, R., Guimarães, F.G., Mahmud, M., Eslami, T.: Stock market forecasting by using a hybrid model of exponential fuzzy time series. Int. J. Approximate Reason. **70**, 79–98 (2016). https://doi.org/10.1016/j.ijar.2015.12.011
30. White, T.: Hadoop: The Definitive Guide. O'Reilly Media, Inc., Sebastopol (2012)
31. Yu, H.K.: Weighted fuzzy time series models for TAIEX forecasting. Phys. A: Stat. Mech. Appl. **349**(3), 609–624 (2005). https://doi.org/10.1016/j.physa.2004.11.006
32. Zhang, S., et al.: Two-factor high-order fuzzy-trend FTS model based on BSO-FCM and improved KA for TAIEX stock forecastin. Nonlinear Dyn. (2018). https://doi.org/10.1007/s11071-018-4433-5
33. Zhou, L., Pan, S., Wang, J., Vasilakos, A.V.: Machine learning on big data: opportunities and challenges. Neurocomputing **237** (2017). https://doi.org/10.1016/j.neucom.2017.01.026

Internet of Things and Mobility

Mobility Aware RPL (MARPL): Mobility to RPL on Neighbor Variability

Vinícius de Figueiredo Marques[✉] and Janine Kniess

Programa de Pós-Graduação em Computação Aplicada,
Universidade do Estado de Santa Catarina, Joinville, SC, Brazil
vinicius.marques@edu.udesc.br, janine@udesc.br

Abstract. Low Power and Lossy Network (LLN) is a common type
of wireless network in IoT applications. LLN communication patterns
usually require an efficient routing protocol. The IPv6 Routing Protocol
for Low-Power and Lossy Network (RPL) is considered to be a possible
standard routing protocol for LLNs. However, RPL was developed for
static networks and node mobility decreases RPL overall performance.
These are the aims of the Mobility Aware RPL (MARPL), presented
in this paper. MARPL provides a mobility detection mechanism based
on neighbor variability. Performance evaluation results obtained by the
Cooja Simulator confirm the effectiveness of MARPL regarding DODAG
Disconnection prevention, Packet Delivery Rate, Packet Delivery Delay
and Overhead when compared to other protocols.

Keywords: Low Power and Lossy Networks ·
Wireless sensor network · Routing protocol · RPL · Mobility support

1 Introduction

Internet of Things (IoT) is a concept that aims to include wireless connectivity for day-to-day devices in order to enable many forms of smart applications. The motivation for such applications is the analysis of a huge amount of data collect by devices with internet connection. So information could be extracted from these data to enhance decision making and planning [13]. An IoT device is commonly composed by a sensing and wireless communication component. The sensing component is responsible for data collection, while the communication component might differs in terms of radio range and transmission power depending on the IoT application requirements [18]. The main characteristics of radio technologies used by IoT devices are short transmission range and low power consumption, since many IoT devices may be battery powered [18].

Low Power and Lossy Network (LLN) is a common type of network formed by IoT devices [15]. These devices also operates with low range radio technology, such as the IEEE 802.15.4, in order to be energy efficient [7]. The usage of low range radio technology demands a hop-by-hop communication model, which in

© Springer Nature Switzerland AG 2019
R. Miani et al. (Eds.): GPC 2019, LNCS 11484, pp. 59–73, 2019.
https://doi.org/10.1007/978-3-030-19223-5_5

turn demands an efficient routing protocol. IPv6 Routing Protocol for Low-Power and Lossy Networks (RPL) is a routing protocol for LLNs designed by the IETF group [17]. The motivation for the RPL design was the lack of a proper routing protocol for LLNs. RPL is compatible with IPv6 through the 6LoWPAN adaptation layer [17]. RPL is intended to become a standard routing protocol for data collection LLN applications.

Many IoT application domains, such as smart health and smart city, may have both static and mobile devices in the network [9]. Accordingly, the complexity of the network management is increased. Mobility demands a resilient routing protocol to handle frequent topology changes [19]. A routing protocol for LLN should have efficient mechanisms for rapid mobility detection, so it may diminish packet loss caused by the mobility of devices and minimize disconnection effects. The RPL routing protocol was initially designed for static LLN topologies. Therefore it faces some issues when used in mobile topologies, such as low packet delivery rate. Nevertheless, RPL can be enhanced to become well suited for mobile scenarios as well [6]. Some of the RPL issues are related to the lack of a mobility detection mechanism and efficient preferred parent selection in which mobility is taken into account.

Many routing protocols have been proposed to cope with absence of a mobility support for RPL [1,2,4,11] and [10]. Nevertheless, the majority of them differentiate the nodes as mobile or static only. MARPL can be used in scenarios where all nodes can move around, remaining static for some periods. Also, a mobility monitoring mechanism based on nodes neighbor variability is not exploited by the analysed related work. We defend the idea that neighborhood monitoring may provide an efficient way for the node detect its mobility and consequently, enhance RPL performance in mobile LLN. Thus, in order to increase Packet Delivery Rate while maintaining low overhead, we propose the Mobility Aware RPL (MARPL), a mobility support for the RPL routing protocol based on neighbor variability. MARPL brings the following main contributions:

- A metric related to node mobility called Neighbor Variability;
- A mechanism for mobility detection through the proposed metric, Neighbor Variability;
- A preferred parent unavailability prevention mechanism;
- A Trickle adjustment mechanism to increase the transmission of control messages only when it's necessary to minimize malicious disconnection effects.
- A route selection mechanism that takes node mobility into account.

The road map of this paper is organized as follows. Section 2 shows details about RPL and the issues faced by it when applied to mobile network topologies. Section 3 presents RPL mobility support proposals found in the literature. Section 4 depicts a mobility support for RPL, MARPL, proposed by the authors of this paper. The results of MARPL performance analysis are shown at Sect. 5. Finally, Sect. 6 presents the conclusions and future work.

2   RPL Mobility Issues

RPL was originally developed for static networks. However, mobility support is a requirement for a plenty of IoT application domains such as smart health and smart cities [9]. RPL faces a series of performance challenges when there are mobile nodes in the topology such as: packet loss and frequent disconnections. Nevertheless, RPL can be adapted for a better mobility support [6].

Devices executing RPL can perform three types of roles in a LLN: a root, a router or a host node [17]. A root node receives all data collected inside the LLN. A router and host node are responsible for data collection, but only a router node can forward packets towards the root node (i.e. a root node in the LLN). The RPL topology is based on a Directed Acyclic Graph (DAG). DAG is a graph with no cycles and all its edges are oriented toward one or more root nodes [17].

A Destination-Oriented DAG (DODAG) is a DAG rooted at a single root node. RPL has three control packet: DODAG Information Object (DIO), Destination Advertisement Object (DAO) and a DODAG Information Solicitation (DIS). DIO is used by RPL to construct and maintain a DODAG topology. When a node joins a DODAG, it does so by selecting a neighbor node with the best route towards the root node. In RPL, route quality is assess based on a rank value every node has when joined to a DODAG. This rank is a distance metric that indicates how far a node is from the root node. Therefore, the best route is the route with smaller rank [17]. After joining a DODAG, a node sends a DAO message to the selected neighbor with best rank. This neighbor with the best route towards the root node is called preferred parent in the RPL terminology. DIS is utilized for a node to request DIO messages from its neighbors to assess the possible routes towards the root node.

RPL has a proactive route discovery and topology construction approach through a periodic DIO transmission. The construction of a RPL DODAG is initiated by DODAG root nodes [17]. DIO control packet dissemination in RPL is controlled by the Trickle algorithm [16].

Trickle is an algorithm for DIO dissemination in RPL in a simple, robust and scalable manner [16]. Trickle has two mechanisms to achieve it: (i) when an inconsistency in the network is detected (e.g. loop), Trickle increases the signaling rate of messages as a way of solving the inconsistency. By contrast, Trickle exponentially decreases control message transmissions when the network is stable in order to save node energy; (ii) Trickle has a suppression mechanism in which DIO transmission is suppressed when its content is considered trivial [16].

In RPL, DIO propagation by the Trickle algorithm is configured through three parameters: I_{min}, I_{max} and k. I_{min} specifies the minimum period of time the suppression of DIO transmission can last. I_{max} regulates the maximum period of DIO suppression. k is the redundancy factor that is used to verify if a message can be transmitted at a specific time [16]. Trickle's transmission suppression is adjusted by the variable I. I value is selected randomly in the closed set $[I_{min}, I_{max}]$ and grows exponentially until it reaches I_{max} [16]. In MARPL, the Trickle adjustment is applied in the variable I, reducing it by half at any moment a mobile node is identified in the neighbor.

The suppression period regulated by the Trickle algorithm influences the performance of the RPL routing protocol in mobile topologies. When the suppression period is too long, nodes might not be able to detect a preferred parent disconnection efficiently since there are less control messages being propagated in the network [6]. Another issue with long periods of DIO suppression is that the DODAG will take longer to update its topology and, therefore, DODAG disconnection effects are aggravated.

It was found in the analysis of related works that most of the issues the RPL routing protocol faces when dealing with mobility are: the lack of efficient mechanisms for DIO and DIS control messages transmission for DODAG disconnection detection; a mechanism for mobility monitoring; and preferred parent selection in which it takes node mobility into consideration.

2.1 Preferred Parent Unavailability Detection

Figure 1a illustrates the RPL default operation mode when dealing with mobile nodes in the network topology. There are three nodes: one mobile and its two neighbor nodes, **A** and **B**. Assuming that mobile node has node **A** as its preferred parent, the mobile node still inside the radio range of node **A** while sending the first data packet. As depicted at Fig. 1a, the mobile node moves outside the range of node **A**'s communication radio. From then on, all data packet sent from the mobile node to its preferred parent, **A**, is lost. This is because RPL does not uses a mechanism for disconnection detection. The mobile node will keep to try

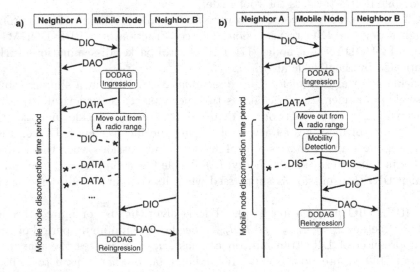

Fig. 1. (a) RPL message exchange without mobility support. (b) MARPL mobility support for RPL.

to send packets to node **A** until it receives a DIO messages from another node in the topology and the rank of this node is lesser than **A**'s rank. Otherwise, the mobile node will still consider node **A** as its preferred parent. As Fig. 1a depicts, the mobile node re-enters the DODAG only when it receives a DIO message from another node, **B**. By the means of simplicity, in this example, it is assumed that the rank of node **B** is lesser then node **A**.

The behavior of the Mobility Aware RPL (MARPL) is illustrated in Fig. 1b. When the mobile node moves out of node **A**'s radio range, MARPL's mobility management of the mobile node detects its movement. The canonical RPL specification does not specify how DIS control messages can be used to detect or avoid preferred parent unavailability. MARPL uses DIS messages when it detects the unavailability of the preferred parent due to mobility. This is performed through sending DIS messages to all its neighbors. The RPL canonical specification states that it might reset the Trickle's timer. Therefore, the mobile node could receive DIO messages from the potential new parents in the neighborhood of the node, see Fig. 1b. Therefore, the mobile node could re-enter the DODAG. It's expected that such mechanism could improve the RPL performance in terms of packet delivery rate. For example, compare the mobile node disconnection time period in Fig. 1b in contrast with Fig. 1a.

The usage of DIS messages to detect or avoid preferred parent unavailability may improve RPL performance in terms of reconnection delay or packet delivery rate. Nevertheless, Trickle adjustment might be necessary to improve RPL performance even further in mobile topologies. As mentioned before, RPL utilizes the Trickle timer for the dissemination of DIO messages. DIO is a RPL control message responsible for the DODAG construction and maintenance. In MARPL, Trickle is adjusted by dividing the suppression time by half when a mobile node is detected in the neighborhood. Consequently, it is expected that it could improve the responsiveness of MARPL in a mobile LLN. MARPL is detailed in Sect. 4.

3   Related Work

As stated at Sect. 2, the main issues regarding RPL when dealing with mobility are the lack of a mobility detection mechanism and link disconnection detection or prevention.

In [2], the authors argued that when a node disconnects from its preferred parent because of mobility, it might wait for too long to receive a DIO message. Therefore, increasing disconnection time and packet loss. In RPL, a node can update its preferred parent by receiving a DIO message from another candidate parent with lower rank [17]. [2] proposes a reverse Trickle algorithm that the DIO suppression time starts short and increases over time. The main rationale behind this idea is that mobile node connects to a preferred parent and it remains connected for a considerable amount of time. A drawback of [2] proposal is that it depends on the existence of static nodes. In contrast, MARPL makes no distinction between mobiles and static nodes, since mobiles nodes can stay static for a period of time.

In [4], the authors proposed a RPL extension named Mobile Compliant RPL (mRPL). mRPL utilizes a handoff mechanism called SmartHop [5]. The authors showed that mRPL enables the exchange of preferred parent efficiently with low overhead and power consumption. mRPL is a proactive preferred parent unavailability prediction mechanism. Therefore, it enables frequently control message exchange in order to assess if the preferred parent still connected. Nevertheless, it's expected that mRPL increases the network overhead in order to perform a fast disconnection identification.

In [11], the authors proposes MoRoRo, a mobility support mechanism for RPL. With MoRoRo, the node mobility can be detected based on packet loss rate by the increase of control message to assess link quality. [6] argues that packet loss is usual in LLN for its lossy links. Therefore, MoRoRo approach increases packet loss and leads to greater overhead. Nevertheless, [11] argues that the utilization of proactive handoff mechanisms in LLN (e.g. such as mRPL) is too aggressive because it generally performs detailed link analysis to detect preferred parent unavailability.

In [1], the authors proposed an enhancement for mRPL through a mobility prediction mechanism. Such mechanism seeks to solve two issues: the high RSSI interference from the environment and the costs of the increased overhead caused by proactive preferred parent unavailability proposal, such as mRPL. [1] mechanism is based on the following assumption: static nodes are required in the topology and their positions are known by the mobile nodes before the network starts to execute. This assumption may not be realistic for every LLN application scenario. Besides that, the authors' proposal has another drawback related to the processing power required by the static nodes in order to process the mobility predicting model.

In [10], the authors proposed a reverse-Trickle timer based on the Received Signal Strength Indication (RSSI) called Dynamic RPL (D-RPL). Every node executing D-RPL keeps track of the RSSI from the last two packet message for every single local-link neighbor node. It could be a control or data packet. Upon reception of a new packet, a node measures the RSSI and compare it to the last measurement from the same neighbor node. If the new RSSI plus a redundancy constant K_{RSSI} is lesser then the last RSSI, the reverse-Trickle timer is executed. The node also sends a local-link multicast DIS to all its neighbors. Otherwise, the default Trickle is executed.

Section 4 presents more details about MARPL, a proposal of mobility support for RPL. D-RPL and mRPL were implemented and compared against MARPL. These protocols were chosen for comparison because it is the most similar to the approach proposed in this paper. Details about the obtained results are show at Sect. 5.

4   Mobility Aware RPL

This section details the Mobility Aware RPL (MARPL) protocol. The design of MARPL encompass a mobility detection and a preferred parent unavailability detection mechanisms. Also, an enhancement to the RPL trickle timer.

As mentioned before, many IoT application domains requires a LLN with both static and mobile nodes. Thus, the routing protocol should be resilient enough to handle constant topology changes caused by node mobility. MARPL is compatible with the canonical RPL. Therefore, both MARPL and RPL can coexist in the same LLN. MARPL is composed by three mechanisms: (i) **mobility detection through the metric Neighbor Variability (γ)**; (ii) **preferred parent unavailability detection** and; (iii) **Trickle adjustment**. Algorithm 1 demonstrates the MARPL mechanisms.

Algorithm 1. MARPL Protocol

1: **procedure** MOBILITY_MONITORING
2:     start $T_{monitoring}$
3:     **if** received a packet **then**   ▷ data or control packet
4:         update sender IP, γ and RSSI in the neighbor table   ▷ if control packet
5:         **if** packet is a DIS or DAO from child node **then**
6:             TRICKLE_ADJUSTMENT
7:         **if** packet is DIO **then**
8:             $neighbor_{new\_rank} \leftarrow \alpha * neighbor_{old\_rank} + \beta * \gamma$
9:     **if** $T_{monitoring}$ expires **then**
10:         **if** $max\{var\{\Delta p_i\}_{i=1}^{y}\} > K_\gamma$ **then**   ▷ if there's a greater variance then K_γ
11:             $K_\gamma = max\{var\{\Delta p_i\}_{i=1}^{y}\}$ ▷ update K_γ with the greatest var
12:         $\gamma \leftarrow var\{\Delta p_i\}_{i=1}^{y}/K_\gamma$
13:         **if** received no packet from the preferred parent **then**   ▷ data or control
14:             **if** $\gamma > 0$ **then**
15:                 send DIS to neighbors
16:         restart $T_{monitoring}$
17: **procedure** TRICKLE_ADJUSTMENT
18:     $\gamma_{packet} \leftarrow \gamma$ from control packet   ▷ DIO, DIS or DAO
19:     **if** $\gamma_{packet} > \gamma$ **then**
20:         $I \leftarrow I/2$
21:         **if** $I < I_{min}$ **then**
22:             $I \leftarrow I_{min}$

As depicted in Algorithm 1, when a node first enters a DODAG, MARPL starts the $T_{monitoring}$ timer (line 2) in order to monitor the node mobility. $T_{monitoring}$ operates based on the rate of sensor data generation (i.e. the frequency of measurements made by the sensor). The frequency of sensor data generation may vary depending on the application characteristics.

At every data or control packet reception, MARPL updates its neighbor table with the packet sender IP, the proposed metric Neighbor Variability (γ) and the Received Signal Strength Indication (RSSI) (line 4). If the received packet is a DIS or DAO control message, MARPL analyses if it's necessary to adjust the Trickle timer (line 6). If the received packet is a DIO message, MARPL updates the neighbor's rank with its γ (line 8) by the Eq. 1.

$$neighbor_{new\_rank} = \alpha * neighbor_{old\_rank} + \beta * \gamma \tag{1}$$

In RPL, a preferred parent is selected by its rank value. The rank value is related by the distance of the preferred parent candidate to the root node. A rank value is calculated by a RPL objective function. MARPL updates the rank of a candidate parent with its γ value since γ is a metric related to the node mobility. The metric γ is updated by Eq. 2. Thus, it's expected that by using γ in the preferred parent selection, static nodes will have greater probability to be selected. Equation 1 shows how the rank value is updated. MARPL utilizes two weight parameters: α for the rank calculated by the RPL objective function and β for the Neighbor Variability metric.

The metric γ is derived by the variance of all the positive RSSI variations (i.e. $\Delta p_i \mid \Delta p_i > 0$) from every neighbor node $i \mid i \subset [1, y]$, y being all neighbors with two consecutive RSSI measurements, over a threshold K_γ. The RSSI (p) variation for every neighbor (i) is calculated by Eq. 3. K_γ is the maximum variance ever calculated by the node during its execution as depicted in Eq. 4 (Algorithm 1, lines 10 and 11).

The first step for Trickle's adjustment (Algorithm 1 line 17) is to read metric γ from the control packet (i.e. identified by γ_{packet} at line 18). If γ_{packet} is greater than the node's γ (line 19), the Trickle's variable I is reduced by half (line 20). It's important to make sure that $I >= I_{min}$ (line 21 and 22), since the following is a requirement for Trickle to work: $I \subset [I_{min}, I_{max}]$.

The MARPL Trickle adjustment mechanism is inspired by [10] and is executed in order to temporary increase DIO transmissions. It's expected that such increase might improve MARPL overall performance in terms of packet delivery rate through the prevention of further disconnections.

At every $T_{monitoring}$ expiration (Algorithm 1, line 9), MARPL updates the proposed metric Neighbor Variability (γ) (line 12). Using γ, a sensor node can identify its mobility. $T_{monitoring}$ execution time is adjusted by the frequency of sensor data generation. Consequently, it's expected that $T_{monitoring}$ execution time is sufficient to enable a node to received packets from all of its neighbors.

$$\gamma = \frac{var\{\Delta p_i\}_{i=1}^{y}}{K_\gamma} \mid y > 0, \Delta p_i > 0, K_\gamma > 0 \tag{2}$$

$$\Delta p_i = ||p_{i-1}|| - ||p_i|| \tag{3}$$

$$K_\gamma = max\{var\{\Delta p_i\}_{i=1}^{y}\} \tag{4}$$

For a better understanding of the rationale behind metric γ calculation, consider Fig. 2, an example of γ calculation. There are three different $T_{monitoring}$ periods: Fig. 2a, b and c. As can be seen in Fig. 2a, the mobile node **A** initially has three neighbors. **A**'s γ is set to 0 since there's no entries in its neighbor table with two consecutive RSSI measurements (p_{i-1} and p_i). Since there hasn't been calculated any variance yet, K_γ has no value. In Fig. 2b, node **A** moved and there are RSSI variations of neighbor **B**, **C** and **D**, besides the new neighbor **E**. The variations of neighbors **C** and **D** are positive (5 and 20 respectively). Therefore, γ can be calculated. Since it's the first time the variance (var) is calculated, K_γ will be set with the initial variance value. In Fig. 2b, the variance and K_γ have the same, 56, since it's the first time a RSSI variance is calculated. Thus, γ is updated to 1, $\frac{var}{K_\gamma} = 1$. In Fig. 2c, node **A** moved again. This time, it has three neighbors with RSSI variation. Nevertheless, only two of them (**D** and **E**) has positive variation (8 and 20 respectively). At Fig. 2c the variance is 36. Since $36 < 56$, K_γ is not updated and γ is updated to 0.64. It's possible to assess that at Fig. 2c, **A** neighbor varied less then at Fig. 2b. Thus, MARPL assumes that the mobile node **A** moved less at 2c.

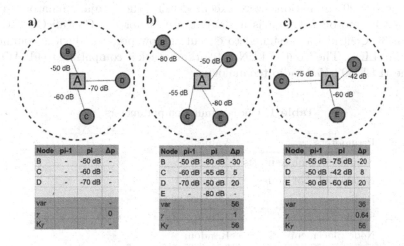

Fig. 2. MARPL γ calculation example.

Link disconnection prevention is critical in topologies with mobile nodes since disconnections will be frequent. RPL does not specify any preferred parent unavailability mechanism [17]. The RPL specification suggests the use of an external mechanism for this task [17]. Hence, if no packet from the preferred parent was received after $T_{monitoring}$ expiration (Algorithm 1, line 13) and node's $\gamma > 0$ (line 14), MARPL sends a DIS message to all the neighbor sensor nodes (line 15) to assess information about the available candidate parents. After that, $T_{monitoring}$ is started again (line 16).

Section 5 presents a performance analysis of MARPL against the canonical RPL specification [17], mRPL [4] and D-RPL [10].

5   Simulation Results and Analysis

This section presents a performance analysis of MARPL compared to the protocols, RPL [17], mRPL [4] and D-RPL [10]. mRPL and D-RPL where chosen by the following reasons: mRPL [4] is a proactive RPL mobility support proposal. In other words, it tries to identify as fast as possible the preferred parent unavailability to re-establish DODAG connection. mRPL aims to achieve this by making the sensor node to send periodic DIS messages to its preferred parent, while monitoring the reception of DIO messages in return. In contrast, MARPL doesn't try to monitor link disconnections since it utilizes Trickle's adjustments based on node mobility to diminish disconnections. D-RPL, proposed by [10], utilizes a reverse Trickle adjustment so that each time a sensor node identifies a RSSI variation, the Trickle suppression time is reduced by half. Differently, MARPL's reverse Trickle adjustment stands on the node's neighbor variability monitoring.

A total of 20 simulations were executed using the Cooja simulator [14] for each routing protocol. Cooja is a simulation tool for the Contiki Operational System [3]. Contiki was designed to execute in low powered devices commonly utilized in LLNs. The Contiki LLN networking stack is compatible to 6LoWPAN and the IEEE 802.15.4 radio technology.

Table 1. Cooja simulation parameters.

Parameters	Values
Number of mobile nodes	50
Number of root nodes	1, 2 and 3
Radio	CC2420 [8]
Simulation time	10 min
Node placement	Random
Mobility model	Steady-State Random Waypoint
Maximum node velocity	3 m/s
Maximum pause time	40 and 20 s
Data generation rate	8 s
Transmission medium	*Unit Disk Graph Medium* (UDGM)
Radio transmission range	50 m
Simulation area	300 m x 300 m
$T_{monitoring}$	8 s
α	1
β	1

Table 1 presents the parameters used in the simulations. The Steady-State Random Waypoint [12] mobility model was used to simulate node mobility. The Steady-State Random Waypoint model extends the Random Waypoint model to enable a time period of pause for the node [12]. All sensor nodes are mobile, but they can remain static for a period of time. Every node is randomly distributed in the simulation area and a new simulation seed is generated at every execution.

We simulated a LLN with a total of 50 sensor nodes within an area of 300 m of width and 300 of height. The number of root nodes varies from 1 up to 3 the time of pause was set in 40 s. We also simulated a scenario with 3 root nodes and 20 s of pause time to asses how the protocols would perform when dealing with more mobility in the topology.

The simulation analysis was performed in terms of: (i) **Packet Delivery Rate (PDR):** that means the rate of received data packets over sent data packets; (ii) **Packet Delivery Delay (PDD):** the time needed for a data packet to travel from the router to the root node; (iii) **DODAG Disconnections:** the number of DODAG disconnections caused by the node mobility. This metric enables to evaluate how good a protocol could prevent disconnections; (iv) **DODAG Reconnection Delay:** the time needed for a DODAG disconnection to be solved; (v) **Overhead:** the rate of control packets of a routing protocol over the total of control packets transmitted to the network.

We present simulation results varying the number of root nodes for every evaluated RPL based routing protocol (1 *Root*, 2 *Roots* and 3 *Roots* in the plots). Such simulations were executed with maximum node velocity of 3 m/s and pause time of 40 s. We also simulate LLN scenarios with a maximum pause time of 20 s and 3 Roots. These cenarios are presented in figures as 3 *Roots* (*). Reducing the time of pause increases the mobility in the LLN.

Figure 3 depicts the simulations results in terms of Packet Delivery Rate in milliseconds. In all simulated scenarios, MARPL presented the best performance in terms of PDR, 5.98% with 1 root node, 11.24% with 2 root nodes, 16.63% with 3 root nodes and 18.03% with 3 root nodes and maximum pause time of 20 s. As can be seen in Fig. 3, the PDR for all the protocol increases as the number of root nodes in the topology also increases when the time of pause is 40 s. When time of pause is 20 s, only MARPL presented a increase in PDR (3 *Roots* (*) in the plots). RPL, mRPL and D-RPL had a decrease in PDR when there's a increase of node mobility. This result is explained by the MARPL usage of the metric Neighbor Variability for Trickle adjustments and route selection. By doing so, MARPL enables the selection of routes with less mobility, therefore, increasing PDR even in more mobile LLNs. MARPL had also better performance in terms of delay with the smallest delays in almost all the evaluated scenarios depicted in Fig. 4. (36045 ms, 29057 ms, 26759 ms and 26912). It's also noticeable that packet delay decreases as the number of root node increases for all the evaluated routing protocols. Except for mRPL, since there's no statistical difference between the results of 1 Root, 2 Roots and 3 Roots.

Figure 5 depicts the results in terms of overhead. mRPL, D-RPL and MARPL presented greater overhead when compared with RPL. Nevertheless, no significant statistical difference was found in terms of overhead between the usage of 1, 2 or 3 root nodes in the LLN topology for any of the evaluated routing protocol. Among the RPL mobility support proposals, MARPL had the smallest average overhead (19.95% for 1 Root, 18.89% for 2 Roots, 18.81% for 3 Roots and 18.51% for 3 Roots and time of pause as 20 s). This result is justified because MARPL's mechanism of Trickle adjustment based on node mobility. Therefore, MARPL only increases control packet transmission when it's necessary to prevent link disconnections.

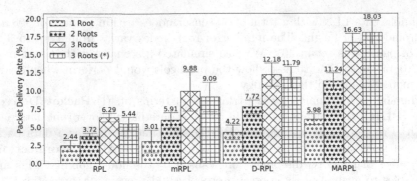

Fig. 3. Packet delivery rate.

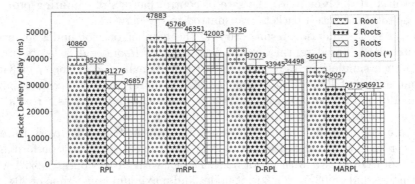

Fig. 4. Packet delivery delay.

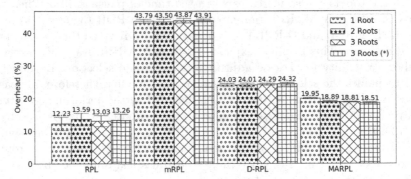

Fig. 5. Overhead.

By analyzing Figs. 6 and 7, we conclude that there is a relationship of DODAG Disconnections and DODAG Reconnection Delays. It's noticeable that there's a inverse correlation between the number of DODAG Disconnections and DODAG Reconnection Delays. It's possible to analyze the capacity of a routing protocol to prevent link disconnections by the number of

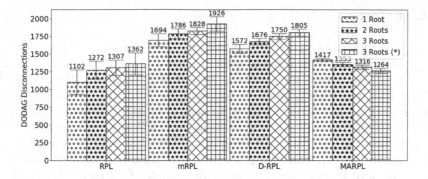

Fig. 6. DODAG disconnections.

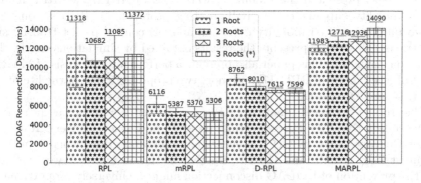

Fig. 7. DODAG reconnection delay.

DODAG Disconnections. It's also possible to analyze how fast a routing protocol is capable to detect a link disconnection by DODAG Reconnection Delays. Therefore, we can compare two different approaches to solve link disconnections: either to prevent link disconnections or to detect it as fast as possible. mRPL and D-RPL tries to detect link disconnection as soon as it happens. Therefore, both had the smallest DODAG Reconnection Delay, Fig. 7. In contrast, they had the greatest number DODAG Disconnections. An important result is the fact that while RPL, mRPL and D-RPL increases the disconnections when the number of root nodes also increases. On the contrary, MARPL decreases it, see Fig. 6. Another relevant result is related to the simulation with 3 *Roots* (∗) and 20 s of pause. Since, when there's more mobility in the topology, RPL, mRPL and D-RPL increase the number of DODAG Disconnections, MARPL presented lesser disconnections when dealing with a LLN with increased mobility. Therefore, we conclude that MARPL is better suited to mobile LLNs. MARPL's link disconnection prevention approach might be a better solution since it had better PDR and delay while maintaining lower overhead when comparing it against other evaluated proposals.

6   Conclusion

RPL is a routing protocol for Low Power and Lossy Networks (LLNs), a common type of network formed by Internet of Things (IoT) applications. Mobility support is a requirement for a wide range of IoT applications. Regardless the fact that RPL was initially intended for static LLNs (i.e. LLNs composed only by static devices) it can be enhanced to include mobility support capabilities. Node mobility increases link disconnections and consequently increases packet loss. RPL faces a series of issues when dealing with mobile nodes. Natively, RPL doesn't have a way of detecting when a node is moving, nor a way of identifying when a link with its preferred parent is unavailable. This paper discussed the issues RPL faces when it deals with mobile nodes and approaches to solve them.

This paper presented the Mobility Aware RPL (MARPL). MARPL intends to add mobility support to the RPL routing protocol. MARPL is composed by two mechanisms: (i) mobility detection and (ii) control packet transmission adjustment. This paper presents the results obtained by simulations executed in the Cooja simulator. This paper also presents a performance analysis of MARPL proposal, the canonical RPL [17] and more two proposals found in the literature: mRPL [4] and D-RPL [10].

The results indicates that MARPL has better performance in relation to Overhead, DODAG Disconnection prevention, Packet Delivery Rate and Packet Delivery Delay. MARPL prevents more disconnections when comparing it against RPL, mRPL and D-RPL. By the simulation analysis, we concluded that the prevention of DODAG disconnection might be inversely proportional to the delay of DODAG reconnection. It means that, efforts to prevent link disconnections may increase reconnection delay. Since MARPL presented better PDR in comparison with other proposals, we believe that disconnection prevention is more important than disconnection detection to face frequent link disconnections caused by node mobility.

It was concluded that further studies can be done to improve MARPL transmission delay while preserving good PDR and Overhead results. Other further improvements are in terms of diminish the DODAG Reconnection Delay while keeping a small number of disconnections. MARPL outperforms all the three proposals in terms of Packet Delivery Delay. Nevertheless, an overhead increase is expected because of the node mobility management requires a high number of control messages since the topology will need to be updated more frequently. We believe that it's necessary for the RPL mobility management to only increase such control message transmissions in specific moments. MARPL only increases control message transmission when a node has mobile nodes connected to it in its neighborhood. It causes the DODAG topology to be updated when needed only. Thereby, preventing disconnections from happening.

References

1. Bouaziz, M., Rachedi, A., Belghith, A.: EKF-MRPL advanced mobility support routing protocol for internet of mobile things: movement prediction approach. Future Gener. Comput. Syst. **93**, 19–24 (2017)
2. Cobarzan, C., Montavont, J., Noel, T.: Analysis and performance evaluation of RPL under mobility. In: Computers and Communication (ISCC), pp. 1–6 (2014)
3. Dunkels, A., et al.: The Contiki OS: the operating system for the Internet of Things (2011). http://www.contikios.org. Accessed Dec 2018
4. Fotouhi, H., Moreira, D., Alves, M.: mRPL: boosting mobility in the Internet of Things. Ad Hoc Netw. **26**, 17–35 (2015)
5. Fotouhi, Hossein, Zuniga, Marco, Alves, Mário, Koubaa, Anis, Marrón, Pedro: Smart-HOP: a reliable handoff mechanism for mobile wireless sensor networks. In: Picco, Gian Pietro, Heinzelman, Wendi (eds.) EWSN 2012. LNCS, vol. 7158, pp. 131–146. Springer, Heidelberg (2012). https://doi.org/10.1007/978-3-642-28169-3_9
6. Gara, F., Saad, L.B., Hamida, E.B., Tourancheau, B., Ayed, R.B.: An adaptive timer for RPL to handle mobility in wireless sensor networks. In: 2016 International Wireless Communications and Mobile Computing Conference (IWCMC), pp. 678–683, Paphos, Cyprus (2016)
7. Gubbi, J., Buyya, R., Marusic, S., Palaniswami, M.: Internet of Things (IoT): a vision, architectural elements, and future directions. Future Gener. Comput. Syst. **29**(7), 1645–1660 (2013)
8. Instruments, T.: CC2420 datasheet. Reference SWRS041B, pp. 1–93, December 2007. http://www.ti.com/product/CC2420
9. Iova, O., Picco, P., Istomin, T., Kiraly, C.: RPL: the routing standard for the Internet of Things... or is it? IEEE Commun. Mag. **54**(12), 16–22 (2016)
10. Kharrufa, H., Al-Kashoash, H., Al-Nidawi, Y., Mosquera, M.Q., Kemp, A.H.: Dynamic RPL for multi-hop routing in IoT applications. In: Wireless On-demand Network Systems and Services (WONS), pp. 100–103. IEEE, Jackson (2017)
11. Ko, J., Chang, M.: MoMoRo providing mobility support for low-power wireless applications. IEEE Syst. J. **9**(2), 585–594 (2015). https://doi.org/10.1109/JSYST.2014.2299592
12. Navidi, W., Camp, T.: Stationary distributions for the random waypoint mobility model. IEEE Trans. Mobile Comput. **1**, 99–108 (2004)
13. Oppitz, M., Tomsu, P.: Internet of Things. Inventing the Cloud Century, pp. 435–469. Springer, Cham (2018). https://doi.org/10.1007/978-3-319-61161-7_16
14. Osterlind, F., Dunkels, A., Eriksson, J., Finne, N., Voigt, T.: Cross-level sensor network simulation with COOJA. In: 2006 31st IEEE Conference on Local Computer Networks, pp. 641–648. IEEE, Tampa (2006)
15. Paul, P.V., Saraswathi, R.: The Internet of Things–a comprehensive survey. In: 2017 International Conference on Computation of Power, Energy Information and Communication (ICCPEIC), pp. 421–426. IEEE, Melmaruvathur, India (2017)
16. The trickle algorithm: RFC 6206. No. RFC 6206, pp. 1–13 (2011)
17. RFC 6550: RPL: IPv6 routing protocol for low-power and lossy networks. No. RFC 6550, pp. 1–157 (2012)
18. Sethi, P., Sarangi, S.R.: Internet of Things: architectures, protocols, and applications. J. Electr. Comput. Eng. **2017**, 1–26 (2017)
19. Zhao, M., Kumar, A., Chong, P.H.J., Lu, R.: A comprehensive study of RPL and P2P-RPL routing protocols: implementation, challenges and opportunities. Peer Peer Netw. Appl. **10**(5), 1232–1256 (2017)

A Method Based on Dispersion Analysis for Data Reduction in WSN

Samuel Oliveira[1,2(✉)], Janine Kniess[2], and Vinicius Marques[2]

[1] Department of Exact and Technological Sciences (DCET),
Federal University of Amapá (UNIFAP), Macapá, AP, Brazil
`samuel.oliveira@unifap.br`
[2] Graduate Program in Applied Computing (PPGCA),
Santa Catarina State University (UDESC), Joinville, SC, Brazil
`janine.kniess@udesc.br, vinicius.marques@edu.udesc.br`

Abstract. Wireless Sensor Networks (WSN) are commonly used to collect observations of real-world phenomena at regular time intervals. Generally, sensor nodes rely on limited power sources and some studies indicate that the main source of energy consumption is related to data transmission. In this paper, we propose an approach to reduce data transmissions in sensor nodes based on sensor data dispersion analysis. This approach aims to avoid transmitting measurements whose values present low dispersion. Simulations were carried out in the Castalia Simulator and the results were promising in reducing data transmissions while maintaining data accuracy and low energy consumption.

Keywords: WSN · Dispersion analysis · Data reduction

1 Introduction

In Wireless Sensor Networks (WSN), commonly used in the context of Internet of Things (IoT), sensor nodes usually have limited storage space and consume large amounts of power. Therefore, it is common for sensor nodes to send the data collected immediately to the base stations, called sink nodes, which are responsible for forwarding the messages to their final destination. Since WSNs are usually composed by a great number of sensor nodes, data transmission is a dominant factor for communication overhead as well as for power consumption.

[1] points out that more than 80% of total energy consumption in WSN may be related to data transmission. Thus, the reduction of data transmissions in WSNs can prolong their life time. In addition, [1] emphasizes that reducing data transmissions in WSNs not only results in energy savings, but also results in reducing network bandwidth consumption. It allows a more efficient use of the available resources.

In this paper, we present the following contributions: (i) **A Method for Reducing Data Transmissions in WSNs**; (ii) **Algorithm for Initialization Phase**; (iii) **Data Reconstruction Algorithm**. The method for Data

© Springer Nature Switzerland AG 2019
R. Miani et al. (Eds.): GPC 2019, LNCS 11484, pp. 74–88, 2019.
https://doi.org/10.1007/978-3-030-19223-5_6

Reduction targets the sensor nodes acting in monitoring applications, such as, temperature monitoring, CO_2 control, among others. The method is based on the dispersion analysis of sensor readings, which aims to identify and to avoid sending sets of measurements with values that demonstrate low dispersion. In this case, only a normalized value corresponding to the whole set is sent. This reduction is intended to use the network resources efficiently, such as bandwidth and energy, while maintaining high accuracy in the data collected by the sensors. The Algorithm for the Initialization Phase is used to define a value that will be used as the maximum acceptable limit so that two or more measurements are considered to have small dispersion and if they need to be transmitted. The Data Reconstruction Algorithm aims to reconstruct the normalized data, optimized by the sensors, in order to retrieve the original data set at its final destination.

This paper is structured as follows: In Sect. 2, we provide a brief overview of related works. In Sect. 3, we present the proposed approach. Such approach contains a dispersion analysis algorithm for reducing the number of data transmissions and an algorithm for data reconstruction. The performance evaluation and simulations descriptions are included in Sect. 4. Finally, in Sect. 5, we conclude the paper and describe future directions.

2   Background and Related Work

This section briefly discusses some of the related work that deal with the problem of reducing data transmission in monitoring applications, based on three main categories: Data Prediction, Data Aggregation and Compressing Sensing (CS).

Data Prediction is a technique that aims to estimate future values based on historical data. Based on this principle, the measurements history from a particular sensor node can be used by the sink node in order to predict future measurements. In this case, the goal is to prevent the sensor node from sending a data that can be predicted by the sink, considering a certain level of accuracy.

In [4], the authors adopt the Dual Prediction Scheme (DPS). DPS applies prediction algorithms both in the sensor and sink nodes, in order to predict the value of future measurements. When the prediction on the sensor reaches high accuracy, the original data is not sent. Instead, the sink node forwards the predicted value, thus providing less overhead in the internal network communication. Results shows that when using the DPS added to data aggregation techniques, it is possible to save up to 92% of the energy consumed by the data transmissions.

The Adaptive Method for Data Reduction (AMDR), proposed by [6], is based on the Least Mean Square (LMS) algorithm, combining two LMS filters of different sizes to estimate the values collected by sensor nodes. This estimation is performed both in sensor nodes and sink nodes, so that the sensor nodes need to transmit only their values that deviate significantly from the predicted values. It was found that AMDR reached a high reduction (around 95%) in data transmissions.

Data Aggregation is a technique commonly used in WSNs aiming to aggregate data coming from different sensor nodes. In this approach, some specific nodes are defined as aggregators. Aggregators are responsible for collecting data from different sensors and to send it all at once, rather than simply retransmitting it individually. This technique reduces the number of transmitted packets in the network and energy consumption.

In [17], the algorithm Continuous Enhancement Routing (CER) is proposed. CER uses the Biased Random Key Genetic Algorithm (BRKGA) to compute the routing tree of a WSN. CER seeks to find routing trees close to the optimal one, performing data aggregation for the longest time possible. The results showed that CER generates higher overhead when compared to the Shortest Path Tree (SPT) algorithm because it creates a high number of routing trees. Therefore, it results in an expressive amount of control packets.

In [10], on the other hand, a method denominated Lifetime Balanced Data Aggregation (LBA) was presented. The main objective of LBA is to extend the lifetime of the network considering its dynamism and heterogeneity. LBA also aims to guarantee the minimum delay in the data delivery. The results show that LBA has better performance when all the nodes initiate their activities with the same amount of energy in their batteries.

Signal processing techniques have also been explored in WSNs, such as, the Compressive Sensing technique. This technique applies a measurement matrix $\Phi \in \mathbb{R}^{m \times n}$ onto a n-dimensional signal vector $x = (x_1, ..., x_n)^T$ to obtain an m-dimensional signal $y \in \mathbb{R}^m$. The data reconstruction can be performed through the Restricted Isometry Property (RIP), which guarantees recovery of x from of the compressed signal y if $m \geq k \log n/k$.

In [12], the authors utilizes the principle of adaptive sampling to transmit only the measurements that indicate a significant change in the collected data. This approach takes advantage of the spatial and temporal correlation between the data collected by the sensors in order to achieve greater compression. The authors used a stochastic model based on Bayesian Inference to define the set of measurements to be transmitted by the sensor node. The data reconstruction is performed by the sink through the Belief Propagation Algorithm. [12] approach achieved better results than Basis Pursuit and Joint-BP methods in terms of accuracy of data reconstruction and energy consumption.

In [7], the authors proposed a compressive and adaptive data collection scheme based on the adaptive adjustment of the frequency in which the measurements are performed by the sensor. They also proposed a data reconstruction algorithm based on the adaptive version of the greedy algorithm called Stagewise Orthogonal Matching Pursuit (StOMP). StOMP adjusts the scatter limit (parameter) based on the reconstruction error. The results showed that the method achieves greater accuracy in the reconstruction and lower power consumption when compared to the Principal Component Analysis (PCA) method. The PCA method is also used for signal reconstruction in Compressive Sensing.

Although the described works present good results regarding the reduction of data transmission in WSNs, some limitations can be discussed. In works based on Data Prediction and Compressive Sensing, it is expected that the sink node has large amounts of energy and high processing power. In aggregation-based works, the delay can be a determining factor, since an aggregator node must wait for the arrival of packets coming from other sensors to be aggregated. The data reduction technique proposed in this work aims to achieve data reduction by exploring the dispersion analysis of the data collected by the sensors. Such technique also aims to reduce energy and bandwidth consumption. In addition, the data reconstruction algorithm proposed in this work aims to reconstruct the data originally collected by the sensors, and normalized by the sink node, in order to present the exact number of measurements at the final destination.

3   Data Reduction Approach

In WSN applications, the sensor nodes generally perform measurements of variables from the physical environment with a predefined frequency. As a result, an orderly data collection is created. For example, this collection may be called S, beginning at a point in time t_0, and following up to a final time t_n. Specifically, $S = \{s_0, s_1, s_2, ..., s_n\}$, in which the n-th element is a pair $s_n = (V_n, t_n)$. The first element of the pair, V_n, indicates the value of the variable detected by the sensor (for example: temperature value), while the second element of the pair, t_n, indicates the time in which the reading occurred.

According to [5], the measurements performed by the sensors in monitoring applications often return very similar or even identical values. Although this behavior may not be prevalent in all types of monitoring applications, it is possible to explore minor periods of low dispersion in sensor data in order to reduce the number of data transmissions. Thus, the method proposed in this work is based on the sensor data dispersion analysis, which aims to identify measurements sets with values that show low dispersion level. That is, values close to each other.

3.1   Algorithm for Reducing Data Transmissions in WSN

The approach for reducing data transmissions on sensor nodes works as explained in the following. Suppose two or more measurements of a particular sensor node demonstrate a certain level of similarity (low dispersion) according to a predefined dispersion measure. The sensor node maintains temporarily this set of values in a variable in order to avoid transmitting all the values. Next, the first and last measurement from this set will be transmitted by the sensor node in one message. The sensor node will also transmit the number of measurements of this set. The transmitted data will be used afterwards by the Data Reconstruction Algorithm. From then on, the variable used to store the set of measurements can be erased and the analysis of the collected values is resumed by the sensor in order to find new sets of measurements with low dispersion level.

The dispersion measure is represented by a non-negative real number. It is zero when the data are equal. The dispersion measure value increases as the data diverge. In the context of this work, the dispersion analysis is performed at each measurement of the sensor nodes. The dispersion measure is represented by the Manhattan Distance, expressed in Eq. 3.1, calculated between V_i e V_{i-1}.

$$D_{V_i,V_{i-1}} = |V_i - V_{i-1}| \tag{3.1}$$

In order to allow the sensor node to be able to identify a set of measurements with low dispersion, a parameter called D_{max} is defined. This parameter represents the maximum acceptable limit for the distance between collected values.

The proposed method for data reduction based on the dispersion analysis is presented in Algorithm 3.1.

Algorithm 3.1. Data Reduction Based on Dispersion Analysis

1: $FirstReadings[]$ ▷ First measurements from sensor
2: $N \leftarrow 50$ ▷ Number of measurements in the Initialization Phase. Ex: 50
3: $N_V \leftarrow 1$ ▷ Counter of measurements not transmitted
4: $N_{max} \leftarrow 21$ ▷ Maximum number of transmissions avoided. Ex: 21
5: $D_{max} \leftarrow$ GetDMaxValue($firstReadings[], N$) ▷ Defines D_{max} value
6: $V_{i-1} \leftarrow FirstReadings[N-1]$
7: $first_V \leftarrow V_{i-1}$
8: **while** True **do**
9:    $V_i \leftarrow$ GetSensorValue()
10:   **if** $|V_i - V_{i-1}| \leq D_{max}$ **and** $N_V < N_{max}$ **then**
11:     $last_V \leftarrow V_i$
12:     $N_V \leftarrow N_V + 1$
13:   **else**
14:     **if** $N_V > 1$ **then**
15:       SendDataToSink($(first_V, last_V, N_V)$) ▷ Data Trasmission (Tuple)
16:       $first_V \leftarrow V_i$
17:     **else**
18:       SendDataToSink((V_{i-1})) ▷ Data Trasmission (Single Measurement)
19:       $first_V \leftarrow V_i$
20:     **end if**
21:     $N_V \leftarrow 1$
22:   **end if**
23:   $V_{i-1} \leftarrow V_i$
24: **end while**

If the distance between the value of the measurements V_i and V_{i-1} is less than or equal to D_{max}, then the measurement V_i will not be transmitted, but will be stored temporarily in a variable, named $last_V$ (line 11). In addition, a counter N_V is incremented (line 12). This procedure will be repeated as long as the condition $D_{V_i,V_{i-1}} <= D_{max}$ is satisfied (line 10). In other words, this procedure will be repeated until the distance between the value of a given measurement and the value of its predecessor measurement is equal or greater than D_{max}. In this case, a tuple is transmitted (line 15) containing the first and last measurement of this set as well as the variable (N_V). N_V will be used by the Data Reconstruction Algorithm, discussed in Subsect. 3.3.

The number of measurements with low dispersion level on a sensor node can be very large. To prevent a sensor from storing a very large number of measurements, as well as avoiding a high delay in sending the data, a parameter called N_{max} is defined. N_{max} is used to define a maximum number of measurements in a set with low dispersion level. The N_{max} tuning depends on the requirements of each monitoring application in relation to the delivery delay. The lower the desired delay, the smaller the value of N_{max}. Consequently, less reduction is achieved. A taxonomy for the choice of N_{max} according to the different types of application is proposed in Sect. 3.2.

The initial phase of the Algorithm 3.1 comprises the collection of the first measurements of the sensor node. This data is used to find the ideal value for D_{max} through the function GETDMAXVALUE() (line 5), whose details will be discussed in the next section.

3.2 Initialization Phase: Tuning D_{max}

In order to make a proper tuning of D_{max}, an algorithm is proposed to analyze the first measurements of a sensor node and perform this choice automatically (Algorithm 3.2). For this task, a parameter called e_{max} is defined, which represents the maximum acceptable error in data reconstruction. This parameter must be adjusted according to the requirements of each application.

The algorithm for tuning D_{max} is presented in Algorithm 3.2.

Based on the first measurements from a particular sensor node, the algorithm for tuning D_{max} generates a reduced dataset through the function DATAREDUCTION() which is an adaptation of the Algorithm 3.1. In this case, the D_{max} parameter must start with a low value, so that it can be increased until it finds an optimal value. Then, this new dataset is reconstructed through the function DATARECONSTRUCTION(), which is an adaptation of the Algorithm 3.3, presented in Sect. 3.3. Then, the reconstructed dataset is compared with the original dataset. If the error obtained in the data reconstruction is less than e_{max}, repeat the procedure by raising the value of D_{max}. That is, the value of D_{max} will be raised while the error obtained in the reconstruction is less than or equal to the maximum acceptable error.

It is important to emphasize that the raise of D_{max} value not necessarily implies on the raise of the error. The parameter N_{max}, presented in the Sect. 3.1, may prevent reaching a higher level of reduction, and hence, a raise in the error. Thus, if the obtained error never reaches the maximum acceptable error, the repetition structure (while) can be broken after a predetermined number of iterations (ex. 100) through the variables *flag* and *counter*.

The error obtained in data reconstruction is determined by calculating the Mean Absolute Error (MAE). When MAE is equal to or greater than e_{max}, the final value of D_{max} will be returned.

Defining a value for the maximum acceptable error is crucial for the value of D_{max} to be chosen. In [9] it is emphasized that some monitoring applications are critical and require high accuracy and low message delivery delays. Based on this, a taxonomy was created in order to classify different application types according to their requirements, assigning specific values for N_{max} and e_{max}. Specifically, we created three classes of monitoring applications (0, 1 and 2) which are based on their requirements related to the delay in the message transmissions and the maximum acceptable error in data reconstruction. Class 0 is less delay tolerant and requires more accuracy in the reconstructed data. Class 2, however, requires a lower level of accuracy and is more delay tolerant. Class 1 has intermediate values between classes 0 and 2. In Sect. 4 we present an example of the classification of real datasets used in the experiments according to the proposed taxonomy.

Algorithm 3.2. Tuning D_{max}

1: **function** GETDMAXVALUE($FirstReadings[], N$)
2:     $D_{max} \leftarrow 0.01$ ▷ D_{max} initial value. Ex: 0.01
3:     $MAE \leftarrow 0$ ▷ Mean Absolute Error
4:     $e_{max} \leftarrow 0.5$ ▷ Maximum acceptable error. Ex: 0.5
5:     $flag \leftarrow 0$
6:     $counter \leftarrow 0$
7:     **while** $MAE \leq e_{max}$ **do**
8:         **if** $counter > 100$ **then**   ▷ A control for preventing infinite loops
9:             break
10:        **end if**
11:        $ReducedData \leftarrow$ DATAREDUCTION($FirstReadings[], N, D_{max}$)
12:        $ReconstructedData \leftarrow$ DATARECONSTRUCTION($ReducedData[], N$)
13:        $MAE = (\sum_{i=0}^{n} |FirstReadings[i] - ReconstructedData[i]|)/n$
14:        **if** $flag == EAM$ **then**
15:            $counter \leftarrow counter + 1$
16:        **else**
17:            $counter \leftarrow 1$
18:        **end if**
19:        $D_{max} \leftarrow D_{max} + 0.01$
20:        $flag \leftarrow MAE$
21:    **end while**
22:    **return** $D_{max} - 0.02$
23: **end function**

3.3   Data Reconstruction Algorithm

An important issue is to ensure that the data sent by the sensor nodes shows the correct frequency at which they were detected. With this aim, we propose the Data Reconstruction Algorithm, presented in Algorithm 3.3.

The Algorithm 3.3 is based on the asymptotic mean of a measurements set with low dispersion level. That is, the Data Reconstruction Algorithm is responsible for defining evenly spaced values between two limits. These limits are represented by the first and the second element from the tuple sent by the sensor node (first and last measurements from a set of measurements with low dispersion level).

Algorithm 3.3. Data Reconstruction

1: **function** DATARECONSTRUCTION($start, end, num$)
2:     $output = []$
3:     $delta \leftarrow (end - start)/(num - 1)$
4:     **for** $i < num$ **do**
5:         $output.append(start + delta * i)$
6:     **end for**
7:     $output.append(end)$
8:     **return** $output$
9: **end function**
10: **while** True **do**
11:     $V_i \leftarrow$ RECEIVESENSORDATA()
12:     **if** V_i is Tuple **then**
13:         $temp \leftarrow$ DATARECONSTRUCTION($V_i[0], V_i[1], V_i[2]$)
14:         **for** $i < V_i[2]$ **do**
15:             $dataset.append(temp[i])$
16:         **end for**
17:     **else**
18:         $dataset.append(V_i)$
19:     **end if**
20: **end while**

Assuming that the final destination receives the optimized sensor data, as described in the Algorithm 3.1, it will be verified whether the received data is an isolated measurement or a tuple (line 12). When the data is a tuple, evenly spaced values between $V_i[0]$ and $V_i[1]$ will be created, according the third element from the tuple, $V_i[2]$. In this way, the reconstructed data set will consist of the same amount of sensor measurements, although not all of them have been transmitted.

4   Simulations, Results and Discussions

According to the previous section, the approach proposed in this work is based on the analysis of the dispersion of the data collected by sensors, avoiding to transmit measurements with low dispersion level. In this section, we present a performance evaluation of the Data Reduction and Reconstruction algorithms in relation to the following metrics: **Number of Transmitted Packages** and **Energy consumption**.

The performance evaluation was divided into two steps. In the first step the potential of data reduction and data reconstruction of the proposed approach was evaluated by using datasets from five real-world monitoring applications publicly available. Also, in the first step, a comparison was made with a state-of-the-art work (baseline) based on the Dual Prediction Scheme with Least Mean Square (LMS) filters, proposed by [6]. We have implemented the baseline in order to reproduce similar results.

The choice of this work for comparison with the proposed approach was due to the fact that it is a recent work, with results that show a high level of reduction in the data transmission, surpassing other state-of-the-art approaches found in the literature, such as [4,8,14]. In the second step, the energy consumption and the number of data transmissions of sensor nodes was evaluated through the Castalia Simulator[1]. More details on network simulations will be covered in Subsect. 4.3.

4.1   Datasets

In the experiments of the proposed approach we used datasets from five real-world applications that perform monitoring through sensors. They are:

- (#1) Monitoring of air compressors from dental chairs [2]. Data from humidity sensors applied in air compressors to perform predictive maintenance.
- (#2) Data from smart meters (Low Carbon London Project) [15]. Data from energy consumption of 5.567 households in London - UK;
- (#3) Water quality monitoring data for the Burnett River (Australia) [13]. Data collection regarding the estuarine water quality;
- (#4) Air Quality data from Intel Berkeley Research Laboratory (IBRL) [11]. This dataset comes from 54 Mica2Dot sensors with weather boards;
- (#5) Air Quality Data - University of California, Irvine (UCI) [16]. Dataset available on the UCI Machine Learning Repository site[2].

In Table 1 we present details about the datasets used in this work, as well as its classification according to the taxonomy described in Sect. 3.3. The datasets are divided into classes (0, 1 and 2) and the parameters N_{max} and e_{max} are adjusted accordingly.

4.2   Analysis on Data Reduction and Data Reconstruction

The Algorithms 3.1, 3.2 and 3.3 were implemented in the C++ programming language, as well as the baseline method. The original datasets were used as the program input. In the output, in turn, reconstructed datasets are returned. Hence, it is possible to identify the number of transmissions avoided in each dataset, as well as to gauge the accuracy of the reconstructed data.

In Table 2 are described the results found in the experiments related to data reduction both in the proposed approach (Dispersion Analysis) and the baseline. The value of D_{max} was automatically adjusted according to the Algorithm 3.2 (see Sect. 3.2).

Figure 1 shows the results obtained in the experiments with the proposed method based on dispersion analysis, as well as the results obtained with the baseline through a bars chart.

---

[1] https://github.com/boulis/Castalia.
[2] https://archive.ics.uci.edu/ml/datasets.html.

Table 1. Details regarding the datasets

#	Sensed parameters	Sampling rate	Period	Num. of samples	Source	Class	N_{max}	e_{max}
#1	Temperature	±2 s	±1 year	3.970.215	[2]	0	15	0,25
	Humidity	±2 s	±1 year	3.970.215	[2]	0	15	0,25
	Dew-point	±2 s	±1 year	3.970.215	[2]	0	15	0,25
#2	kWh/hh (per half hour)	30 min	1 year	17.458	[15]	0	15	0,25
#3	pH	30 min	1 year	14.332	[13]	1	30	0,35
	Dissolved oxygen (mgl)	30 min	1 year	14.332	[13]	1	30	0,35
#4	Temperature	±30 s	4 days	30.507	[11]	2	45	0,50
	Humidity	±30 s	4 days	30.507	[11]	2	45	0,50
	Light	±30 s	4 days	30.507	[11]	2	45	0,50
	Voltage	±30 s	4 days	30.507	[11]	2	45	0,50
#5	Temperature	1 h	1 year	9.357	[16]	2	45	0,50
	Relative humidity	1 h	1 year	9.357	[16]	2	45	0,50
	Absolute humidity	1 h	1 year	9.357	[16]	2	45	0,50

Concerning the method based on dispersion analysis, the results show that the amount of reduction to be achieved depends on the dispersion level in the datasets. Datasets with highly dispersed values reaches a smaller reduction, for instance, the dataset #2, which reached only 10.65% of reduction. On the other hand, less dispersed datasets achieves greater reduction, such as the datasets #1 (all), #3 (all), #4 (temperature, humidity and voltage) and #5 (absolute humidity), which reached up to 91%, 96%, 97% and 97% of reduction, respectively.

The results show that the proposed approach achieves better results in most cases. It is important to emphasize that the baseline also have limitations in dealing with highly dispersed data. For instance, in the dataset #2, no transmission could be avoided. In dataset #5 (temperature and humidity), the baseline achieved was up to 6% and 3% respectively. The proposed approach, on the other hand, achieved 69% and 61% in the same datasets.

4.3   Energy Consumption Analysis

In order to evaluate the energy impact of the proposed approach on sensor nodes, simulations were carried out in the Castalia simulator. Thus, a WSN with 55 nodes equipped with the CC2420 2.4 GHz IEEE 802.15.4 ZigBee-Ready RF Transceiver[3] radio was reproduced, being only 1 sink node. The sensors were distributed randomly through the parameter *SN.deployment*, in an area of 150 m × 150 m. One sink, in turn, was positioned in the center area.

---

[3] http://www.ti.com/product/CC2420.

Table 2. Data reduction results

#	Sensed parameters	D_{max}	Reduction (%)		MAE	
			D.A	Baseline	D.A	Baseline
#1	Temperature	1.000	91.75%	91.13%	0.024	0.118
	Humidity	1.000	91.99%	92.79%	0.017	0.110
	Dew-point	1.000	91.83%	91.66%	0.022	0.064
#2	kWh/hh (per half hour)	1.000	10.65%	0%	0.017	0.000
#3	pH	1.020	96.73%	98.36%	0.043	0.089
	Dissolved oxygen (mgl)	1.110	96.60%	67.53%	0.240	0.095
#4	Temperature	1.060	97.81%	93.51%	0.072	0.205
	Humidity	1.220	97.73%	85.90%	0.181	0.171
	Light	1.000	86.29%	66.28%	0.030	0.015
	Voltage	1.000	97.82%	99.95%	0.005	0.034
#5	Temperature	1.210	69.50%	6.40%	0.451	0.009
	Relative humidity	2.569	51.08%	3.13%	0.344	0.464
	Absolute humidity	1.070	97.62%	95.18%	0.097	0.155

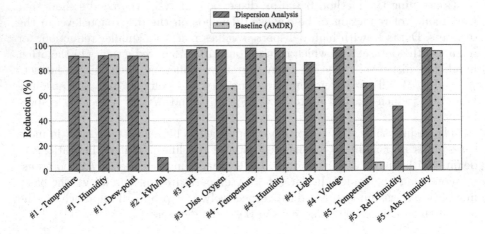

Fig. 1. Results

Regarding the CC2420 radio, its range is 50 m and the bandwidth is 250 Kbps. In RX mode, 0.062 joules/second are consumed. In TX mode, 0.057 joules/second are consumed and in Idle mode, 0.014 joules/second are consumed.

The Castalia simulator is divided into modules. Among them, stand out: application module, communication module and physical layer module. In the communication module, the implementation of the Low Energy Adaptive Clustering Hierarchy (LEACH) [3] algorithm was used. In the application module, we created an application named *DataReduction*, which contains the implementation of Algorithms 3.1, 3.2 and 3.3. We also created an application named *BaselineAMDR* which contains the implementation of the baseline method. The energy consumption of the *DataReduction* application has been compared to the *BaselineAMDR* and another application named *ValueReporting (General)*, which is available in Castalia, however, no data reduction technique is applied. In the physical layer module, in turn, the IBRL dataset [11] was included. Specifically, data from 54 sensor nodes, from 06 to 09 March 2004, totaling an average of 8.640 readings for each sensor node.

It is important to highlight that, in the simulations, when the amount of data transmission is reduced, the sensors tend to stay longer in the receive mode (RX), which can cause a high increase in energy consumption. Considering this fact, we only show in the results the energy consumed when the nodes are in transmit mode (TX).

In the simulation, a 12 s interval has been defined between the data transmissions through the parameter *minSampleInterval*. A number of 30 simulations were performed for each experiment. Figure 2 presents the results related to energy consumption from sensor nodes using *DataReduction, BaselineAMDR* and ValueReporting (General) applications. Figure 3, in turn, presents the number of data transmissions carried out by the sensor nodes during the simulations.

Figures 2(a) and 3(a) present the results obtained in the total time of the simulations (103680 s). Figures 2(b) and 3(b), on the other hand, present the results obtained in the simulations over time.

In the Figs. 2 and 3, it is noted that the *DataReduction* application obtained the best results, decreasing the data transmissions up to 84%, which means that only 15% of the sensed values were actually transmitted to the sink node approximately, consuming only 86.91 J.

The Mean Absolute Error was also evaluated in the simulations. In *DataReduction* application, we collected the data sent by the nodes in order to use it as the input of the Data Reconstruction Algorithm (Algorithm 3.3). Thus, it is possible to gauge the error obtained in the final data from each sensor. In *BaselineAMDR* application, we collected the data sent by the sensor nodes, as well as the predicted values by the LMS algorithm in order to make a comparison with the real data and determine the Mean Absolute Error. Figure 4 presents a boxplot diagram showing the Mean Absolute Error obtained in the 54 sensor nodes used in the simulations.

Regarding the proposed approach, it can be observed in the results presented in Fig. 4 that the error obtained in the data reconstruction is quite lower than the maximum acceptable error (0.5). In none of the cases the maximum acceptable error was exceeded. In the baseline method, on the other hand, the error obtained in the final data was greater than the error obtained in the proposed approach. However, in none of the cases the maximum acceptable error was exceeded. Consequently, it can be concluded that the data reduction method based on the dispersion analysis can keep a certain level of accuracy in the sensor data, reducing the energy consumption from sensor nodes, and contributing to extend the the network lifetime.

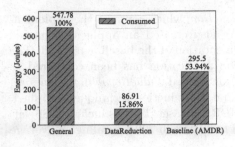
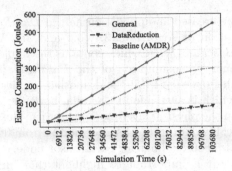

(a) Energy consumption   (b) Energy consumption over time

Fig. 2. Energy consumption evaluation

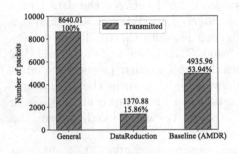
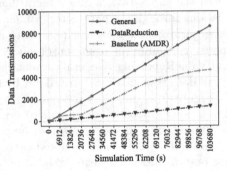

(a) Data transmission   (b) Data transmission over time

Fig. 3. Data transmission evaluation

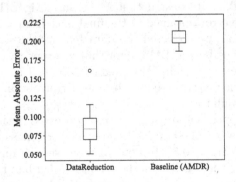

Fig. 4. Mean absolute error

5   Conclusions and Future Work

In this work, we proposed an approach for reducing the number of data transmissions in the context of Wireless Sensor Networks. The main objective of this approach is to prevent sensor nodes from transmitting measurements whose values show low dispersion (variability/scattering) within an acceptable maximum limit.

To achieve this goal, three algorithms were proposed. They are: Algorithm for Data Reduction based on dispersion analysis, Algorithm for the initialization phase (parameter adjustment) and Algorithm for Data Reconstruction based on asymptotic mean.

The experiments were based on the use of real sensor data and were conducted in two steps. The first step aimed at evaluating the performance of the reduction and reconstruction algorithms in order to gauge the amount of reduction achieved in each dataset as well as the error obtained in the reconstructions. In the second step, the energy consumption of the sensors was evaluated through the implementation of the proposed approach in the Castalia simulator. We also provided, in the two steps, a comparison between the proposed approach and a selected baseline method named *Adaptive Method for Data Reduction* [6].

Results presented in Sect. 4 shows that the method proposed in this work reached a high level of reduction in data transmissions, up to 97%. Regarding the simulations, the results showed that the proposed approach obtained a reduction in data transmissions up to 84%, as well as a low energy consumption of the nodes.

As future work prospects, it is suggested to investigate new forms of data reconstruction in order to propose a more effective method that will make it possible to decrease the number of data transmissions while maintaining a low error level during the reconstruction phase.

References

1. Alsheikh, M.A., Lin, S., Niyato, D., Tan, H.P.: Rate-distortion balanced data compression for wireless sensor networks. IEEE Sens. J. **16**(12), 5072–5083 (2016)
2. Castañeda, W.A.C.: Metodologia de gestão ubíqua para tecnologia médico-hospitalar utilizando tecnologias pervasivas. Ph.D. thesis, Universidade Federal de Santa Catarina (2016)
3. Chen, Y., Shen, C., Zhang, K., Wang, H., Gao, Q.: Leach algorithm based on energy consumption equilibrium. In: 2018 International Conference on Intelligent Transportation, Big Data Smart City (ICITBS), pp. 677–680, January 2018
4. Dias, G.M., Bellalta, B., Oechsner, S.: Using data prediction techniques to reduce data transmissions in the IoT. In: 2016 IEEE 3rd World Forum on Internet of Things (WF-IoT). IEEE, December 2016
5. El-Telbany, M.E., Maged, M.A.: Exploiting sparsity in wireless sensor networks for energy saving: a comparative study. Int. J. Appl. Eng. Res. **12**(4), 452–460 (2017)
6. Fathy, Y., Barnaghi, P., Tafazolli, R.: An adaptive method for data reduction in the internet of things. In: Proceedings of IEEE 4th World Forum on Internet of Things. IEEE (2018)

7. Huang, Z., Li, M., Song, Y., Zhang, Y., Chen, Z.: Adaptive compressive data gathering for wireless sensor networks. In: 2017 3rd IEEE International Conference on Computer and Communications (ICCC), pp. 362–367, December 2017

8. Jaber, A., Taam, M.A., Makhoul, A., Jaoude, C.A., Zahwe, O., Harb, H.: Reducing the data transmission in sensor networks through Kruskal-Wallis model. In: 2017 IEEE 13th International Conference on Wireless and Mobile Computing, Networking and Communications (WiMob). IEEE, October 2017

9. Karim, S.: Energy efficiency in wireless sensor networks, through data compression. Master's thesis, University of Oslo (2017)

10. Li, Z., Zhang, W., Qiao, D., Peng, Y.: Lifetime balanced data aggregation for the internet of things. Comput. Electr. Eng. **58**, 244–264 (2017)

11. Madden, S.: Intel Lab Data (2004). http://db.lcs.mit.edu/labdata/labdata.html. Accessed 15 Mar 2019

12. Masoum, A., Meratnia, N., Havinga, P.J.: A distributed compressive sensing technique for data gathering in wireless sensor networks. Procedia Comput. Sci. **21**, 207–216 (2013). The 4th International Conference on Emerging Ubiquitous Systems and Pervasive Networks (EUSPN-2013) and the 3rd International Conference on Current and Future Trends of Information and Communication Technologies in Healthcare (ICTH)

13. Queensland Government: Ambient estuarine water quality monitoring data (includes near real-time sites) - 2012 to present day (2015). https://data.qld.gov.au/dataset/ambient-estuarine-water-quality-monitoring-data-near-real-time-sites-2012-to-present-day. Accessed 15 Mar 2019

14. Santini, S., Romer, K.: An adaptive strategy for quality-based data reduction in wireless sensor networks. In: Proceedings of the 3rd International Conference on Networked Sensing Systems (INSS 2006), pp. 29–36 (2006)

15. UK Power Networks: SmartMeter Energy Consumption Data in London Households (2015). https://data.london.gov.uk/dataset/smartmeter-energy-use-data-in-london-households. Accessed 15 Mar 2019

16. Vito, S.D., Massera, E., Piga, M., Martinotto, L., Francia, G.D.: On field calibration of an electronic nose for benzene estimation in an urban pollution monitoring scenario. Sens. Actuators B: Chem. **129**(2), 750–757 (2008)

17. Zegarra, E.T., Schouery, R.C.S., Miyazawa, F.K., Villas, L.A.: A continuous enhancement routing solution aware of data aggregation for wireless sensor networks. In: 2016 IEEE 15th International Symposium on Network Computing and Applications (NCA), pp. 93–100, October 2016

Autonomic IoT Battery Management with Fog Computing

Hugo Vaz Sampaio[✉], Ana Luiza Cordova de Jesus,
Ricardo do Nascimento Boing, and Carlos Becker Westphall

Universidade Federal de Santa Catarina, Florianopolis, Brazil
hvazsampaio@gmail.com

Abstract. Internet of Things (IoT) is the connection of any object to the internet, to generate useful information about its own state or surrounding environment. IoT allows new products and services to be applied in different areas, such as smart cities, industry, smart homes, environment monitoring, smart cars, heath monitoring and others. Fog computing emerges to meet the Quality of Service requirements, of low latency real time IoT systems, that Cloud Computing cannot guarantee. This paper presents a Fire Alarm fog System, for a Smart Home, with the development of an IoT device hardware. A fog system is also developed with a website, that displays the sensor values, and the estimated battery life of the IoT device. Calculations were done with a variation of sleep-time of the IoT device, the results shows an increase of 2.5 times of battery lifespan.

Keywords: Fog computing · IoT · Zigbee · Battery management · Smart homes

1 Introduction

Internet of Things (IoT) can be defined as the connection of any object to the internet, to generate useful information about its own state or surrounding environment [9]. Any object may be connected to a device with sensors to capture data, and actuators. A microcontroller is used to manage the sensors and actuators, as well as communicating with a network interface to send and receive information. IoT devices can be battery powered, thus IoT systems must consider that IoT devices may have hardware limitations, such as processing, memory and power restrictions. IoT can be applied in different areas, such as smart cities, industry, smart homes, environment monitoring, smart cars, heath monitoring and others.

IoT allows new applications and services, creating new, but not limited to, network connection, security and access paradigms, for example in a real time IoT system. Cloud computing (CC) was designed to process data in batch, and could be used to handle big data generated from the IoT system [20]. However

© Springer Nature Switzerland AG 2019
R. Miani et al. (Eds.): GPC 2019, LNCS 11484, pp. 89–103, 2019.
https://doi.org/10.1007/978-3-030-19223-5_7

CC cannot guarantee low-latency for real-time applications that requires high Quality of Service (QoS) [13]. Location awareness, support for seamless mobility and ubiquitous coverage are also not fully supported by CC solutions.

Thus Fog Computing emerges as a solution to allow low latency applications for real time IoT systems. Fog computing is a distributed computing paradigm that acts as an intermediate layer in between Cloud datacentres and IoT devices/sensors, to extend the Cloud systems and services physically closer to the user [11].

A fog system may be distributed between the fog nodes, and it is used to filter unnecessary IoT data sent to the Cloud. A fog application consists of a multi-layered system where data is generated on the IoT layer, then sent to be processed in the fog, and forwarded to the cloud.

A Smart environment fog system may have multiple different systems and services running. This paper proposes an IoT fire alarm system using a battery powered IoT device for a Smart Home. The IoT Fire Alarm system is developed with the concept of Fog computing [11]. In a Smart environment there may be a large number of nodes, [18] and [17] develops a wireless sensor network, for a greenhouse smart environment, and analyses it with network of queues theory to determine the maximum number of nodes a large scale system can hold while guaranteeing an acceptable waiting time.

The proposed IoT Fire Alarm System developed on this paper is divided in two parts. In the first part the IoT device hardware is developed with a micro-controller, sensors, actuators and an antenna, to detect and inform an emergency fire condition. In the second part, the autonomic IoT battery estimation system is developed using a fog server.

2   Related Work

2.1   Energy Consumption

Energy saving in IoT devices, especially when integrating with Fog Computing, can be seen from several angles. First, it should be kept in mind that not all applications take advantage of the use of Fog Computing - applications and services that require many downloads, updates or need computations that are considered too heavy will save more energy when sent to the Cloud, without trying to perform these tasks at the edge of the network beforehand [12]. In this case, it is best to focus on real-time and low latency applications when it is decided to take advantage of the Fog's differentiated characteristics.

A common technique used in cloud computing, idle power consumption, is not so easily achieved with Fog, due to the existence of fewer features like CPU, storage and RAM in Fog when compared to the Cloud. Thus, it is more difficult to use the same techniques to save energy, so that if Fog servers become inactive for long periods of time Fog can not be as efficient at saving energy as when comparing with Cloud [12]. That way, one needs to think about other possible ways to save energy when integrating Fog and Internet of Things.

Another important issue when it comes to energy savings using Internet of Things is the fact that many IoT devices rely on batteries to function and are also connected to wireless networks. For users of these devices, a long service life of a device is considered important; that is, the battery-dependent device must be able to last for many years [7]. The use of Wi-Fi, for example, is a protocol commonly used in IoT devices; its use can allow the connection of an estimated Internet device in one year using two AA type alkaline batteries when using efficient energy management [15].

2.2 Using Network Protocols to Save Energy

Network protocols, although it is not considered the main source of energy expenditure on Iot devices, can play an important role in identifying sources of energy consumption and inefficiency in a device [4].

The use of network protocols such as Bluetooth and ZigBee can be good options for energy savings in Fog Computing [12]. It should be kept in mind, however, that different IoT devices can use different technologies in their favor for greater energy savings. For example, ZigBee can be used in sensors, actuators and even smart LED lamps, but is not suitable for high bandwidth devices such as security cameras [7].

Even the use of routing protocols such as IPv4 or IPv6 can present an energy expenditure when connecting IoT devices to the Internet [22]. Thus, it is necessary to use protocols such as 6LoWPAN (IPv6 over Low-Power Wireless Personal Area Networks) or 6GLAD (Global to Link-layer Address Translation for 6LoW-PAN Overhead Reduction), where it is also possible to perform the compression of addressing headers that, depending on parameters such as packet size, network topology, communication scope, among others, can decrease up to 38% of the energy consumption in smart device batteries [22].

2.3 Home Automation

Home automation, or smart houses, is one of the areas where IoT can be applied. The use of intelligent objects, with communication technologies, creates a network of intelligent devices used as infrastructure for systems and services. A smart home may have different automation systems such as door access control, fire alarm system, water or electricity consumption management, and others, that can be used to improve the quality of life of the inhabitants of a residence. Home automation uses radio technologies such as bluetooth, Wi-Fi, and other network protocols, to connect household devices such as lights, doors, curtains, fan, frigde, oven, among others, and make use of them more intelligently. The most simple and one of the most used examples is the use of intelligent lamps that can be switched on, off and have their luminosity controlled through the use of apps on mobile devices such as a cellphone [8].

The use of home automation can be integrated using Fog Computing with IoT. With the growth of IoT devices, and consequently the existence of more domestic devices that can be considered intelligent, it is necessary to think about cases of energy saving with this types of devices [21]. [16] paper surveys the most common hardware used to develop an IoT device, comparing the existing IoT supported hardware platforms and microcontrollers.

3   IoT Fire Alarm Device

In this paper a fire alarm system, for a smart home, is developed with an IoT device and a fog server. The IoT device sensors the environment conditions then forward these values to the fog server. The proposed Iot device was designed to be used in a kitchen of a smart home.

The Iot Fire Alarm device hardware was developed with, an Arduino Uno [2] ATmega328p microcontroller [3], a DHT11 [1] air temperature and humidity sensor, a MQ-2 gas and smoke sensor, and a flame sensor. The microcontroller captures values of the sensors, connected to analogical ports of the Arduino, then data are transferred to the fog using an Xbee Zigbee antenna. In case an emergency fire condition is detected, a buzzer and a LED light are used as sound and visual actuators.

In order to capture the sensors data values, a program was created using the C language and uploaded to the microcontroller of the Arduino UNO board. The program captures the values of smoke and gas, air temperature, as well as the existence of flames, and sends to the zigbee antenna. The antenna then forwards a packet to the fog containing the sensor values.

Initial calibration of the sensors were performed, in the university lab, with DHT11 air sensor indicating temperature values in Celcius degree (°C) scale, the MQ-2 gas/smoke sensor indicated 4% gas concentration at normal room conditions, and the flame sensor indicates presence of flame light waves, and returns true or false.

The physical connections of the IoT device are shown in Fig. 1. The power port of sensors and actuators modules are connected to the microcontroller digital ports, this allows to switch on and off each module independently. The digital ports have a maximum output current of 20 Mah, but the MQ-2 sensor requires 160 Mah. The microcontroller 5 V port has a maximum output current of 200 Mah. A transistor bridges a connection between the 5 V port and MQ-2 power port, and a digital port controls the transistor, used to switch on and off the MQ-2 sensor. The zigbee antenna connects to the microcontroller's RX and TX serial ports.

An emergency fire condition is defined, in this paper, when three conditions are met: Air temperature higher than 35 °C, gas concentration above 4% and presence of flame light waves. With these values it was created a list of possible conditions for the IoT device, presented in Table 1, when the values of sensors varies.

In a home kitchen context, general heat sources may be from an oven, stove or microwave. If the fire system only detects high temperature, it could mean that hot air was released after opening the oven, or a hot pressure cooker release. If the system only detects a high concentration of gases, it could be a gas leak in

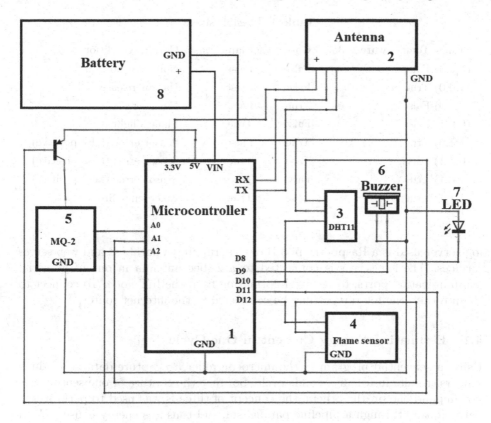

Fig. 1. IoT fire alarm physical connections.

the kitchen, and if the system only detects flame light waves, it could be flames from the stove, a match or lighter.

There are three conditions on Table 1 that could also indicate an emergency fire state. These are a warning states, that can turn into an emergency state, if it continues for a long period of time. If the system detects a high concentration of gas/smoke with flame, then there could be a fire, but the air sensor might not be working. The second condition is when the system detects high air temperature and flames. There could be a fire and a malfunction on the gas sensor. The third condition is when high temperature and smoke are detected, but not the flames. A high density smoke may block the light flame waves from reaching the flame sensor, thus being a warning state.

4   Fog Fire Alarm System

The IoT device sends data to the fog, where it will be stored in the database. The data are processed and exhibited in a website, developed to show the alarm sensor values, estimated node battery life, and manage the sleep-time cycle. The

Table 1. Possible states

States	Temperature > 35 °C	Gas > 4%	Flame sensor	Current condition
(0,0,0)	False	False	False	Normal condition
(1,0,0)	True	False	False	Hot air release
(0,1,0)	False	True	False	Gas leak
(0,0,1)	False	False	True	Flames light
(1,1,0)	True	True	False	Sensor error (false positive)
(0,1,1)	False	True	True	Sensor error (false positive)
(1,0,1)	True	False	True	Sensor error (false positive)
(1,1,1)	True	True	True	Emergency fire

fog server used is a Raspberry pi 3 B device, running a database and web server services. The fog server is connected to a zigbee antenna in one of its serial communication ports, to receive information from the IoT node. To connect to the internet, the fog server must be connected to the internet router.

4.1 Estimating Energy Current in One Cycle

Using a sequential program in the microcontroller, to capture data of all three sensors, results in a four seconds cycle. So, that the capture of one sensor does not depend one on the others, the concept of threads was used to perform the data capture through a pipeline parallelism, and thus less energy is used. With this, a minimum cycle of 2 s was defined, due to the limitation of the response time of the DHT11 sensor.

In order to calculate the energy current of the prototype, it is necessary to use the values of each of the modules used in it. The energy current values of the modules are given in milliamperes (mA), per hour and per second, are shown in Table 2.

Table 2. Energy current per module

Module	Current per hour	Current per second
DHT11 Sensor	0.3 mA	0.00008333 mA
MQ-2 Sensor	160 mA	0.04444 mA
Flame Sensor	0.4 mA	0.0001111 mA
Arduino's microprocessor (sleep-mode)	0.0001 mA	0.000000027778 mA
Arduino's microprocessor (active mode)	0.3 mA	0.00008333 mA
XBee ZigBee Antenna (send mode)	33 mA	0.0091666 mA
XBee ZigBee Antenna (receive mode)	28 mA	0.00777778 mA
XBee ZigBee Antenna (sleep-mode)	0.0001 mA	0.0000002778 mA

Considering that the DHT11 sensor spends 0.3 mA per hour [1], the MQ-2 sensor spends 160 mA per hour [10], and that the flame sensor spends 0.4 mA per hour, it can be calculated that the sensors expend 160.7 mA per hour when powered. With this, we can calculate the energy current of the sensors, in addition to the 0.3 mA current of the Arduino microprocessor [3].

Each sensor has different response times: two seconds for DHT11 [1], one second for MQ-2 [10] and 1 s for the flame sensor. Thus, each sensor needs to stay powered for at least the response time, but there is no need for energy expenditure when they are not sending data to the Fog.

Knowing these values, and considering that the sensors are only active during its own response time, so it is possible to calculate the energy current used in one cycle of the IoT node, as being:

$$\text{IoT cycle} = \text{active mode} + \text{sleep-mode} \tag{1}$$

The active part of the cycle considers the current used by the microcontroller and sensors, to capture sensors values, and the antenna to receive and send information. In sleep-mode the sensors are turned off, while the antenna and microcontroller are in sleep-mode to save energy.

The data capture depends on the response time of each of the sensors, times its current, in addition to the microcontroler of the Arduino itself. It is considered that the microcontroller will only be turned on for 2 s in one cycle. With that, the current spent in capturing the sensors value is:

$$\text{Data capture} = \text{DHT11} + \text{MQ-2} + \text{flame sensor} + \text{microcontroller} \tag{2}$$

$$\text{Data capture} = 0,0449 \, \text{mA/cycle} \tag{3}$$

After finalizing the sensors data capture, the data is sent in a packet to the coordinator node. For this calculation, it was considered an average packet size of 25 bytes (or 200 bits). The IoT node was developed with an Xbee Zigbee [5] antenna, that has a transmission speed of 250 kbps. The time antenna spent for sending one packet is:

$$\text{Time to send one packet} = \frac{200}{250000} = 0.0008 \, \text{s, or } 0.8 \, \text{ms.} \tag{4}$$

With this time result, we multiply the energy value spent by the XBee antenna for data transmission. With this calculation, we have the current spent per packet.

$$\text{Current/packet} = 0.0008 \, \text{s} * 0.0091666 \, \text{mA} = 0.00000733328 \, \text{mA/packet} \tag{5}$$

During the active cycle, the antenna is switched on in receive mode and available to receive control messages from the fog. The antenna will switch to send mode only while sending a packet. Inn this paper, a packet takes 0.8 ms to be sent to the fog, this means the antenna will be on send mode for 0.08% of the time in a second and on receive mode for 99.92% of the time. With this, we can calculate the current used while on receive mode:

$$\text{Current in receive mode} = 0.00778\,\text{mA/s} * 1.9992\,\text{s} = 0.0155\,\text{mA/cycle} \quad (6)$$

Considering the time that the IoT node will be awake in a cycle, we have the value of energy current in a cycle as the sum of the results in Eqs. 3, 5 and 6:

$$\text{Active cycle (mA)} = 0,0449 + (0.00000733328 + 0.0155) = 0.0604\,\text{mA} \quad (7)$$

After sending the packet, the IoT node enters sleep-mode. The energy current is calculated with the values of the microprocessor and the XBee antenna, both in sleep mode, according to Table 2:

$$\text{Sleep-mode cycle} = (0,00000002778\,\text{mA} + 0,0000002778\,\text{mA}) * T \quad (8)$$

The variable T is a time variable in seconds, and it is controlled using the fog system. In order to change the cycle interval, the value of T can be modified by the use of control messages sent to the IoT node. At the end of the cycle the data is sent to Fog, and then both the antenna and Arduino enter sleep mode. Figure 2 demonstrates this situation.

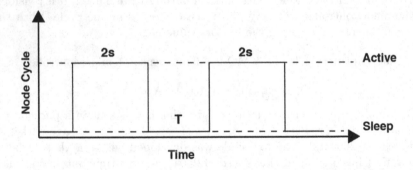

Fig. 2. Energy expenditure of the IoT in time

There is, however, a limit associated with the maximum time of T. According to normative instruction IN012/DAT/CBMSC of the State Fire Brigade in the state of Santa Catarina, Brazil, it was defined that electronic devices used for fire alarms, must have a maximum response time to be accepted within the safety standards established by law. The maximum response time for the detection of flames by a fire alarm device is 5 s [19]. Considering this value, and considering that the existing time duration of the IoT cycle is 2 s, the maximum time the node can be in sleep mode is 3 s. Table 3 compares energy expenditure estimates by changing the sleep-mode T-time values of the Arduino microprocessor and the XBee antenna.

Another important value to be calculated is in relation to the lifetime of a battery used in the IoT device. The fog system will autonomously estimate the

Table 3. Cycle current altering the time value of T

Mode	1 s	2 s	3 s
Sleep (mA)	0.0000003056	0.0000006112	0.0000009168
Active (mA)	0.0604	0.0604	0.0604
Total per cycle (mA)	0.0604003056	0.0604006112	0.0604009168

battery energy considering values of Table 3. Batteries with easy access in the market have around 2,000 mA, and can also vary between 2.100 and 2.500 mA each. The calculation to estimate how many cycles that each battery can handle is as follows:

$$\text{Battery cycles estimation} = \frac{\text{Battery power}}{\text{cycle current}} \tag{9}$$

The number of cycles a battery can withstand is multiplied by the its cycle time, that is, a minimum cycle time of two seconds and maximum of five seconds. The estimated time in hours, per battery, is calculated as follows:

$$\text{Lifespan estimation in hours} = \frac{\text{Battery cycle estimation * Cycle time}}{3600} \tag{10}$$

Table 4 shows the rounded number of cycles that each battery can live with the energy current of the IoT node, while varying the sleep-mode time.

Table 4. Lifespan in cycles and hours

Lifespan	Cycles			Hours		
Battery (mA)	2000	2100	2500	2000	2100	2500
T 0	33,087	34,742	41,359	18.38	19.30	22.97
T 1	33,087	34,741	41,359	27.57	28.95	34.46
T 2	33,087	34,741	41,359	36.76	38.60	45.95
T 3	33,087	34,741	41,358	45.95	48.25	57.44

The resulting lifespan of the IoT node will be available for display through a monitoring system site running in the fog. For example, Fig. 3 shows the result of the calculations if the sleep-mode time T was 0 s (i.e. if there the sleep-mode was not in use), while using a battery with a power of 2000 mA.

It is possible to notice a large difference in the lifespan of the batteries when varying T time the IoT node. The results indicates that with a 2500 mA battery and T with three seconds sleep mode, the IoT node will run for 57.44 h, or 57 h and 26 min. The MQ-2 sensor is the module that drains the most battery.

It then would be interesting to modify the IoT node to use different combinations of two sensors, but still be able to identify an emergency fire condition.

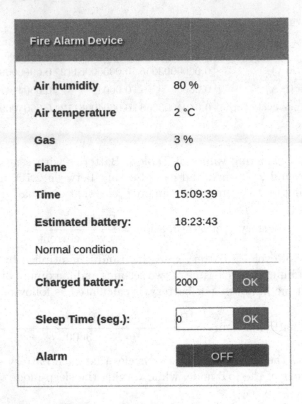

Fig. 3. Estimated lifespan with 0 s of sleep-mode.

Table 5. Lifespan in hours when varying T

Lifespan	T 0			T 3		
Battery (mA)	2000	2100	2500	2000	2100	2500
DHT11 and MQ-2	18.41	19.33	23.01	46.04	48.34	57.54
Flames and MQ-2	18.43	19.35	23.04	46.08	48.38	57.60
Flames and DHT11	69.43	72.91	86.80	173.60	182.27	217.00

For brevity, these options are exemplified in Table 5 using a sleep-mode T time of 0 and 3 s.

It's very noticeable how the presence of the MQ-2 sensor influences the energy current when present in the IoT node. The lifespan of an IoT device can be almost 4 times longer without a gas sensor. One possibility that would allow to continue using a gas sensor, instead of using only the flame sensors and the DHT11 sensor, would be to make use of another gas sensor, such as MQ-9 [10], which captures burning smoke, and has a lower energy value of 70 mA.

4.2   Emergency Mode

Previous estimates are based on situations where no fire was detected. To consider an emergency situation, the behavior of the sensors must be different. First, in an emergency situation, as opposed to a normal operating situation, the physical warnings of the fire alarm, buzzer and LED must be turned on to serve as a more concrete form of communication to the user. In addition, all IoT node sensors must be switched on during the time of the emergency situation - not only for the 2 s of the cycle, as previously defined (in this case, there is no cycle, only continuous consumption per second) - so that the data is constantly being captured during the emergency situation until the user sends a message to turn off the physical alarms - that is, when the IoT node receives a message from the Fog to turn off the alarms.

The energy expenditure values of the physical warnings of the IoT device (buzzer and LED) are shown in Table 6.

Table 6. Energy current per actuator

Module	Current per hour	Current per second
Buzzer	25 mA	0.00694444 mA
LED	20 mA	0.00555556 mA

With this, it is possible to estimate the battery life of the IoT device when in an emergency situation, and the amount of energy current when compared to the normal operation of the IoT device. It's important to note that the other values used in the calculation, such as energy current values of the sensors and the XBee ZigBee antenna, continue with the same values as in Table 2.

While in emergency mode (EM), the antenna, microprocessor and sensors will be active constantly, that is, we disconsider the cycles:

$$EM = sensors + antenna + microcontroller + actuators = 234 \, mA \qquad (11)$$

Table 7. Lifespan in hours on emergency mode

Lifespan with actuators	Emergency mode in hours		
Battery (mA)	2000	2100	2500
DHT11, flames and MQ-2	8.54	8.97	10.68
DHT11 and MQ-2	8.56	8.99	10.70
Flames and MQ-2	8.55	8.98	10.69
Flames and DHT11	27.03	20.34	33.78

Table 7 shows the battery estimation of the nodes on Table 5, when added with a buzzer and LED actuators, while on emergency mode with different batteries. At this mode, the lifespan of an IoT device can vary over three times without the gas sensor. Figure 4 shows a screen of the system, with the estimated battery on an emergency situation.

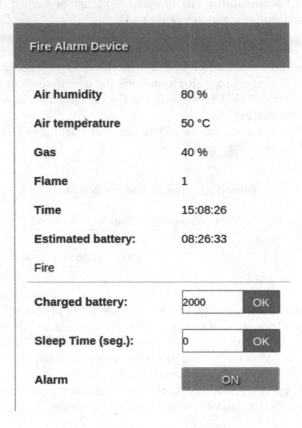

Fig. 4. Estimated lifespan on emergency mode.

4.3 Comparison of Battery Lifespan with Other Network Protocols

In the energy calculations performed previously, it was considered that the antenna used in the IoT node would be the XBee antenna, which in turn uses the ZigBee protocol to communicate. However, it would also be possible to use other commonly used network protocols, such as Wi-Fi and Bluetooth. For this, it would be necessary to replace the XBee antenna with the XBee Wi-Fi antenna or the Bluetooth module 4.0 BLE, respectively.

The XBee Wi-Fi antenna allows data to be sent via Wi-Fi, and can send data with up to 72 Mbps [6]. The energy current values when using the XBee Wi-Fi antenna are given in Table 8.

Table 8. Energy current per antenna module.

Module	Current per hour	Current per second
XBee Wi-Fi Antenna (send mode)	309 mA	0.08583333 mA
XBee Wi-Fi Antenna (receive mode)	100 mA	0.02777777 mA
XBee Wi-Fi Antenna (sleep-mode)	0.006 mA	0.00000166666 mA
Bluetooth 4.0 BLE (Active mode)	8.5 mA	0.00236111 mA
Bluetooth 4.0 BLE (sleep-mode)	1.5 mA	0.000416 mA

The other values involved in the calculation (such as the Arduino microcontroller and the sensors current) still remains the same. The energy expenditure of the IoT node, if the XBee Wi-Fi or bluetooth antenna was used, is shown in Table 9, by varying the sleep-mode time values of the IoT node and the battery power used. For the estimation of the lifespan in emergency situation, The total IoT node current using wifi will be approximately 306 mA, and with bluetooth 214,4 mA.

Table 9. Lifespan in hours with WiFi or Bluetooth modules

Lifespan in hours		Normal mode			Emergency mode		
–	Battery (mA)	2000	2100	2500	2000	2100	2500
Xbee Wifi	T 0	10.879	11.423	13.599	6.636	6.862	8.170
	T 1	16.319	17.135	20.399	–	–	–
	T 2	21.759	22.847	27.199	–	–	–
	T 3	27.198	28.558	33.998	–	–	–
Bluetooth BLE 4.0	T 0	22.396	23.516	27.995	9.324	9.790	11.655
	T 1	33.595	35.274	41.993	–	–	–
	T 2	44.793	47.032	55.991	–	–	–
	T 3	55.991	58.790	69.989	–	–	–

Compared to the use of the ZigBee XBee antenna, the use of Wi-Fi to send the data is not optimal - on the contrary, the lifespan of the different batteries is less than when compared to the use of the ZigBee protocol. The current draw on receive mode is four times higher, and on send mode is over nine times.

With the use of the Bluetooth 4.0 BLE module it is possible to send the data captured by the IoT node with the Bluetooth protocol, but its main disadvantage is the distance allowed by the module, of only 100 m inside a closed environment [14]. Unlike the XBee ZigBee and Wi-Fi antennas, the Bluetooth 4.0 BLE module has no differentiation of energy expenditure for sending and receiving data.

5   Conclusion and Future Work

When compared to the values obtained in the estimation of energy expenditure using the XBee ZigBee antenna, the use of the Bluetooth 4.0 BLE module, and consequently the use of the Bluetooth network protocol, presents a greater energy saving of the batteries - that is, a greater battery lifespan in all cases. This is mainly due to the fact that the module does not have different energy values in cases of sending and transmitting data, as does both ZigBee and Wi-Fi XBee antennas, as well as lower values of the module spent when active.

Using a regular 2000 mA battery, the IoT alarm device will work continuously for 18 h, and up to 45 h with a 3 s sleep-cycle. This is an increase of up to 2.5 times, in the battery lifespan, when using sleep conditions. Although there is a considerable increase on estimated battery time, that is still less than two days working, and changing batteries every two days may turn this fire alarm system costly, especially if multiple IoT devices are used. With these results, we propose that this IoT fire alarm device should be powered in an outlet, and the battery system should guarantee the system working, even if there is an power outage. Although a power outage may not last over 18 h, several power outages may occur over a long period of time, such as one year.

As future work, we consider that the home IoT devices are connected to an outlet power source, so the system will be upgraded to estimate, in Watts (W), how much power does an IoT device spend per hour, or kW/h, and the monthly energy cost considering local energy provider rates and currency. This new function will allow to estimate the total monthly cost of the IoT devices, in a smart home, when applying a sleep-cycle in the IoT to save energy and lower costs.

Acknowledgements. This work was partially supported by the Research and Innovation Support Foundation of the State of Santa Catarina (FAPESC) under grant 23038.013359/2017-71.

References

1. Aosong: DHT11 product manual (2018). http://akizukidenshi.com/download/ds/aosong/DHT11.pdf
2. Arduino: Arduino UNO board technical specifications (2018). https://store.arduino.cc/usa/arduino-uno-rev3
3. ATMEL: ATMEGA 328P microcontroller technical specifications. https://pdf1.alldatasheet.com/datasheet-pdf/view/241077/ATMEL/ATMEGA328P.html
4. Biason, A., et al.: EC-CENTRIC: an energy-and context-centric perspective on IoT systems and protocol design. IEEE Access **5**, 6894–6908 (2017). https://doi.org/10.1109/ACCESS.2017.2692522
5. Digi: Zigbee XBee antenna specifications. https://www.digi.com/products/embedded-systems/rf-modules/2-4-ghz-modules/xbee-zigbee
6. Digi: Digi Xbee wi-fi (2018). https://www.digi.com/products/xbee-rf-solutions/2-4-ghz-modules/xbee-wi-fi#specifications

7. Friedli, M., Kaufmann, L., Paganini, F., Kyburz, R.: Energy efficiency of the Internet of Things (2016). https://www.iea-4e.org/document/384/energy-efficiency-of-the-internet-of-things-technology-and-energy-assessment-report
8. Ghazal, B., Kherfan, M., Chahine, K., Khatib, K.: Multi control chandelier operations using Xbee for home automation. In: Technological Advances in Electrical, Electronics and Computer Engineering (TAEECE), pp. 107–111. IEEE (2015). https://doi.org/10.1109/TAEECE.2015.7113609
9. Gupta, H., Dastjerdi, A.V., Ghosh, S.K., Buyya, R.: iFogSim: a toolkit for modeling and simulation of resource management techniques in internet of things, edge and fog computing environments. CoRR (2016). http://arxiv.org/abs/1606.02007
10. Hanwei, E.: MQ-9 semiconductor sensor for co/combustible gas (2018). https://img.filipeflop.com/files/download/Sensor_de_gas_MQ-9.pdf
11. Iorga, M., Feldman, L., Barton, R., Martin, M.J., Goren, N., Mahmoudi, C.: Fog computing conceptual model (2018). https://doi.org/10.6028/NIST.SP.500-325
12. Jalali, F., Khodadustan, S., Gray, C., Hinton, K., Suits, F.: Greening IoT with fog: a survey. In: 1st IEEE International Conference on Edge Computing, pp. 25–31. IEEE, Honolulu (2017). https://doi.org/10.1109/IEEE.EDGE.2017.13
13. Mahmud, R., Kotagiri, R., Buyya, R.: Fog computing: a taxonomy, survey and future directions. In: Di Martino, B., Li, K.-C., Yang, L.T., Esposito, A. (eds.) Internet of Everything. IT, pp. 103–130. Springer, Singapore (2018). https://doi.org/10.1007/978-981-10-5861-5_5
14. OSOYOO: Bluetooth 4.0 BLE module datasheet (2016). http://osoyoo.com/wp-content/uploads/2016/10/OSOYOO-HM-10-Bluetooth-Module.pdf
15. Perera, C., Qin, Y., Estrella, J., Reiff-Marganiec, S., Vasilakos, A.: Fog computing for sustainable smart cities: a survey. ACM Comput. Surv. (CSUR) **50**(3), 32 (2017). https://arxiv.org/pdf/1703.07079.pdf
16. Ray, P.P.: A survey on Internet of Things architectures. J. King Saud Univ. Comput. Inf. Sci. **30**(3), 291–319 (2018)
17. Sampaio, H., Motoyama, S.: Implementation of a greenhouse monitoring system using hierarchical wireless sensor network. In: 9th Latin-American Conference on Communications (LATINCOM), pp. 1–6. IEEE (2017). https://doi.org/10.1109/LATINCOM.2017.8240156
18. Sampaio, H., Motoyama, S.: Sensor nodes estimation for a greenhouse monitoring system using hierarchical wireless network. In: 25th International Conference on Software, Telecommunications and Computer Networks (SoftCOM), pp. 1–5. IEEE (2017). https://doi.org/10.23919/SOFTCOM.2017.8115582
19. Fire Detection, Santa Catarina State: IN 012/DAT/CBMSC-sistema de alarme e deteccao de incendio (2014). http://www.cbm.sc.gov.br/dat/images/arquivo_pdf/IN/IN_29_06_2014/IN_12.pdf
20. Sharma, S.K., Wang, X.: Live data analytics with collaborative edge and cloud processing in wireless IoT networks. IEEE Access **5**, 4621–4635 (2017). https://doi.org/10.1109/ACCESS.2017.2682640
21. Stojkoska, B., Trivodaliev, K.: A review of Internet of Things for smart home: challenges and solutions. J. Cleaner Prod. **140**, 1454–1464 (2017). https://doi.org/10.1016/j.jclepro.2016.10.006
22. Zimmermann, A.: Arquitetura para ganho de eficiencia energetica em redes de sensores sem fios de proxima geração (2008). https://repositorio.ufsc.br/handle/123456789/91383

Evaluating Post-quantum Signatures
for IoT Devices

Jéssica Carneiro(✉) ⓘ and Leonardo B. Oliveira

Federal University of Minas Gerais, Belo Horizonte, MG 31270-901, Brazil
{jessicacarneiro,leob}@dcc.ufmg.br

Abstract. With the advent of quantum computing, traditional digital signatures schemes such as RSA, DSA, and ECDSA will become insecure thanks to Shor's algorithm which will break them in polynomial time. Thus, cryptosystems resilient to quantum computing must be considered, especially for devices in the Internet of Things which limitations may hinder the use of secure cryptosystems. An alternative is the use of hash-based signatures which are post-quantum and provide a flexible trade-off between performance (both storage and processing time) and security level adaptable to a device's restrictions. This paper presents a straightforward background on basic hash-based signatures, an implementation of hash-based signatures schemes, specifically Winternitz and Merkle Signature Scheme, on an Arduino Due platform, and a performance evaluation. Our results show that hash-based signatures are feasible for IoT-like devices.

Keywords: Quantum cryptography · IoT security ·
Hash-based signatures

1 Introduction

Digital signatures associate information to an entity – i.e., a person, an institution, or a device. They provide authentication, data integrity, and non-repudiation [16] of messages exchanged in a network. Currently, digital signatures are widely applied in Web services, personal computers, IoT devices, etc. Some digital signature algorithms such as RSA [18], DSA [9], and ECDSA [14] are among the most extensively known and adopted cryptosystems nowadays [5].

The above-cited algorithms have their security paved in the inherent hardness of mathematical problems such as the integer factorization (RSA), discrete logarithms (DSA), and discrete logarithms over elliptic curves (ECDSA). However, the development of polynomial time algorithms for quantum computers to solve such problems [21] made them insecure under the threat of quantum computing. Hence, quantum-resistant alternatives to those digital signature schemes must be considered.

L. B. Oliveira—Also, a visiting associate professor at Stanford University.

© Springer Nature Switzerland AG 2019
R. Miani et al. (Eds.): GPC 2019, LNCS 11484, pp. 104–114, 2019.
https://doi.org/10.1007/978-3-030-19223-5_8

Moreover, it is paramount to evaluate post-quantum cryptosystems suitable for devices of the Internet of Things due to the expected increase of such devices[1]. IoT devices count on limited resources which impose a significant restriction to which cryptosystems are viable for these platforms. Hash-based signatures (HBS) represent a reasonable alternative for IoT devices since they only require a one-way function [5], such as cryptographic hash functions, and not expensive operations as in RSA and ECDSA.

HBS allow a trade-off between performance (both in storage and processing time) and security level [11]. Also, in the case of the employed hash function become insecure – as in the advent of a collision be found, it is trivial to replace it, which provides a certain flexibility to the signatures. Besides, their security relies only on the collision resistance property of the hash function chose [5] which is well-understood by the security community.

The option for HBS in this work is due to their fast execution and better-understood security parameters [7] in comparison to other post-quantum alternatives such as lattice-based cryptography. Also, the HBS requires less computational power since it only requires one-way functions. Therefore, a resource-constrained device with hardware to compute AES, for instance, can be easily adapted to run an HBS scheme.

The paper's structure and main contributions of this work are:

1. A simple and straight-forward explanation of the functioning of HBS in Sect. 2;
2. The discussion about the implementation of Winternitz (W-OTS) and Merkle (MSS) schemes in Sect. 3;
3. The performance evaluation regarding storage, processing, and communication in Sect. 4;
4. A gathering of works in post-quantum cryptography for resource-constrained devices in Sect. 5.

2 Background

The Hash-based signatures were created by Merkle [17]. Although they exist for about 40 years, they only gained attention recently as a post-quantum alternative to the currently adopted signature schemes. Their construction only requires the existence of one-way functions and their security relies on the collision resistance property of the chosen function.

Among the many and main advantages of HBS are:

1. The implementation simplicity;
2. Their well-understood security [7];
3. Their keys and signatures are smaller than other post-quantum alternatives (e.g. lattice-based cryptography) and can be smaller compared to classical computing alternatives for the same security level such as RSA [19];

---

[1] http://www.gartner.com/newsroom/id/2636073.

4. The time spent generating signatures and verifying them is competitive even in comparison to traditional schemes [12].

Some disadvantages include the limited number of signatures that can be generated with a key and the impossibility to use them for encryption, which makes HBS a cryptosystem exclusively for digital signatures.

2.1   Types of HBS

HBS schemes are divided into three distinct types: one-time signatures (OTS), few-time signatures, and multi-time signatures (MTS). The first allows the generation of a single signature per pair of keys, that is each private key can sign a single message before being discarded. Therefore, the OTS are not useful in practice. However, OTS are used in the construction of MTS schemes that allow a larger number of signatures. The second type, few-time signatures, is not very discussed in the literature and will not be discussed in this paper.

Figure 1 shows how a signature is generated using the scheme called LD-OTS, the simplest OTS in the literature. In the Fig., n represents the size of the output produced by the hash function f in bits, SK is the private key – or signing key, PK is the public key and b_i is the i-th bit in the hashed message that will be signed for $0 \leq i < n$. SK is a sequence of bits, each of size n, selected randomly. We obtain PK by applying f to each sequence of SK. The signature is calculated by selecting a sequence $sk_{i,0}$ from SK if the i-th bit is 0 or $sk_{i,1}$ if it is 1. As one can see, a OTS scheme reveals part of its private key, therefore, a second signature could present an adversary with the whole SK. So, a LD-OTS SK should be discarded after one utilization. Also, the security level of the HBS presented is defined as $n/2$ [7].

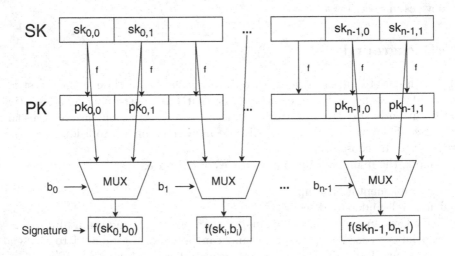

Fig. 1. Signature generation in LD-OTS.

To verify a LD-OTS signature, a similar process is conducted. However, for each bit in the hashed message, we obtain the respective sequence (according to b_i binary value) from PK instead of SK. Then, f is calculated over all sk_i, n sequences in the signature and compared to the sequences selected in the previous step (from PK). Since $f(SK) = PK$, both results should be equal for a signature to be valid for the corresponding message.

2.2 WOTS

It is noticeable that LD-OTS keys have a considerable large size $(2n^2)$. This occurs because each bit in the message is signed individually – a sequence from SK with n bits is selected for each bit in the message. The W-OTS scheme, however, decreases the key size allowing more bits to be signed simultaneously. A parameter w defines the number of bits signed together. This improvement can be accomplished by increasing the number of executions of f, namely, processing time. From w and n these other following parameters are defined:

$$t_1 = \left\lceil \frac{n}{w} \right\rceil, t_2 = \left\lceil \frac{\lceil log_2 t_1 \rceil + 1 + w}{w} \right\rceil, t = t_1 + t_2 \tag{1}$$

The private key SK is composed of t sequences of bits with size n. The public key PK is generated by applying f $2^w - 1$ times to SK. For the signature generation we calculate the message hash as for LD-OTS, resulting in $f(M) = B = (b_0, b_1, ..., b_{n-1})$. B is then divided into t_1 sequences of size w as in $B = b_{t-1}||...||b_{t-t_1}$, where $||$ stands for concatenation. Following, each b_i is considered an integer of value between 0 e $2^w - 1$ and a checksum C is computed.

$$C = \sum_{i=t-t_1}^{t-1} (2^w - b_i) \tag{2}$$

Afterward, C is divided into t_2 sequences of bits with size w as in $C = b_{t_2-1}||...||b_0$. If the size of B and C are not divisible by w, zeros are padded at the beginning of the sequence. Finally, the signature SIG is calculated using $B||C$:

$$SIG = (f^{b_{t-1}}(sk_{t-1}), ..., f^{b_1}(sk_1), f^{b_0}(sk_0)) \tag{3}$$

The signature is verified through the calculation of the checksum again as described previously and by comparing the signature hash computed bellow with the public key.

$$(f^{2^w-1-b_{t-1}}(sig_{t-1}), ..., f^{2^w-1-b_0}(sig_0)) = (pk_{t-1}, ..., pk_0) \tag{4}$$

2.3 MSS

The scheme MSS, which is our example of a MTS scheme, uses a binary tree of hashes (Merkle tree) to sign up to 2^h messages where h is the tree's height.

Figure 2 shows a tree that allows the signature of 8 messages. There are generated 2^h OTS keys and the hash of these public keys $PK_0, ..., PK_{2^h}$ are stored in tree's leaves. Each node above the leaves is computed by hashing its both left and right child together in this order. The public key in a MSS scheme is the tree's root. Therefore, to verify a signature, the verifier should receive the OTS public key used for that particular message, the index of the used OTS key and all nodes in the verification path to allow the root's calculation. A signature MSS is valid if the OTS verification results are valid and also if the reconstruction of the tree results in the same known root (the public key).

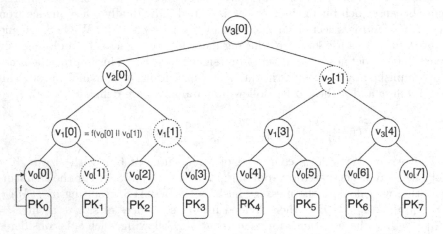

Fig. 2. MSS h = 3. Dashed-dashed nodes are used in calculating the root in a signature with $v_0[0]$.

3   Implementation

The implementation of the HBS schemes presented in this paper (W-OTS and MSS) were made in C using the cryptographic library RELIC[2]. The HBS were implemented following the specifications and algorithms defined in [5] and described in Sect. 2 of this work.

To generate the keys we used a pseudorandom number generator (PRNG) implemented in RELIC. Through this approach, there is no need to store all of the MSS OTS keys, but only the seed for the PRNG would suffice to generate the OTS keys as needed. This improvement saves storage without incurring in significantly more processing costs.

The implementation was designed to allow for the cryptographic hash function used to be easily replaced. The excerpt below presents a generic function to calculate a message's hash. As it can be observed, the hash function can be

---

[2] https://github.com/relic-toolkit.

selected in compiling time by using macros. The RELIC's implementation of SHA-2 was the one used in the code.

```
1   void hash_msg(uint8_t out[MD_LEN],
2                 uint8_t *msg, size_t size)
3   {
4   #if MD_MAP == SHONE
5     md_map_shone(out,msg,size);
6   #elif MD_MAP == SH224
7     md_map_sh224(out,msg,size);
8   #elif MD_MAP == SH256
9     md_map_sh256(out,msg,size);
10  #elif MD_MAP == SH384
11    md_map_sh384(out,msg,size);
12  #elif MD_MAP == SH512
13    md_map_sh512(out,msg,size);
14  #endif
15  }
```

4 Results

4.1 Analytic Evaluations

Analytic evaluations were performed according to the definitions in [5]. The Tables 1 and 2 presents the trade-off between memory (signature and key size) and processing (number of executions of the hash function) in the W-OTS scheme accordingly to the choice of the parameter w for SHA256 and SHA512 respectively. The key size decreases linearly while the number of evaluations of f increases exponentially. Therefore, it is paramount to find the trade-off that satisfies the device's constraints.

Table 1. Signature size × processing time (SHA256)

w	Key/sig. (bytes)	Execution of SHA256
2	4,256	399
4	2,144	1,005
8	1,088	8,670
16	576	117,9630

Table 3 shows the analytic evaluation of MSS scheme considering $w = 4$ and the use of SHA256 function, which provides a 128-bit security level. The signature size is different from the tables presented before for W-OTS alone since some Merkle's tree nodes are added for the MSS public key can be validated.

Table 2. Signature size × processing time (SHA512)

w	Key/sig. size (bytes)	Execution of SHA512
2	16,768	786
4	8,384	1,965
8	4,224	16,830
16	2,176	2,228,190

Table 3. Key/Signature size × tree height

h	Key/sig. size (bytes)	Number of sig.
14	2,592	2,720
16	2,656	65,536
18	2,720	262,144

4.2   Experimental Evaluations

The experimental evaluations were developed for the Arduino Due platform which contains an ATSAM3X8E 84 MHz processor unit, 96 kB of SRAM memory, and 512 kB of Flash memory. The experiments were performed 100 times for each operation (key generation, signature generation, and signature verification). The Fig. 3(a) and (b) presents the time per operation using the functions SHA256, SHA384, and SHA512 implemented in RELIC's library. The chosen values for w were 2 and 4 since these values allow an acceptable key size for Arduino Due without an impractical increase in execution time for the platform.

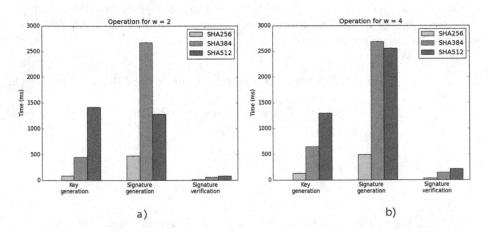

Fig. 3. Time per operation in W-OTS.

Figure 4 presents the time per operation for MSS using W-OTS. The larger cost for MSS is the key generation since it is necessary to generate all OTS keys to compute the PK through the computation of a Merkle tree. For small h values it is possible to generate the keys in the resource-constrained device itself, however, for larger trees it would be impractical. The signature generation and verification operations have the majority of their costs related to the OTS scheme costs. This occurs because generating and validating the authentication path is cheap since only h nodes are used compared to the OTS-related costs.

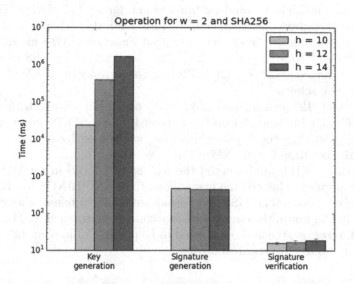

Fig. 4. Time per operation in MSS.

5   Related Work

The work of [2] presents a panorama of the post-quantum cryptography including HBS, code-based cryptography, lattice-based cryptography, and multivariate-quadratic-equations cryptography. Other works that introduce a general perspective on post-quantum cryptosystems are [1,3,6].

There are works that implement post-quantum cryptosystems cited in Sect. 1 for resource constrained-devices. An implementation of multivariate quadratic cryptosystems for wireless sensor networks is presented in [15]. A code-based cryptosystems implementation is presented in [4]. Also, the work of [22] presents lattice-based cryptography as a suitable alternative for IoT devices due to its efficiency and strong security guarantees.

In the literature, there are also works that implement and evaluate HBS in resource-constrained devices such as smart cards with 8-bits processors [19] and

16-bit [12], AVR ATxmega processors [8], and ARM Cortex M3 micro-controllers [13]. However, there are still few papers about this topic.

The MSS and W-OTS schemes were implemented in smart cards with 8-bit processors of the AT90SCxxx family using AES block cipher in [19]. The authors showed that their implementation for smart cards results in a smaller code compared to RSA for that platform, also it was more efficient than RSA and had a similar performance compared to ECDSA. However, in this paper, the keys were not generated directly in the device due to its severe limitations. The scheme XMSS is implemented in [10] for IoT motes. XMSS presents lots of hash operations, which could be burdensome for an IoT device. Therefore, they propose a lightweight sign/verify solution for this scheme by using the Keccak-400 hash function in eXtended Output Function (XOF) mode. Another HBS implementation is the work of [20]. They implemented a MSS scheme on a Pyboard IoT device with STM32F405RG microcontroller using LD-OTS as the OTS underlying scheme.

The work of [12] presents a version based on XMSS for which they named XMSS$^+$ and their implementation for a 16-bit Infineon SLE78 smart card. The problem of generating the keys, in this case, was solved by reducing the time spent in this operation for the XMSS$^+$.

The authors of [13] implemented the scheme SPHINCS in an ARM Cortex M3 microcontroller. This scheme is stateless, that is, SPHINCS has no records of the last key used, unlike MSS. The disadvantage of stateless schemes is that their keys are significantly larger than stateful schemes (such as MSS and its variations). However, the authors showed to be possible to implement a stateless scheme in a resource-constrained device.

6   Conclusion

The present work demonstrated the applicability of HBS in resource-constrained IoT devices as an alternative to traditional signature schemes in the post-quantum period. The HBS should be considered as possible substitutes for RSA, DSA, ECDSA, and others. Also, their well-understood security level and their easy implementation give the HBS advantages in relation to other post-quantum cryptosystems. It is paramount, as stressed before, to consider and study new alternatives to prevent the security implications of large-scale quantum computers in functioning.

For future works, we will implement other HBS schemes for evaluation and comparison to the already implemented schemes. Besides, other metrics can be used in evaluations such as power consumption, code size, and the number of cycles an IoT device processor needs to perform the operations.

Acknowledgment. This work was partially supported by FAPEMIG, CNPq, CAPES, and RNP. We would also like to thank Rafael Misoczki.

References

1. Barreto, P.S.L.M., et al.: A panorama of post-quantum cryptography. In: Koç, Ç.K. (ed.) Open Problems in Mathematics and Computational Science, pp. 387–439. Springer, Cham (2014). https://doi.org/10.1007/978-3-319-10683-0_16
2. Bernstein, D.J.: Introduction to post-quantum cryptography. In: Bernstein, D.J., Buchmann, J., Dahmen, E. (eds.) Post-quantum cryptography, pp. 1–14. Springer, Heidelberg (2009). https://doi.org/10.1007/978-3-540-88702-7_1
3. Bernstein, D.J.: Post-quantum cryptography. In: van Tilborg, H.C.A., Jajodia, S. (eds.) Encyclopedia of Cryptography and Security, pp. 949–950. Springer, Heidelberg (2011). https://doi.org/10.1007/978-1-4419-5906-5
4. Biasi, F.P., Barreto, P.S., Misoczki, R., Ruggiero, W.V.: Scaling efficient code-based cryptosystems for embedded platforms. J. Cryptogr. Eng. 4(2), 123–134 (2014)
5. Buchmann, J., Dahmen, E., Szydlo, M.: Hash-based digital signature schemes. In: Bernstein, D.J., Buchmann, J., Dahmen, E. (eds.) Post-Quantum Cryptography, pp. 35–93. Springer, Heidelberg (2009). https://doi.org/10.1007/978-3-540-88702-7_3
6. Buchmann, J., Ding, J. (eds.): PQCrypto 2008. LNCS, vol. 5299. Springer, Heidelberg (2008). https://doi.org/10.1007/978-3-540-88403-3
7. Buchmann, J., Dahmen, E., Ereth, S., Hülsing, A., Rückert, M.: On the security of the Winternitz one-time signature scheme. In: Nitaj, A., Pointcheval, D. (eds.) AFRICACRYPT 2011. LNCS, vol. 6737, pp. 363–378. Springer, Heidelberg (2011). https://doi.org/10.1007/978-3-642-21969-6_23
8. Eisenbarth, T., von Maurich, I., Ye, X.: Faster hash-based signatures with bounded leakage. In: Lange, T., Lauter, K., Lisoněk, P. (eds.) SAC 2013. LNCS, vol. 8282, pp. 223–243. Springer, Heidelberg (2014). https://doi.org/10.1007/978-3-662-43414-7_12
9. ElGamal, T.: A public key cryptosystem and a signature scheme based on discrete logarithms. IEEE Trans. Inf. Theory 31(4), 469–472 (1985)
10. Ghosh, S., Misoczki, R., Sastry, M.R.: Lightweight post-quantum-secure digital signature approach for IoT motes
11. Hülsing, A.: W-OTS+ – shorter signatures for hash-based signature schemes. In: Youssef, A., Nitaj, A., Hassanien, A.E. (eds.) AFRICACRYPT 2013. LNCS, vol. 7918, pp. 173–188. Springer, Heidelberg (2013). https://doi.org/10.1007/978-3-642-38553-7_10
12. Hülsing, A., Busold, C., Buchmann, J.: Forward secure signatures on smart cards. In: Knudsen, L.R., Wu, H. (eds.) SAC 2012. LNCS, vol. 7707, pp. 66–80. Springer, Heidelberg (2013). https://doi.org/10.1007/978-3-642-35999-6_5
13. Hülsing, A., Rijneveld, J., Schwabe, P.: ARMed SPHINCS: computing a 41 KB signature in 16 KB of RAM (2016)
14. Johnson, D., Menezes, A., Vanstone, S.: The elliptic curve digital signature algorithm (ECDSA). Int. J. Inf. Secur. 1(1), 36–63 (2001)
15. Maia, R.J.M., Barreto, P.S.L.M., de Oliveira, B.T.: Implementation of multivariate quadratic quasigroup for wireless sensor network. In: Gavrilova, M.L., Tan, C.J.K., Moreno, E.D. (eds.) Transactions on Computational Science XI. LNCS, vol. 6480, pp. 64–78. Springer, Heidelberg (2010). https://doi.org/10.1007/978-3-642-17697-5_4
16. Menezes, A.J., Van Oorschot, P.C., Vanstone, S.A.: Handbook of Applied Cryptography. CRC Press, Boca Raton (1996)

17. Merkle, R.C.: A certified digital signature. In: Brassard, G. (ed.) CRYPTO 1989. LNCS, vol. 435, pp. 218–238. Springer, New York (1990). https://doi.org/10.1007/0-387-34805-0_21

18. Rivest, R.L., Shamir, A., Adleman, L.: A method for obtaining digital signatures and public-key cryptosystems. Commun. ACM **21**(2), 120–126 (1978)

19. Rohde, S., Eisenbarth, T., Dahmen, E., Buchmann, J., Paar, C.: Fast hash-based signatures on constrained devices. In: Grimaud, G., Standaert, F.-X. (eds.) CARDIS 2008. LNCS, vol. 5189, pp. 104–117. Springer, Heidelberg (2008). https://doi.org/10.1007/978-3-540-85893-5_8

20. Saldamli, G., Ertaul, L., Kodirangaiah, B.: Post-quantum cryptography on IoT: Merkle's tree authentication. In: Proceedings of the International Conference on Wireless Networks (ICWN), pp. 35–41. The Steering Committee of The World Congress in Computer Science, Computer Engineering and Applied Computing (2018)

21. Shor, P.W.: Algorithms for quantum computation: discrete logarithms and factoring. In: 1994 Proceedings of 35th Annual Symposium on Foundations of Computer Science, pp. 124–134. IEEE (1994)

22. Xu, R., Cheng, C., Qin, Y., Jiang, T.: Lighting the way to a smart world: lattice-based cryptography for internet of things. arXiv preprint arXiv:1805.04880 (2018)

Performance Analysis of a System for Vehicle Identification Using LoRa and RFID

Marcelo G. Griese and João H. Kleinschmidt[(✉)]

Federal University of ABC, Santo André, SP, Brazil
joao.kleinschmdt@ufabc.edu.br

Abstract. This paper proposes a system for vehicle identification using RFID and Low Power Wide Area Networks (LPWAN). Vehicle plates are identified with RFID tags and this information is sent to a cloud server using LoRa links. We developed a proof of concept of the proposed architecture to study the feasibility of using LoRa for the transmission of vehicle data. We analyzed the performance of the system in real urban environments with different parameters of the LoRa transmission. The results obtained shows the system may achieve reasonable performance in terms of packet error rate and message throughput. The system showed LoRa is a viable technology to be applied in this context and other applications of Intelligent Transport Systems.

Keywords: Vehicle identification · LoRa · RFID · LPWAN

1 Introduction

Vehicle inspection has always been a challenge for government agencies, which have always tried to find ways to facilitate this activity. The model of identification of vehicles through plates fixed in the front and back of the cars is adopted worldwide, only varying its patterns of numbering and sequencing. In recent years, cameras installed in the roads are being used for electronic surveillance using the character recognition of the plates through images obtained by cameras in the roads. However, these plate identification systems using cameras are vulnerable to weather conditions, dirt and traffic conditions. In such conditions, the efficiency of these systems in the vehicle identification is not adequate. Many vehicle identification systems are being proposed to use radio frequency identification technology (RFID), which may increase the efficiency of the systems [1–5].

Combining this efficiency with reduced equipment costs, RFID has become popular in the last decade in the identification of vehicles in commercial applications such as access control in parking lots and automatic toll collection. However, besides monitoring, these systems could act with other objectives, inserting the traffic monitoring in an Internet of Things (IoT) context [2, 6]. The basic concept of IoT is the connectivity of objects or things, so the information is sent from the environment in which these objects are inserted to a central monitor station or cloud which is able to make decisions more efficiently. This is a typical scenario of a smart city, which makes use of the technology to improve the urban infrastructure, making it more efficient and increasing the quality of life of people. Among the applications of smart cities, we could cite the

R. Miani et al. (Eds.): GPC 2019, LNCS 11484, pp. 115–127, 2019.
https://doi.org/10.1007/978-3-030-19223-5_9

monitoring and control of public lighting, monitoring of river levels, water and energy distribution systems and monitoring and control of road traffic.

The ease of creating devices and applications with IoT concepts has grown the demand for technologies capable of performing a communication between machines, known as Machine-to-Machine (M2M). Thus, since the emergence of the IoT concept there is a technological race to find the best solution for the connectivity of these devices. There is already a large telephony industry covering 3G, 4G and 5G technologies. Although it is possible to use these technologies developed for mobile telephony in IoT applications, they are not always the most suitable for all applications, either by cost or by offering a higher data rate than the applications need. Many IoT applications and smart cities, such as public lighting, smart grids, pollution monitoring, agriculture, among others, send some tens of bytes of data every few minutes or even hours. Another important feature in IoT applications is power consumption, as these devices typically are battery powered and require some energy-efficient data transmission technology, which is not the case for the traditional long-range technologies used for Internet access. Technologies for local and personal wireless networks such as Bluetooth, ZigBee and Wi-Fi can also be used in IoT applications, but with a low transmission range of up to a few tens of meters [6].

In recent years, several communication technologies known as Low Power Wide Area Networks (LPWAN) have been developed, which have two main characteristics: long distance communication and low energy consumption [7–10]. Among these technologies we can highlight LoRa, Sigfox, Weightless and NB-IoT, among others. They have great potential to meet the demand for IoT applications in industry and cities [11–15]. One of the most promising technologies that has been studied in the literature is LoRa [16, 17]. LoRa is a protocol developed and patented by Semtech Corporation [18, 19]. In a LoRa network, the devices send information to a gateway, which in turn can connect to an application server on the Internet. The LoRa protocol can operate in unlicensed frequency bands.

Several works propose the use of RFID for vehicle inspection and related applications, such as traffic control or stolen vehicle detection [1–5]. In these works, data collected by RFID readers are either stored on the device itself or sent to a server with long range wireless radios such as 4G technologies or low range like ZigBee. However, these works do not consider LPWANs to send the data. In this paper we propose a system for vehicle inspection with RFID and LoRa for data transmission. RFID tags are placed on vehicle license plates and readings made by the RFID reader are sent by a LoRa end node to a LoRa gateway. This gateway is connected to the Internet and sends the data to a server in the cloud. This work analyzes the performance of the data transmission with LoRa technology using different physical layer parameters. We analyze the packet error rate and throughput in an urban environment in the metropolitan region of São Paulo, Brazil. The paper is structured as follows: Sect. 2 describes the main features of LoRa and RFID technology; Sect. 3 presents the proposed system and test scenarios. Section 4 shows the results obtained and Sect. 5 makes the final considerations.

2   LoRa and RFID

LoRa is a wireless technology developed by Semtech [18, 19] to operate in the sub-GHz frequency bands, such as 433 MHz, 868 MHz (Europe) and 915 MHz (United States and Brazil). LoRa allows to reach transmission range of several kilometers with low energy consumption. The physical layer is called LoRa [16] and the upper layers form the LoRaWAN standard (open standard developed by LoRa Alliance) [17]. A LoRa network consists of end devices and gateways, forming a star topology. End devices can communicate with the gateways, which are connected to a LoRa server with IP network access. LoRaWAN defines security features and a medium access protocol so that multiple devices can communicate with a gateway which uses LoRa modulation. The payload in a packet is up to 255 bytes, reaching data rates up to 50 Kbps. In this work, only the radio layer (LoRa) will be addressed.

LoRa employs a modulation called chirp spread spectrum and has three parameters for modulation customization: spreading factor (SF), bandwidth (BW) and coding rate (CR). The spreading factor (SF) specifies the number of symbols sent for each information bit and its value is in the order of 2^{SF}; if SF = 6, we have 64 chips/symbol. In LoRa this parameter can be adjusted from 6 to 12. When SF = 12 there are 4096 chips/symbol. The higher the SF, the greater the transmission time of data, but its noise immunity will also be greater.

The bandwidth (BW) parameter is related to the transmission rate and the maximum transmission range, or receiver sensitivity. A higher bandwidth leads to a higher transmission rate and a shorter time to send a message. However, the sensitivity of the receiver is lower (and also the distance achieved by the transmission). The coding rate (CR) uses forward error correction (FEC) and can be configured with 4/5, 4/6, 4/7 or 4/8 rates, that is, adding redundancy bits to the transmitted data. The more bits are transmitted, the less susceptible to errors is the packet, but in the cost of increasing the transmission time (time on air defined by LoRa). The data transmission rate is dependent on the parameters SF, BW and CR, and can be calculated using Eq. 1:

$$R_b = SF. \frac{\left[\frac{4}{4+CR}\right]}{\left[\frac{2^{SF}}{BW}\right]}.1000 \tag{1}$$

Figure 1 shows the LoRa packet format, which is defined by three fields. The first is a preamble used to synchronize the receiver with the data received from the transmitter. It is required for both the transmitter and the receiver to be configured with the same value of SF. The size of the preamble is variable and can be configured. The second field is an optional header which contains information related to the payload: the number of bytes, the coding rate and also information whether the data is protected by CRC (Cyclic Redundancy Check) code or not. The header is optional, since it may be omitted if this information is previously configured in the receiver. The header itself also has a CRC code. The third field is the payload of the message with two optional bytes of the CRC code. The maximum data size is 256 bytes.

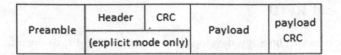

Fig. 1. LoRa packet format

The radio frequency identification technology (RFID) enables the reading of information contained in electronic tags, which are fixed to the objects to be identified [1, 3–5]. The electronic tag is composed of a microprocessor and an antenna. The tag can be active, when it has an internal battery to operate, or passive, when it has no internal battery and works with the radio wave energy emitted by the reader. The reader is the device which emits the radio waves and collects the response sent by the electronic tag. The tag receives the energy of the reader via an attached antenna and modulates the radio frequency signal to send the information to the reader. All readers are able to read and write on electronic tags. The EPC Gen2 (Electronic Product Code Generation 2) standard has a 96-bit numbering pattern and a set of standardizations defining the physical and logical characteristics of the communication between the reader and the tag. In this work we use the RFID-UHF (Ultra High Frequency), which operates in the frequency of 860–960 MHz with a range up to 10 m. This is the frequency band usually used in the identification of vehicles.

3   Implemented System

The proposed architecture is shown in Fig. 2. The RFID tag could be placed on the car plate or other specific part of the vehicle. The local controller is a device equipped with a RFID reader and a LoRa end device. This controller is able to read the tag which contains the information about the vehicle, such as the number of the plate, and then send the information to a LoRa gateway. This gateway is connected to the Internet and sends the information to a database in the cloud. Then the data received may be stored for future analysis. Several studies show RFID tags may be read with high accuracy even when vehicles are moving in high speeds [1].

We implemented the proposed controller with Arduino Mega microcontroller, RFID reader, LoRa shield and a battery (Fig. 3). The RFID-UHF antenna has an integrated reader which communicates with the tags and sends the information to the Arduino via serial communication. The microcontroller has a LoRa shield to communicate with the gateway and send the information obtained by the RFID reader.

In order to build a functional prototype that could be installed in real surveillance locations, the Arduino Mega board with the LoRa shield was packed in a plastic enclosure with IP65 degree of protection (Fig. 3a). Also we add an interface to facilitate the tests by using a 4-line display and a numeric keypad that allows monitoring and operating the system without the need of a computer. The basic parameters of the system can be modified, such as LoRa parameters SF, CR and BW. A real-time clock (RTC) module is used to obtain hour, minute and second. This information will be used to record the exact moment of transmission of each message to the LoRa gateway.

Figure 3(c) shows the complete set, in which, in addition a 12 V/12 A battery (Fig. 3b) to power the entire system during street tests for several hours without recharging.

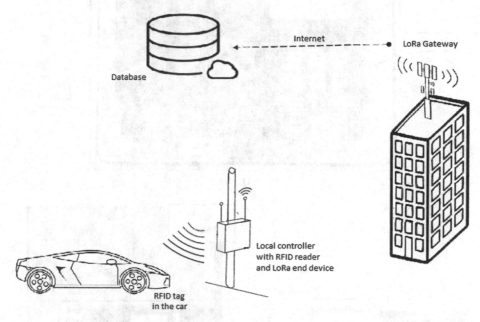

Database

Internet

LoRa Gateway

Local controller
with RFID reader
and LoRa end device

RFID tag
in the car

Fig. 2. System architecture

To implement the LoRa technology we used a gateway and an end device. The transmitter (end device) is an Arduino with a LoRa shield manufactured by Dragino (Fig. 4) operating at 915 MHz. This shield has a LoRa module manufactured by HopeRF Micro-electronics, providing an easy way to physically connect the LoRa module to the Arduino. The LoRa gateway is also manufactured by Dragino, model OLG01, and it has the same LoRa shield hardware, but already incorporated in an architecture based on the Arduino Uno connected to an ATmega328P. In addition, it has additional hardware which allows Internet connectivity via WiFi or Ethernet. The gateway is single channel (915 MHz) and therefore needs to be configured with the same BW, SF and CR parameters of the transmitter before data transmission.

The installation of the LoRa gateway is shown in Fig. 5. It was installed at the top of a 27-storey building which is approximately 80 m high, in the city of São Bernardo do Campo, in the metropolitan region of São Paulo (Brazil). The gateway was connected to the Internet using an Ethernet cable. Thus, the gateway receives the data sent by the LoRa transmitter through the radio interface and forwards it to an application in the cloud over the wired network. This application only receives the data and writes them to a database for later analysis. The data size is 26 bytes, with location information, identification (vehicle plate) and a timestamp (time obtained by the RTC). Both the LoRa shield and the LoRa gateway have a 3 dBi antenna approximately.

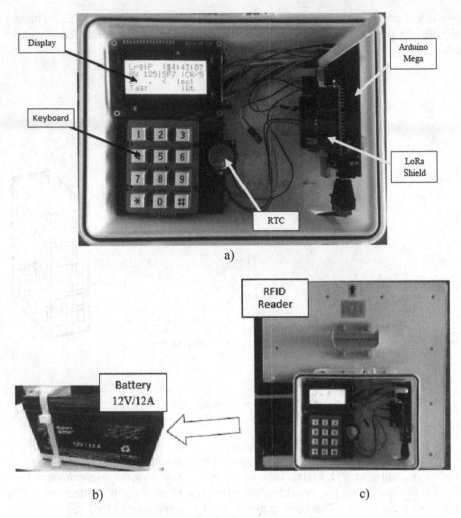

Fig. 3. Prototype

Fig. 4. LoRa transmitter (*end device*)

Fig. 5. LoRa gateway

We choose four points to perform the tests according to the distance to the gateway and the possibility of carrying out the tests without interruptions. Figure 6 shows the positions in the map of the city of São Bernardo and the distance to the gateway. Position 1 is located 500 m from the gateway, inside a park with many trees. The transmitter was placed at a height of 4 m from the ground.

Position 2 is located 1 km from the gateway, in St. José Square. The place also has many trees and is next to Assis Street. The transmitter was placed at a height of 80 cm from the ground, on top of a table. Position 3 is two kilometers from the gateway, at the junction of Piraporinha Avenue and exit 18 of the Anchieta Highway. The transmitter was placed at a height of 1 m from the ground in a traffic light control panel. Position 4 is located three kilometers from the gateway, on the third floor of a building in the São Bernardo Campus of the Federal University of ABC (UFABC). The transmitter was placed at a height of 1.5 m from the ground.

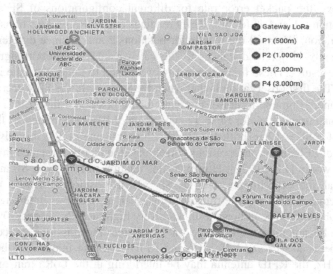

Fig. 6. Position of the tests

The factors and levels used for the tests are specified in Table 1. For each test the RFID antenna reads the values of RFID tags. These tags are positioned close to the antenna, simulating the plates of vehicles. We configure the antenna to send to the controller via serial port one read per second, until it reaches 500 readings for each configuration of Table 1. The factors used were the distance from the transmitter to the gateway and the BW and SF parameters. The choice of value of the parameters considers preliminary tests and similar references [20–22]. In general, low values of SF leads to high packet error rates. So we choose high values of SF (9, 10 and 12), since the application tolerate higher delays but need more reliability. The coding rate is fixed in 4/8, since this configuration has a lower packet error rate. For the bandwidth we choose the most used values in practical applications: 125 and 250 kHz. The data is received by the radio interface of the gateway and sent over the wired network to a computer that works as the LoRa application server. The calculated metrics for performance analysis are the packet error rate (PER) and throughput. PER is calculated using the number of packets that are not received, considering the total packets sent by the end node. The throughput is the number of successful messages delivered in a minute.

Table 1. Factors and levels

Factors	Levels
Distance between end device and LoRa gateway	500 m, 1 km, 2 km and 3 km
Bandwidth (BW)	125 and 250 kHz
Spreading factor (SF)	9, 10 and 12
Coding rate (CR)	4/8

4 Obtained Results

Figure 7 shows the packet error rate for different configurations of SF and BW in different locations (1 and 4) for 500 RFID readings and LoRa packets transmissions in each configuration. We omit the results for positions 2 and 3, since different locations and consequently, different distances to the gateway, do not present significant difference in the results. These first experiments were used to understand the influence of SF and BW. The first observation is that when the SF is high, the PER decreases, since a high SF is more immune to noise. For example, in position 4 the PER is above 40% with SF = 9 and under 30% for SF = 12. The value of BW also influences the PER. As can be seen for SF = 12 in both locations, a higher value of BW usually leads to a higher value of PER. Both observations corroborate the theory presented in Sect. 2 and other related works [11, 21, 22]. However, this relation of PER with SF and BW was not true for all the experiments, such as SF = 10 in position 1. This is probably to additional factors influencing the transmissions, such as obstacles, interference, etc. In general, the obtained PER in these tests were very high, usually around 30%. Both the RFID and LoRa antennas were turned on during the transmissions. Since LoRa use frequencies between 915 and 928 MHz and RFID-UHF use frequencies between 902 and 907.5 MHz, the RFID antenna may be interfering in the LoRa transmissions.

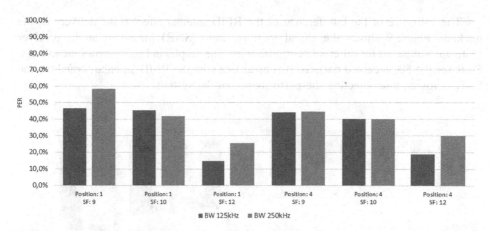

Fig. 7. PER for different configurations

Figure 8 shows the PER for different configurations in position 1, but comparing the results when the RFID antenna is turned on or turned off during LoRa transmissions. For each configuration we send 500 LoRa packets with the information collected by RFID reader. We can see in the results that turning the RFID antenna off during the transmissions of LoRa packets considerably improved the performance. We always obtained values of PER above 30% turning the RFID antenna off. The same observation of Fig. 8 is confirmed: high SF and low BW decreases the PER, thus improving the performance of the system. For SF = 12 and BW = 125 kHz we achieved the better results, with PER below 5%.

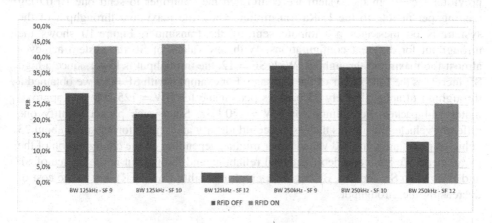

Fig. 8. PER for RFID antenna on and off

The influence of the interference of the RFID antenna affected the delivery of the packets. Figure 9 shows the signal to noise ratio (SNR) measured at the receiver (gateway) obtained for different configurations. The graphs in Fig. 9 shows the average SNR for the 500 received packets. It is clear that with the RFID antenna turned on, the SNR is lower, thus affecting the performance of the system.

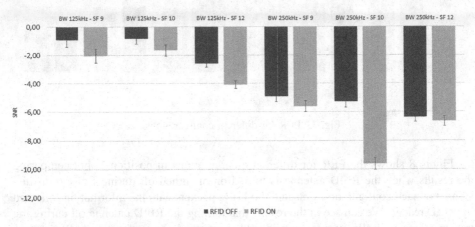

Fig. 9. Signal to noise ratio for different configurations

Another important metric for the proposed system is the throughput. We analyzed the throughput considering the number of successful messages deliverd in a minute. The message contains the information about the identified vehicle, as described in previous section. In the system we configured the controller to send one RFID tag reading per minute to the LoRa transmitter. Thus, the maximum throughput of the system is 60 messages per minute sent by the transmitter. Figure 10 shows the throughput for different configurations. With low values of SF the system achieves almost the maximum throughput. With SF = 12, the throughput is lower, since a high SF increases the time on air of the message. For example, with SF = 12 we obtained a throughput of approximately 23 packets per minute for BW = 125 kHz and approximately 44 packets per minute for BW = 250 kHz. Since each packet identify one different vehicle, this means the system could identify and send information of about 23 vehicles per minute until 60 vehicles per minute, depending on the configuration of the parameters. We have a tradeoff between reliability and throughput in the choice of SF and BW. High SF and low BW achieves high reliability (low PER), but in the cost of decreasing the throughput.

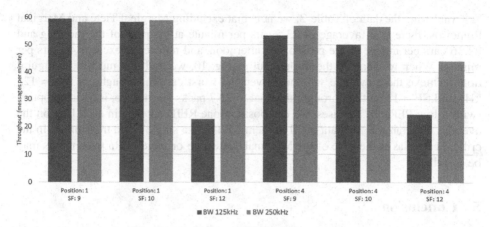

Fig. 10. Throughput for different configurations

The analysis of the results shows LoRa and RFID are possible technologies to be explored in a scenario of vehicle inspection. One question which arise with the analysis of the results is how suitable is this proposed architecture to be implemented in a scenario of vehicle inspection. The Traffic Engineering Company (CET) of São Paulo annually publishes a study with the quantity of vehicles in the main streets and avenues of the city of São Paulo [23]. Table 2 show some points of avenues analyzed by CET during the rush hour in the morning and afternoon. Each collect point indicates where the data is collected (the exact location may be consulted in the report of CET). The data is shown in vehicles per minute, considering the average of 3 h in each location. This number sums all the cars that pass through all the lanes of the avenue, that is, if an avenue has three lanes, the numbers refer to the volume of cars of the three lanes. The volumes of buses, trucks and bicycles, also counted in the report, are not shown in the table.

Table 2. Cars per minute in the streets of São Paulo, Brazil [23]

Local (collection point)	Cars per minute (morning)	Cars per minute (afternoon)
Av. Ipiranga (point 1)	11.63	6.21
Av. Senador Queiroz (point 4)	31.39	14.14
Av. Interlagos (point 2)	19.81	27.31
Av. Washington Luís (point 3)	35.88	45.44
Av. dos Bandeirantes (point 1)	45.31	36.22
Av. Ibirapuera (point 3)	8.15	9.64
Av. Vereador José Diniz (point 1)	25.66	27.57
Est. Do M' Boi Mirim (point 2)	10.07	12.38
Marginal Tietê (point 1)	83.17	100.61
Marginal Pinheiros (point 1)	52.31	56.98

Analyzing the data of Table 2, we note that excluding Marginal Tietê and Marginal Pinheiros, there is an average of 23.5 cars per minute at the peak of the morning and 22.36 cars per minute at the peak of the afternoon, and no avenue exceeds 46 cars per minute. When we analyze the throughput of Fig. 10, we find that most of configurations achieve these average volumes. Even the worst case in throughput, BW = 125 kHz and SF = 12, with a throughput equal to 22.7 packs per minute, is a viable option (with a low PER). In all cases, we can position one RFID antenna in each lane on the avenues and transmit the data of all of them with only a single LoRa transmitter. In the critical cases, as in the case of the Marginal Tietê, two or more LoRa transmitters may be installed.

5   Conclusion

Vehicle inspection is one interesting application of the Internet of Things and smart cities. In this paper we proposed an architecture for this task using LoRa and RFID technologies. The proposed system reads a RFID tag in the plate of a car and this information is sent by LoRa communication to a LoRa gateway connected to the cloud. The results obtained show the performance of the system under different configurations. The results indicate the feasibility of the proposal, although some configurations of the LoRa parameters do not achieve a good performance. The PER with low values of SF may be too high for the application considered, while high SF result in lower PER, but in the cost of lower throughput. The adequate choice of SF, BW and CR must be made, considering their tradeoffs. The proposed system may be applied to other applications of vehicles in smart cities, such as traffic monitoring, parking, stolen vehicles and so on. Future works include analyzing the performance of LoRaWAN in the system, since this protocol adds additional features, such as medium access control and security. Other issue to be investigated is the duty cycle restriction which may limit the number of transmission in a given period.

References

1. Wang, Y., Pretorius, A.J., Abbosh, A.M.: Low-profile antenna with elevated toroid-shaped radiation for on-road reader of RFID-enabled vehicle registration plate. IEEE Trans. Antennas Propag. **64**(4), 1520–1525 (2016)
2. Xiao, L., Wang, Z.: Internet of things: a new application for intelligent traffic monitoring system. J. Netw. **6**(6), 887–894 (2011)
3. Sundar, R., Hebbar, S., Golla, V.: Implementing intelligent traffic control system for congestion control, ambulance clearance, and stolen vehicle detection. IEEE Sens. J. **15**(2), 1109–1113 (2015)
4. Vishnevsky, V., Larionov, A., Ivanov, R.: Architecture of application platform for RFID-enabled traffic law enforcement system. In: 7th International Workshop on Communication Technologies for Vehicles (Nets4Cars-Fall), St. Petersburg, pp. 45–49 (2014)
5. Wang, J., Ni, D., Li, K.: RFID-based vehicle positioning and its applications in connected vehicles. Sensors **14**(3), 4225–4238 (2014). (Basel, Switzerland)

6. Al-Fuqaha, A., Guizani, M., Mohammadi, M., Aledhari, M., Ayyash, M.: Internet of things: a survey on enabling technologies, protocols, and applications. IEEE Commun. Surv. Tutor. **17**(4), 2347–2376 (2015)
7. Centenaro, M., Vangelista, L., Zanella, A., Zorzi, M.: Long-range communications in unlicensed bands: the rising stars in the IoT and smart city scenarios. IEEE Wirel. Commun. **23**(5), 60–67 (2016)
8. Raza, U., Kulkarni, P., Sooriyabandara, M.: Low power wide area networks: an overview. IEEE Commun. Surv. Tutor. **19**(2), 855–873 (2017)
9. Mekki, K., Bajic, E., Chaxel, F., Meyer, F.: A comparative study of LPWAN technologies for large-scale IoT deployment. ICT Express **5**(1), 1–7 (2019)
10. Sinha, R.S., Wei, Y., Hwang, S.H.: A survey on LPWA technology: LoRa and NB-IoT. ICT Express **3**(1), 14–21 (2017)
11. Petäjäjärvi, J., Mikhaylov, K., Yasmin, R., Hämäläinen, M., Iinatti, J.: Evaluation of LoRa LPWAN technology for indoor remote health and wellbeing monitoring. Int. J. Wirel. Inf. Netw. **24**(2), 153–165 (2017)
12. Li, L., Ren, J., Zhu, Q.: On the application of LoRa LPWAN technology in Sailing Monitoring System. In: 13th Annual Conference on Wireless On-Demand Network Systems and Services (WONS), pp. 77–80 (2017)
13. Magrin, D., Centenaro, M., Vangelista, L.: Performance evaluation of LoRa networks in a smart city scenario. In: IEEE International Conference on Communications (ICC), pp. 1–7 (2017)
14. Li, Y., Yan, X., Zeng, L., Wu, H.: Research on water meter reading system based on LoRa communication. In: IEEE International Conference on Smart Grid and Smart Cities (ICSGSC), pp. 248–251 (2017)
15. Sanchez-Iborra, R., Cano, M.D.: State of the art in LPWAN solutions for industrial IoT services. Sensors **16**(5), 708 (2016). (Basel, Switzerland)
16. LoRa-Alliance: LoRA Alliance wide area network for IoT (2015). https://www.loraalliance.org/technology
17. LoRa-Alliance: LoRaWAN specification (2016). https://www.loraalliance.org/lorawan-for-developers
18. Semtech Corporation: LoRa modem designer's guide. Application note AN1200.13 (2013)
19. Semtech Corporation: LoraTM modulation basics. Application note AN1200 (2015)
20. Griese, M.G., Kleinschmidt, J.H.: The impact of physical layer parameters in the performance of LoRa in urban environments (2019, submitted for publication)
21. Petäjäjärvi, J., Mikhaylov, K., Pettissalo, M., Janhunen, J., Iinatti, J.: Performance of a low-power wide-area network based on LoRa technology: doppler robustness, scalability, and coverage. Int. J. Distrib. Sens. Netw. **13**(3), 1–16 (2017)
22. Petrić, T., Goessens, M., Nuaymi, L., Toutain, L., Pelov, A.: Measurements, performance and analysis of LoRa FABIAN, a real-world implementation of LPWAN. In: IEEE 27th Annual International Symposium on Personal, Indoor, and Mobile Radio Communications (PIMRC), pp. 1–7 (2016)
23. Companhia de Engenharia de Tráfego – CET: Mobilidade no Sistema Viário Principal: Volume e Velocidade – 2016, São Paulo (2017). (in Portuguese)

Automating Mockup-Based Usability Testing on the Mobile Device

Silvio Barra[1], Rita Francese[2(✉)], and Michele Risi[2]

[1] University of Cagliari, 09124 Cagliari, CA, Italy
silvio.barra@unica.it
[2] University of Salerno, 84084 Fisciano, SA, Italy
{francese,mrisi}@unisa.it

Abstract. User interface usability is a very relevant aspect, especially for mobile applications. In this paper we propose a methodology for automating user interface usability testing in the early phases of the development process directly on the mobile device. Mockup interfaces are designed, then the way the designer interacts with the interface is compared with the way the end-user interacts with the same interface and the discrepancies between the two usage models are highlighted. The methodology is supported by a mobile tool named PlatoS, which captures a case of use of a mockup in terms of a sequence of actions. On the end-user side, PlatoS captures the user interaction with the mockups and performs the automatic identification of usability problems on the base of the log data. An example of evaluation of an eCommerce mobile prototypes is also presented.

Keywords: Mobile application · Automatic usability evaluation · Mockups

1 Introduction

The importance of Usability in software development is widely recognized. This is specifically true for mobile applications: poor usability and user experience are the main causes of uninstalling the app, and, ultimately, are responsible of the failure of the software product [2,6,25]. Recently, the introduction of usability aspects in all the phases of the development process is increasing, especially in agile methodology [2,3].

User interaction is generally evaluated in experiments involving a human supervisor, who observes the user behavior and annotates the mistakes that each participant performs and the time he needs to conclude a given test [17]. As a result, a lot of time of the human observant is waste to supervise the evaluation tasks, since there is the need of performing an one-to-one evaluation session for each participant. Thus, the adoption of a "play-replay" approach may be very useful to conduct unsupervised field studies [10]. Generally, this usability evaluation modality requires a running system, as in the approach proposed by

© Springer Nature Switzerland AG 2019
R. Miani et al. (Eds.): GPC 2019, LNCS 11484, pp. 128–143, 2019.
https://doi.org/10.1007/978-3-030-19223-5_10

Lettner and Holzmann [10]. However, it is well known that a early detection of usability problems before the source code is written lowers the correction cost [24]. A solution may be to involve the users in the early phases of the development for evaluating prototypes of mockups, which have a low creation cost and are very effective in the early detection of usability problems [19].

The use of the mockups on the user's device and on the field may have several advantages with respect to the laboratory settings [9,27]. Indeed, mobile users use their applications when they are in environment with a high number of stimuli, such as on the train or while they are walking. Thus, the "mobility" aspect has also to be considered when evaluating usability of mobile apps.

In this paper, we propose a methodology for automating user interface usability testing in the early phases of the development process. The Android interfaces are designed in terms of mockups running on the user device. The methodology is based on the comparison of a perfect model (the way the designer interacts with the interface in terms of sequences of operations to perform and the associated accomplishment times) and the user model (model of the user behavior when interacting with the same GUI), and highlights the discrepancies between the two models. The methodology is supported by a tool named PlatoS, which enables the interface designer to integrate Android mockups, edited by using standard modeling tools (e.g., Eclipse or Android Studio) and to capture a case of use of a mockup in terms of a sequence of actions, directly on the mobile device. On the end-user side, PlatoS captures the user interaction with the mockups. It also performs automatic identification of usability problems through a statistical analysis of log data. The methodology presented in this paper is better explained through an example of evaluation of eCommerce mobile application mockups.

This paper is organized as follows: in Sect. 2 we discuss related work concerning usability evaluation approaches based on mockups. In Sect. 3 we present the usability evaluation methodology and the PlatoS architecture. An example of user interface evaluation is reported in Sect. 4. Finally, Sect. 5 concludes the paper with final remarks and outlines future work.

2 Related Work

Mockups of a mobile application are images representing how the app interface should appear when implemented. Their use in agile and model driven development approaches is increasing [20], together with their adoption in Requirement Specification [18].

The use of mockups for evaluating usability in the early development phases has been largely adopted in case of web applications, see [20] as an example. For mobile apps there exist several tools which support the designer in the creation of interactive mockups that can be downloaded on the user mobile device and work in a very similar way to the final application, see for example [12,13]. They generally do not collect the user behavior to perform usability evaluation. There is the need of a human observer who annotates the interaction times and the user problems.

Designer experts generally follow Usability and User Experience guidelines to produce mockups of the needed quality [7]. Often developers during the development lifecycle perform many changes to the original design and the initial effort of the designer is lost. Mockups are exploited in [14] for verifying whether an implemented mobile application corresponds to its original mockup-based design. To this aim computer vision techniques have been adopted. In our approach, the prototype is evolutionary and this problem does not subsist.

The DUE technique [4] divides the mockups into web page zones, (e.g., navigation, general information and data entry). The methodology is supported by a tool which allows the usability expert to identify if the usability guidelines have been respected in each page zone.

Klikker [27] supports usability testing of mobile applications in the early phases of the development process by using web-based mockups. The tasks are visually represented by paths and deviance from the established path are detected. The use of web technologies does not require the users to download any software. Few details have been provided on the analysis of the results. Only qualitative data have been collected in the case study.

3   The Proposed Methodology

The usability methodology we propose is user-centered: end-users actively take part to the design of interactive user interface since the early phases of the development. The methodology is supported by the PlatoS tool, which has a Client-Server architecture, as depicted by the deployment diagram in Fig. 1.

The process is composed of the following four activities:

- *Mockup Design activity.* On the personal computer the interface designer creates the interfaces by using an editing tool such as the one offered by Android Studio and uploads them (as XML documents) on the PlatoS Server (i.e., the Interface Upload component).
- *Task definition and simulation activity.* The designer downloads from the PlatoS server the mockups by using the PlatoS Android app on his mobile device. Then, for each interface he simulates the use of it, while the PlatoS app acquires data concerning the sequences of actions (e.g., which fields should be filled, which button has to be pressed) and takes the times of each action. The collected data are then transferred on the PlatoS server.
- *User Testing activity.* End-users download from the server the user interfaces, the tasks to be performed and the designer times and simulate the use of these interfaces on their mobile device. End-user feedback is collected after every mockup testing and transferred on the server.
- *Problem detection activity.* The user usability metrics [15] are automatically compared to the designer ones through a statistical analysis and a detailed report is created to be available in the designer private area accessible via web. In case the interface has some highlighted problem, the designer analyzes the issue and tries to address it by modifying properly the prototype. Indeed,

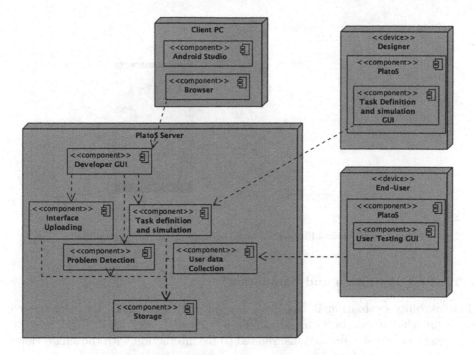

Fig. 1. The PlatoS system architecture.

mockups with poor user performances are send back to the Mockup Design activity to solve the usability problems.

3.1 Mockup Design

The XML interface may be created by using modern IDE's that support Android development, like Android Studio, or by programming editor. The use of real Android interfaces has the advantage of avoiding the problem of aligning the designed interface of a through-away prototype to the final interface implemented by the developers [11].

The Android user interface consists of a hierarchy of objects named *views*. The View class is the basic building block for all user interface components, such as buttons, checkboxes, and text entry fields. On the views the user can perform various actions (*events*), e.g., clicking on a button. Some views, as input text fields (*EditText*), have associated different events, such as hovering over the field and changing the text in the field. The views for a screen are organized in a hierarchy. The root of this hierarchy is a view named *ViewGroup*, which contains the layout of the entire screen. Some view groups are designated as *layouts* because they organize child views in a specific way and are typically used as the root view group.

Figure 2 shown an example of Android interface and the associated XML.

Fig. 2. An Android interface and the associated XML document.

3.2   Task Definition and Simulation

The usability evaluation is based on several predefined tasks the user has to perform when interacts with the mobile interfaces. Each task in turns may be composed of one or more actions, related to the interaction with the single views composing the interface.

Once an interface has been created, the designer imports it on the mobile device by pressing the *Import Layout* button of the PlatoS mobile app, shown in Fig. 3(a). Then he presses the *manage sequence* button, which enables him to select the interface and start the simulation, which records information concerning the correct use of the interface to perform a task. In particular, the developer presses the Start button and uses the interface, e.g., he fills in the input fields, checks the checkboxes and press the required buttons in the correct order. After the simulation, the designed provide a detailed textual description of the performed steps to complete correctly the task. Platos collects the times between the ending time of an action on a view and the ending time of an action of the successive view and associates this time to each view. A table consisting of view id, view type (e.g., TextView, Spinner), priority and duration is automatically filled. Table 3 shows an example of simulation data. Starting from this information the *sequence file* is generated, i.e., an XML file containing the sequence of actions which the user should follows when simulating the use of the considered interface. These data may be checked and modified by the developer by pressing the insert button, shown in Fig. 3(b). When the data insertion ends, pressing the submit button uploads the sequence data related to the selected user interface on the PlatoS server.

3.3   User Testing

The PlatoS's user testing feature is based on a logging process, which works without intervene in the user activity. The application allows end-user to provides

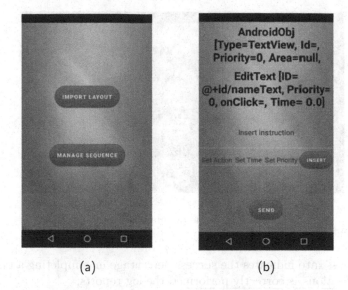

(a)   (b)

Fig. 3. Developer's PlatoS GUI to handle the mockups and the action sequences.

personal information on volunteer base (e.g., such as gender and age, previous smartphone use experience, left-hand or right-hand user), useful to compare performances with different user groups. Then, the list of the interfaces to be tested is shown with the defined tasks. Once selected one of them, PlatoS vocally describes the task to be performed and also shows a textual description of it. An example of simulated interface is shown in Fig. 4. The test begins when the user presses the *Start* button. During the test, PlatoS collects the information related to the interaction with views and it takes into accounts the steps listed in the sequence to detect when the task has been correctly completed. In addition, during the test, by tapping the mobile screen for three seconds the user can access again to the description: this time is not considered in the log.

The Log File. The interaction between the user and the mockup is captured and stored into a log file, which records the following general information:

- interface to be tested
- version of the interface to be tested
- version of PlatoS
- mobile device operating system and model
- simulation date and time
- user data

The action performed by the user on the interface are traced as follows:

Component: ComponentName ID: ComponentID Time: InteractionTime
SuccessRate: %

Fig. 4. An example of simulated interface.

The success rate indicates the success percentage in completing a task; if the sequence of actions is correctly performed the log reports:

| *Result Ok; Time : InteractionTime* |

In case the user jumps some actions or perform them in a wrong order (e.g., pressing submit and then filling in an input filed) the log entry will be:

| *Result Failed; Time : InteractionTime* |

If the user abandons the simulation the log traces all his actions until the ending of the procedure. In this way it is easy to verify where the problem occurs.

3.4 Usability Problem Detection

The aim of PlatoS is to conduct usability testing of mockup Android interfaces without involving expert users or supervisors and to automatize the report of the results. To reach this objective we have to define the usability metrics and a statistical/graphical approach for reporting results.

Usability Metrics. To evaluate the usability problems of a user interface prototype PlatoS collects data concerning the following dimensions: effectiveness, efficiency, and user satisfaction, as suggested by [22] and [23] and largely adopted in literature [8,26].

- *Effectiveness.* It is measured in terms of success rate in completing a task, traced by the Log (see Sect. 3.3).
- *Efficiency.* The time needed to accomplish the task. This time starts after the user has listened the instruction and has pressed the start button and finish when the task ends. The last condition is verified when the sequence of action have been completed or the user abandons the task.
- *User Satisfaction.* The previous two metrics does not collect qualitative and subjective information on the user attitude towards the interface. In particular, after each task the user has to answer the questions reported in Table 1,

Table 1. Post-task user satisfaction questionnaire.

ID	Question
Q1	This description of the task was clear
Q2	I thought the interface analyzed in this task was easy to use
Q3	I was satisfied with the experience of performing this task
Q4	I thought there was too much inconsistency in this interface
Q5	Open comments

adapted from [1], scored by using a 5 points Likert scale, from 1 (strongly disagree) to 5 (strongly agree).

Data Analysis Features. To get the usability reports the developer launches the analysis results feature offered by PlatoS.

Let T_o the optimal time value acquired in Sect. 3.2 and μ_s the average time of the end-user sample.

The objective of our study is to investigate the effort of the end-users when using an User Interface. The research questions we want to answer is:

Is the mean value of the sample performing the test significantly different from a given optimal value?

To achieve our goal, we propose the following null hypotheses:

H_n: when performing an usability evaluation task there is no difference between the optimal effort T_o and μ_s.

Alternative hypotheses for H_n admit a positive difference between μ_s and T_o. This hypothesis is one sided because we postulate that T_o is the optimal value and it is highly unlikely that a sample mean will fall below the optimal value in the null hypothesis. We avoid to make any normality assumption we decide to use the non-parametric Wilcoxon Signed-Rank Test [5] for a one-tailed test and set the criteria for a decision. Results are statistically significant at alpha level $\alpha = 5\%$, where α is the largest probability of committing a Type I error, which rejects the null hypothesis when it is true. If the probability of a Type I error is less than 5% ($p - value < 0.05$), the null hypothesis is rejected; otherwise, the null hypothesis is maintained. When the difference is significant, the hypothesis testing does not provide information about the magnitude of the difference. To this aim, we used the Rosenthal's distance r [16,21] for computing the effect size, $r = Z/\sqrt{N}$, where Z is the test value of the Wilcoxon signed-rank test and N is the total number of the measurements. The effect size is small for $r < 0.3$ (including negative values), medium for $0.3 \leq r < 0.5$ and large for $r \geq 0.5$. For medium and large effect size further analysis are needed.

Result Reporting. PlatoS shows a list of the interfaces, by highlighting in green, orange and red the tasks which have no significant difference, a little, a

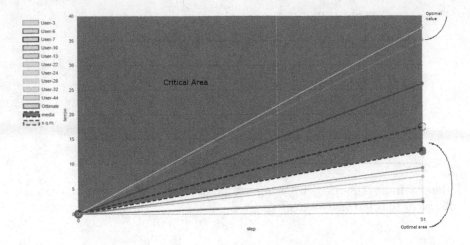

Fig. 5. An example of PlatoS dashboard about a specific task. (color figure online)

medium-large effect size, respectively. The actions with a mediumlarge effect size require further analysis.

For each task PlatoS provides the collected statistic metrics (Efficiency, Effectiveness and User Satisfaction) for the user sample involved in the evaluation. The output is a table for each task, where for each action the action number, effectiveness, the p_value of the efficiency and the distance r (when applicable) are reported, an example is shown in Table 5. It is possible to explore the results by using the PlatoS analytical dashboard. In Fig. 5, the optimal time of a task composed by a single activity is compared with respect to the times of the sample users. It is easy to see that only a user took more time than the optimal value. Figure 6 shows the times of a testing task composed by 7 steps. Each line refers to a user of the sample. It is worth noting that the second and fourth steps should be analyzed because some users took a worst time with respect to the optimal one.

4   An Example of Use

In this section we explain the use of PlatoS for investigating the effectiveness of the proposed automatic usability evaluation approach in detecting usability problems.

Data are collected at an activity granularity level (screen level) in such a way to represent the user navigational behavior.

4.1   The Context

Participants were eight people 25–29 years old, four male and four female. Before selecting a person, we asked him/her questions concerning: (a) their use of smartphone, and (b) if they use the mobile device for eCommerce. People who resulted

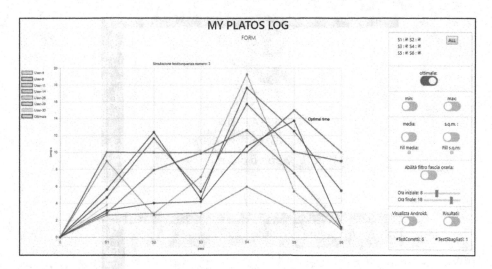

Fig. 6. An example of PlatoS dashboard about a task composed by 7 steps.

smart-users and answered "Yes" to the last question were selected. During the study, participants had to analyze the mockups of an Android application (or experimental object) for a paint eCommerce. We reverse engineered the mockups starting from the interface of an existing eCommerce application. Typical products sold are professional acrylic paint, brushes and knives.

The hardware used for this experiment was a Galaxy Samsung S9 Android device running the Android operating system (version 8.0.0).

4.2 Design

Our study was performed at the University of Salerno in various environments. Before the test started the designer used the interface mockups to be proposed during the end-user evaluation and their log data were collected and stored for successive comparison. The evaluation was composed of three phases.

- Pre-Test. The supervisor briefly described the evaluation aim and the instructions to conduct the test to participants, which have also been informed that the collected data would be managed with confidentially. In addition, they used for five minutes the PlatoS system on a simple user interface.
- Test-Execution. In the second phase, the participants used PlatoS on the selected interfaces. In particular, the participants were asked to perform the following tasks:

Task 1. Add a product to cart by using the interface in Fig. 7(a). This task is composed by a single activity as described in Table 3.

Task 2. Add a product to cart by using the interface shown in Fig. 7(b). In particular, this task requires to add the product by using the + button. Also this task is composed by only one activity as described in Table 3.

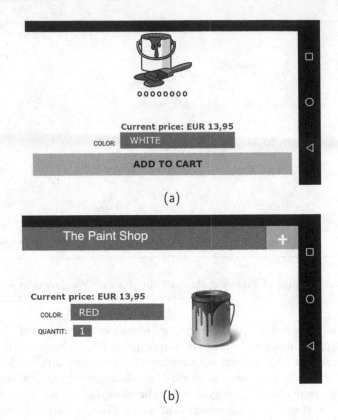

Fig. 7. eCommerce GUIs adopted during the evaluation.

Task 3. Insert registration data (see Fig. 4). Table 3 shows the actions a user has
to perform for registering.

– Post-Test. At the end of the evaluation, users had to fill the Post-Test questionnaire, aiming at collecting usability perception related to the PlatoS system. The usability questionnaire reported in Table 2 is the System Usability
Scale (SUS) [1], widely adopted, scored by using a 5 points Likert scale, from
1 (strongly disagree) to 5 (strongly agree).

4.3   Results

In the following we report the results of the test performed by the end-users.
The times to accomplish Task 1 and Task 2 are reported in Table 4, while the
metrics concerning the same tasks are reported in Table 5. In particular, both
the task were successfully terminated by all the users (Effectiveness). In case of
Task 1, the null hypothesis cannot be rejected ($p\_value > 0.05$). Thus, we can

Table 2. Post-test questionnaire.

ID	Question
P1	The tasks to perform were clear
P2	I found PlatoS unnecessarily complex
P3	I thought PlatoS was easy to use
P4	I think that I would need the support of a technical person to be able to use this system
P5	I found the various functions in this system were well integrated
P6	I thought there was too much inconsistency in this system
P7	I would imagine that most people would learn to use this system very quickly
P8	I found the system very cumbersome to use
P9	I felt very confident using the system
P10	I needed to learn a lot of things before I could get going with this system
P11	Open comments

Table 3. Simulation templates of: the eCommerce interface shown in Fig. 7(a) (Task 1); the eCommerce interface in Fig. 7(b) (Task 2); the eCommerce registration user interface depicted in Fig. 4 (Task 3), where n is the number of chars inserted into the EditText field.

	Operation n.	OperationName	Component	Time
Task 1	1	Add to cart	Button	1.2 s
Task 2	1	Add to cart by pressing the + button	Button	1.5 s
Task 3	1	Insert your name	EditText	0.5 s $*$ n
	2	Insert your surname	EditText	0.5 s $*$ n
	3	Insert your birth date	EditText	0.6 s $*$ n
	4	Select your sex	Spinner	1.4 s
	5	Insert your job	EditText	0.5 s $*$ n
	6	Set the radio button	RadioButton	1.1 s
	7	Add	Button	1.2 s

deduct that the time the user took to accomplish the task was in the complex near to the time set by the designer. On the contrary, for Task 2 we have to reject the null hypothesis ($p\_value = 0.01172$). For verifying the relevance of the difference between the times of the user sample and the time set by the designer we have to examine the effect size in terms of the Rosenthal's distance r. The value $r = 4.25$ denotes a large effect size. This means that the button *"Add to cart"* in Fig. 7(a) is easier to find with respect to the + button on the top right-hand side of Fig. 7(a). Thus, the second interface seems to be less intuitive than the previous one.

Table 4. Simulation results of the eCommerce interface in Fig. 7(a) and (b).

Task	User1	User2	User3	User4	User5	User6	User7	User8
Task 1	1.0418	1.1068	1.7339	1.2587	1.3511	1.2021	1.4993	1.6408
Task 2	1.5874	1.3849	1.8571	3.5398	2.0432	1.9781	1.7059	1.8773

Table 5. Metrics related to the interface in Fig. 7(a) and (b).

	Effectiveness	Efficiency p_value	Distance r
Task 1	100%	0.09766	n.a.
Task 2	100%	**0.01172**	4.25

Table 6. Simulation results of the registration interface shown in Fig. 4.

Task 3	User1	User2	User3	User4	User5	User6	User7	User8
Action 7	1.5901	1.5015	1.8995	1.7874	1.4743	1.4952	2.0259	1.8558

Table 7. Metrics related to the interface in Fig. 4.

	Effectiveness	Efficiency p_value	Distance r
Action 7	100%	**0.003906**	4

All the users completed Task 3. They had some problems with Action 7 pressing the Add button. Tables 6 and 7 show the times related to Action 7 and the corresponding evaluation metrics, respectively. 100% of users pressed the button, but $p\_value = 0.003906$ revealed that the sample employed too much time to press the button with respect to the right time. The effect size r is large. When examining the Add button in Fig. 4, it is possible to note that it has the same color of the background and that it is not clear that it is a button.

The user satisfaction results collected by the Post-Test questionnaire in Table 2 are reported in Fig. 8, where an histogram is associated to each question. They are very positive. In particular, all the participants considered clear the tasks to perform (**P1**), PlatoS is not perceived as complex (**P2**) and results easy to use (**P3**). They agree that there is no need of support for using the system (**P4**) and the system functions were well integrate (**P5**). No inconsistencies were perceived (**P6**), while PlatoS was perceived as easy to learn (**P7**). The system was not perceived as cumbersome (**P8**), while all the participants agree that they were confident when using PlatoS (**P9**). They also considered unnecessary to learn a lot of things to be able to use the system (**P10**). One user was neutral in P2 and P3. He explained in the open comments section: *"The PlatoS colors and buttons are not too much familiar"*.

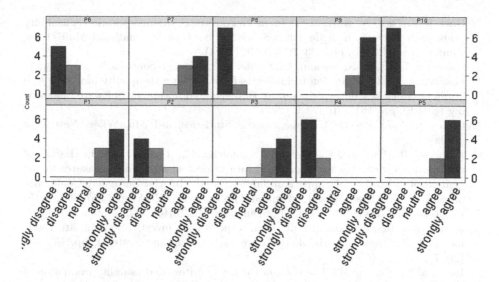

Fig. 8. Post-experiment questionnaire results.

5 Conclusion

In this paper we presented an approach for the detection of usability problems in mobile Android applications in the early stages of development based on the use of native Android mockups. The methodology is based on the automatic detection of the designer and the users' behaviors and their comparison based on statistical approach. An example of use is shown whose results are encouraging.

We are planning to improve the PlatoS interface by following the material design guidelines and to perform a deeper evaluation for better assessing the effectiveness of the proposed approach with respect to traditional supervised usability assessment modalities. As future work, we are also interested in investigating the support which eye-tracking features (and in particular eye-gazing) may offer to remote usability evaluation on the mobile device. Many examples of use of this technology have been provided for web applications, but their adoption in case of mobile apps is still new.

Acknowledgements. We would like to offer our sincere thanks to the experiment participants.

References

1. Brooke, J.: SUS-A quick and dirty usability scale. Usability Eval. Ind. **189**(194), 4–7 (1996)
2. Butt, S.M., Ahmad, W.F.W., Rahim, L.: Handling tradeoffs between agile and usability methods. In: International Conference on Computer and Information Sciences (ICCOINS), pp. 1–6. IEEE (2014)

3. Butt, S.M., Onn, A., Butt, M.M., Inam, N.T., Butt, S.M.: Incorporation of usability evaluation methods in agile software model. In: 17th International Multi-Topic Conference (INMIC), pp. 193–199. IEEE (2014)
4. Cabrejos, L.J.E.R., Kawakami, G., Conte, T.U.: Using a controlled experiment to evaluate usability inspection technologies for improving the quality of mobile web applications earlier in their design. In: Brazilian Symposium on Software Engineering (SBES), pp. 161–170. IEEE (2014)
5. Conover, W.J.: Practical Nonparametric Statistics, 3rd edn. Wiley, New York (1998)
6. Francese, R., Gravino, C., Risi, M., Scanniello, G., Tortora, G.: On the use of requirements measures to predict software project and product measures in the context of android mobile apps: a preliminary study. In: 41st Euromicro Conference on Software Engineering and Advanced Applications (SEAA), pp. 357–364 (2015)
7. Francese, R., Gravino, C., Risi, M., Scanniello, G., Tortora, G.: Mobile app development and management: results from a qualitative investigation. In: 4th International Conference on Mobile Software Engineering and Systems, pp. 133–143 (2017)
8. Ivory, M.Y., Hearst, M.: The state of the art in automated usability evaluation of user interfaces. University of California, Computer Science Division (2000)
9. Kaikkonen, A., Kekäläinen, A., Cankar, M., Kallio, T., Kankainen, A.: Usability testing of mobile applications: a comparison between laboratory and field testing. J. Usability Stud. 1(1), 4–16 (2005)
10. Lettner, F., Holzmann, C.: Automated and unsupervised user interaction logging as basis for usability evaluation of mobile applications. In: 10th International Conference on Advances in Mobile Computing & Multimedia (MoMM), pp. 118–127. ACM (2012)
11. Ligman, J., Pistoia, M., Tripp, O., Thomas, G.: Improving design validation of mobile application user interface implementation. In: 5th International Conference on Mobile Software and Systems, pp. 277–278. ACM (2016)
12. Mockplus. https://www.mockplus.com
13. Moqups. https://moqups.com
14. Moran, K., Li, B., Bernal-Cárdenas, C., Jelf, D., Poshyvanyk, D.: Automated reporting of GUI design violations for mobile apps. arXiv:1802.04732 (2018)
15. Nielsen, J.: Usability metrics: tracking interface improvements. IEEE Softw. 13(6), 12–13 (1996)
16. Pallant, J.: SPSS Survival Manual, 3rd edn. McGrath Hill, Maidenhead (2007)
17. Polson, P.G., Lewis, C., Rieman, J., Wharton, C.: Cognitive walkthroughs: a method for theory-based evaluation of user interfaces. Int. J. Man-Mach. Stud. 36(5), 741–773 (1992)
18. Reggio, G., Leotta, M., Ricca, F.: A method for requirements capture and specification based on disciplined use cases and screen mockups. In: Abrahamsson, P., Corral, L., Oivo, M., Russo, B. (eds.) PROFES 2015. LNCS, vol. 9459, pp. 105–113. Springer, Cham (2015). https://doi.org/10.1007/978-3-319-26844-6_8
19. Ricca, F., Scanniello, G., Torchiano, M., Reggio, G., Astesiano, E.: On the effort of augmenting use cases with screen mockups: results from a preliminary empirical study. In: International Symposium on Empirical Software Engineering and Measurement (ESEM). ACM (2010)
20. Rivero, J.M., Grigera, J., Rossi, G., Luna, E.R., Montero, F., Gaedke, M.: Mockup-driven development: providing agile support for model-driven web engineering. Inf. Softw. Technol. 56(6), 670–687 (2014)

21. Rosenthal, R.: Meta-Analytic Procedures for Social Research, vol. 6. Sage, Newbury (1991)
22. Scholtz, J.: Common industry format for usability test reports. In: CHI - Extended Abstracts on Human Factors in Computing Systems, p. 301. ACM (2000)
23. Stewart, T.: Ergonomic requirements for office work with visual display terminals (VDTs): part 11: guidance on usability. International Organization for Standardization ISO 9241 (1998)
24. Travassos, G., Shull, F., Fredericks, M., Basili, V.R.: Detecting defects in object-oriented designs: using reading techniques to increase software quality. In: ACM Sigplan Notices, vol. 34, pp. 47–56. ACM (1999)
25. Venkatesh, V., Ramesh, V., Massey, A.P.: Understanding usability in mobile commerce. Commun. ACM 46(12), 53–56 (2003)
26. West, R., Lehman, K.: Automated summative usability studies: an empirical evaluation. In: SIGCHI Conference on Human Factors in Computing Systems, pp. 631–639. ACM (2006)
27. Wetzels, M.: Klikker: a method and infrastructure for mining, analysis, and visualisation of user behaviour and usability issues for mobile application development. Glob. J. Comput. Sci. Technol. 18(1) (2018)

Cloud and Related Technologies

Network and Cloudlet Selection
for Computation Offloading
on a Software-Defined Edge Architecture

Bruno Silva[1($\boxtimes$)], Warley Junior[2], and Kelvin Lopes Dias[1]

[1] Informatics Center, Federal University of Pernambuco,
Road Jorn. Anibal Fernandes, Cidade Universitaria,
Recife, PE 50740-560, Brazil
{brs,kld}@cin.ufpe.br
[2] College of Computer and Electrical Engineering,
Federal University of Southern and Southeastern Para,
Marabá, PA 68505-080, Brazil
wmvj@unifesspa.edu.br

Abstract. Edge computing is an emerging paradigm that brings the benefits of the cloud processing closer to the user, thus reducing delays in computational offloading. However, mobile user experience can still be affected due to signal degradation, reduced network throughput, as well as limited edge processing capabilities. To mitigate this problem, this paper proposes a framework to select computational and network resources for offloading operations in a mobile cloudlet environment. The proposed strategy considers the quality of service (QoS) requirements of the application as input to a fuzzy system in order to perform network selection. The selection of computational resources is carried out by a weighted cost function with metrics set by the analytic hierarchy process (AHP) method. A Software Defined Networking (SDN) approach is devised in order to reroute offloading data. Face recognition application were evaluated and achieved gains in terms of reduced processing times of up to 58,58%.

Keywords: Edge computing · Computational offloading ·
Software Defined Networks · Fuzzy logic

1 Introduction

The growth of Internet through wireless technologies has popularized the use of mobile devices such as smartphones, laptops, and tablets. These smart devices have become an essential part of our lives, thus telecom players has been pressed to provide applications to mobile platforms with similar quality to ones served by fixed networks costumers. However, even with technological evolution that have brought improvements to mobile hardware (e.g., CPU, memory, battery, and connectivity), they may not be able to keep up with the exponential increase in

© Springer Nature Switzerland AG 2019
R. Miani et al. (Eds.): GPC 2019, LNCS 11484, pp. 147–161, 2019.
https://doi.org/10.1007/978-3-030-19223-5_11

the Quality of Service (QoS) requirements of applications, due to limitations of dimensions and technical constraints. Mobile Cloud Computing (MCC) emerged as a means of augmenting the mobile devices capabilities, but since it generally relies on public cloud processing for computational offloading, delay-sensitive applications do not perform well [16].

To overcome these limitations, Edge Computing paradigm considers moving cloud services closer to the mobile user. Thus, in addition to extending battery life and mobile device throughput migration of data to the cloud, this proximity feature allows higher QoS than that provided by using MCC. Cloudlets are example of this approach with a virtualized resource environment connected to the Internet, for use of nearby mobile devices via WiFi, providing services with higher bandwidth, lower latency, and increased computational power [9].

Due to user mobility in corporate and campus networks, numerous WiFi access points may be available during ongoing sessions. Thus, it is necessary to determine the appropriate network that guarantee the quality of access to the cloudlet resources, such that upon offloading a task, the device can receive the resulting processing regardless of change of access point. Although there are traditional solutions to address change of access points [2], those handoff decision techniques rely primarily on network parameters (e.g., RSSI, bandwidth), not meeting computation offloading requirements. Cloud-based applications belong to diverse domains (e.g., image processing, real time), and hence, both the execution requirements for the connected cloudlet state and those of the running application itself should be taken into account [8].

Therefore, on the one hand, even keeping user connected to a resource-rich cloudlet environment, mobile applications may suffer degradation due to overloaded access points, poor and unstable wireless connectivity. Conversely, underutilized access points do not benefit users accessing overloaded cloudlets, which may cause increased delays on offloading return to device due to high CPU utilization and lack of memory. Still in relation to the cloudlets, they offer virtual machines (VMs) with different amounts of vCPUs (virtual CPUs), which are directly related to its processing power. In addition, it is also necessary to be aware of the QoS requirements of each type of application. While some applications are more sensitive to changes in the state of the wireless network, others have their execution more influenced by variations of the state of the cloud. Therefore, a framework that encompasses all these requirements is of paramount importance to grant QoS of computation offloading through both network and cloudlet resources selection [17].

This paper proposes and evaluates a framework for selecting access point and cloudlet resources in order to support offloading operations. The contributions of this paper are as follows:

- We propose a algorithm for joint network and virtual machine selection to ensure that the mobile application requirements are met.
- We devise dynamic decision making approaches, using a fuzzy system and the AHP technique, which calculates the cost of offloading and allows the real-time decision for the applications.

To the best of our knowledge, the proposed framework differs from others in the literature, since application-aware, thus customizing the decisions according to its QoS requirements.

This paper is organized as follows: Sect. 2 presents the related works; Sect. 3 presents the system's architecture as well as the interaction between its components; Sect. 4 details the testbed and methodology scenarios; Sect. 5 performance evaluation and analysis of results. Finally, Sect. 6 concludes this paper and also includes plans for future work.

2   Related Work

Previous works proposed solutions to address different aspects of edge computing research. We have defined classified it into three features: (i) selection criteria, (ii) connectivity strategy and (iii) decision mechanism.

The selection criteria define the metrics used to assist in the decision of the best wireless network and cloudlet for execution of computational offloading from the mobile device. Unlike the Lee et al. [6], Khalaj et al. [5] and Ravi et al. [12,13] that considers only the network state connected to the device, the authors Li et al. [7] and Mitra et al. [10] proposed algorithms that use the network and cloud state to assist in decision making. Our proposal is similar to the Saad et al. [14] that considers the network and cloud, as well as the application type. However, the previous work does not include data size to be offloaded as a selection criterion.

Connectivity strategy on wireless networks aims to maintain the mobile device's connection to the cloud environment during the handover between Access Points (APs). Solutions, such as Lee et al. [6] and Khalaj et al. [5] use proxies to manage the connection between the mobile device and cloud. Nonetheless, these solutions have the disadvantage of generating possible overheads and reducing offloading performance. Ravi et al. [12] and Saad et al. [14] interconnect cloudlets with the cloud, where connectivity is guaranteed through discovery and communication modules on the cloudlet-side and connection module on the device-side. Mitra et al. [10] use the Multi-homed Mobile IP (M-MIP) protocol which has high energy consumption due to multihoming. This work uses Open-Flow rules that do not require additional protocols and signaling compared to those already on the network.

The decision mechanism combines metrics for network and cloudlet selection. Mitra et al. [10] uses Multi-Criteria Decision Making method (MCDM) that allows to distribute varied weights for each criteria, but the decision can be affected directly according to the way these weights were defined. On the other hand, Ravi et al. [13] implements fuzzy logic as a secondary criteria (such as, connection time), which is more related to the mobile device state, where the final decision is made. Our proposal uses fuzzy logic, defining different membership functions for each of the criteria, based not only on the application type, but also, for each data size, contributing to dynamic decisions.

In addition to the already highlighted aspect, our work differs from the ones mentioned above due to other characteristics. Unlike the Junior et al. [3], that utilize OpenFlow rules to redirect flows according to the new AP based on wireless coverage, in this proposal, the SDN paradigm is also part of the decision system, redirecting the data flow to the new Virtual Machine (VM) of the selected cloudlet. In addition, in most approaches, decision algorithms are run on the mobile device itself, which may increase energy consumption and, thus reducing battery life-time. In our work, the activities of the algorithm are delegated to the network controller, that also collects some metrics used by network and VM selection strategies. Therefore, to the best of our knowledge, the proposed decision algorithm is the only one that makes decisions using different metrics and thresholds according to the mobile application type.

3   Proposed SDN-EDGE Offloading Architecture

The proposed framework is presented in Fig. 1 and has three main layers. The components, operation and signaling of these layers are presented in more detail below.

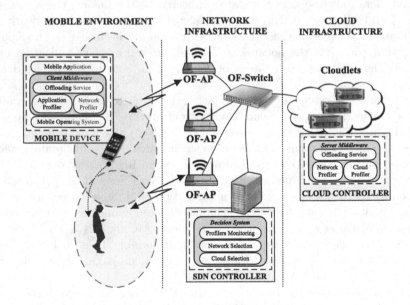

Fig. 1. Three-tier architecture.

3.1   Components

At each layer, a set of components work to meet the requirements necessary to achieve the desired goals of the proposal. Following is a description of each one of them:

- **Mobile Device Layer:** consists of devices running cloud-based applications, via wireless connectivity. A Client Middleware on the device is in charge of locating the cloud resources and managing the offloading executions through the Offloading Service. In addition, for dynamic network state monitoring and application data for decision making, two profilers systems collect information from the running application and the available wireless networks.
- **Network Infrastructure Layer:** comprises all network infrastructure and consists of OpenFlow elements (Switch and APs) responsible for providing the connectivity of mobile devices and the access to the cloud services. These elements are OpenFlow-enabled whose packet routing rules are managed by a SDN Controller. The decision system proposed in this work is implemented by the SDN controller. The elements that make up this system are the profilers bases which receive and store information that serve as input to the network and cloud selection steps. For these two steps, thresholds and criteria were defined, detailed as follows:
  - **Network selection:** the strategy used in the handoff decision is composed of three phases. Initially, information gathering by the profilers in the mobile device occurs. In the decision phase, implemented in the SDN controller, these collected data are initially received and stored in a database. This base feeds the fuzzy system that verifies the characteristics of the running application to load a specific profile of functions and degrees of pertinence, defined by empirical methods, corresponding to it. Unlike other MCDM mechanisms, the fuzzy system allows for customizing the decision based on the expert's experience [11]. Finally, as an output, the system verifies possible candidate networks and chooses the appropriate one for handoff execution.
  - **Cloud selection:** for the offloading cost calculation, the formula used is presented in Eq. 1. It consists of three normalized metrics n through the min-max [4] method. These values are multiplied by their respective weights w, obtained by the AHP [1] method, whose Consistency Ratio (CR)[1] was 0.056.

$$Ct = (wP \times nP) + (wU \times nU) + (wM \times nM) \tag{1}$$

The meaning of the acronyms and the value of their weights are:
  * **Processing Time (P), 0,493:** corresponds to the average processing time obtained through previous measurements, which allows calculating the cost of offloading in VMs with different vCPUs.
  * **CPU utilization (U), 0,311:** corresponds to the percentage of CPU utilization calculated for each VM in the available cloudlets.
  * **Memory utilization (M), 0,196:** refer to the memory percentage being used for each VM and the total time for a request to reach a VM and return to the device, respectively. This criterio will be chosen, according to the highest priority QoS requirement and the classification assigned by the profiler of the application.

---

[1] CR must be less than 0.1 so that the relative weight outputs are considered valid.

– **Cloud Infrastructure Layer:** contains the remote resources, through virtualized environments, accessible by the mobile user through Cloudlets. These
provide VMs that service device requests through Offloading Service of the
Server Middleware. The Network Profiler helps mobile devices get information from wireless networks, and the Cloud Profiler collects cloud state data.
These data are metrics such as percentage usage of processing and memory,
which are sent to the SDN controller.

3.2 Pseudocode of the Proposal Steps and Decision Algorithm

The decision algorithm commands the flow of system activities. It interacts with
the network's mobile devices, cloudlets, and the SDN controller to manage the
OpenFlow rules contained in the wireless network devices, ensuring the routing of
offloading data. A pseudocode to illustrate the whole framework for computation
offloading based on software-defined edge environments is shown below.

Algorithm 1. Pseudocode of the proposal.

---

1 **repeat**
2 $\quad$ $dataMD \leftarrow$ ConnectionMD();
3 $\quad$ **if** $mds[\,]$ ***does not contain*** $dataMD.ip$ **then**
4 $\quad\quad$ $mds[\,] \leftarrow dataMD.ip, dataMD.vm$;
5 $\quad$ **end if**
6 $\quad$ $fuzzyNetworks[\,] \leftarrow$ Fuzzy($dataMD.app, dataMD.net, outNets[\,]$);
7 $\quad$ $ssidCon \leftarrow$ FindFuzzy($dataMD.net, fuzzyNetworks[\,]$);
8 $\quad$ **if** $ssidCon = false$ **then**
9 $\quad\quad$ $ssidSel \leftarrow$ FindNetwork($fuzzyNetworks[\,]$);
10 $\quad$ **else**
11 $\quad\quad$ $ssidSel \leftarrow dataMD.ssid$;
12 $\quad$ **end if**
13 $\quad$ $vms[\,] \leftarrow$ ConnectionVM();
14 $\quad$ $ipLowerCost \leftarrow$ CalculateCost($dataMD.app, vms[\,]$);
15 $\quad$ **if** *($ssidSel = dataMD.ssid$)* **and** *($ipLowerCost = dataMD.vm$)* **then**
16 $\quad\quad$ SendMessage($dataMD.ip, ssidSel$);
17 $\quad$ **else**
18 $\quad\quad$ $mds[\,] \leftarrow dataMD.ip, ipLowerCost$;
19 $\quad\quad$ AddRulesRyu($ssidSel, dataMD.ip, ipLowerCost$);
20 $\quad\quad$ SendMessage($dataMD.ip, ssidSel$);
21 $\quad$ **end if**
22 **until** ∞;

The first activity of the algorithm is to execute the method `ConnectionMD`,
whose function is to initiate a socket to accept the requests of the mobile devices
connected to the APs in the wireless environment. Once a connection to some
device is performed, an object ($dataMD$) containing device information and

metrics is received. Next, a conditional clause (IF) checks the *dms* list for the existence of the "device-VM" mapping. If it does not exist, it is updated using some information from the object sent by the device, namely its IP address and the connected VM connected from Cloudlet. This check is necessary due to the control of the insertion of the rules in the OpenFlow elements, as detailed in the next steps of the pseudocode.

After the initial step of receiving information and control updates, the network selection is started. For this, the `Fuzzy` method is executed, receiving as the first parameter the variable *dataMD.app*, containing information of the application executed by the user, so that the pertinence functions are selected from characteristics. This method also receives network metrics through the variable *dataMD.net*, which contains the signal level of all wireless networks found by the device and the throughput of device's current connected network. The *outNets* list contains the throughput of the other wireless networks captured by the controller through the APs. The return of this method feeds the list *fuzzyNetworks*, containing a boolean value for each network verified by the fuzzy system. If its value is true, it means that it is a candidate network for the mobile device to trigger handoff, and false if it means that it should not be considered in the selection. Then, in line 7, the *ssidCon* variable receives the boolean value returned by the `FindFuzzy` method, which checks if the device's current network has the acceptable characteristics for offloading the application data. Then the conditional IF checks the received value, in case of true, the variable *ssidSet* receives the value of *dataMD.ssid*, indicating at the end of the decision steps, that the device will remain in the current network. If it has received false, the method `FindNetwork` checks in the *fuzzyNetwork* list the name of the network that received favorable value to execute the handoff, being stored in the variable *ssidSet*.

Continuing the execution of the algorithm, the step of selection network resources through cost function (Eq. 1) is started. The metric information for each of the VMs is captured by the profilers and stored in the *vms* list using the `ConnectionVM` method. Then the `CalculateCost` method receives the variable containing the application information *dataMD.app*, and the *vms* list. The value returned in the variable *ipLowerCost*, contains the VM IP of the lowest cost of offloading, calculated by the formula via weights of the AHP.

The last activities of the algorithm are responsible for enabling the operation of the new configuration defined by the decision steps. In line 15, it is checked if the chosen network is equal to the current one connected and if the IP of the VM with less cost is the one of the one that was connected automatically by the device. If these two conditions are met simultaneously, it means that no routing rules are added by the decision system, and the `SendMessage` method returns to the mobile device that handoff is not required. In case some condition is not met, it is necessary to insert new OpenFlow rules in the devices so that the offloading data is routed correctly. To do this, the list *mds* is updated with the new IP of the VM selected by the algorithm, and the method `AddRulesRyu` receives the variable *ssidSet*, to indicate to which AP should be inserted the rules. The variables *dataMD.ip* and *ipLowerCost* indicate the fields of the source and destination IPs of the packet. Finally, the `SendMessage` method this time, will return to the device the name of the target network.

4   Testbed and Methodology

In this section, we present the methodology and results of the experiments carried out to evaluate the proposed system. Thus, details of the experimental environment and benchmark applications are described.

Experimental Environment: For the evaluation of the proposed system the real environment was used, where it is represented in Fig. 2. The environment has three access points (OF-AP) with standard firmware replaced by OpenWrt (running OpenFlow), the Ryu SDN controller and some servers where the cloudlet service operates through the OpenStack cloud manager, containing the VMs available with the Offloading Service.

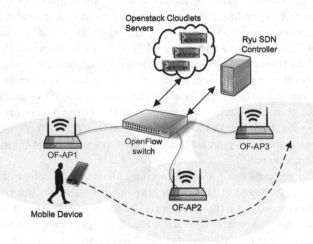

Fig. 2. Experimental environment.

Mobile Application: It was used in the tests an application in the Android platform, developed by the authors: **BenchFace** is an application for face detection and uses Haar features based on cascading classifiers, a method proposed by the researchers in [15]. The algorithm for face detection uses a machine learning approach. It trains cascade functions with a set of positive images (images containing faces) and negative images (images that do not have faces). The application consists of a single image with 78 faces at different angles. At the end of the execution, the application displays the number of detected faces and elapsed time to detect them on the screen. Figure 3 shows the application screen described.

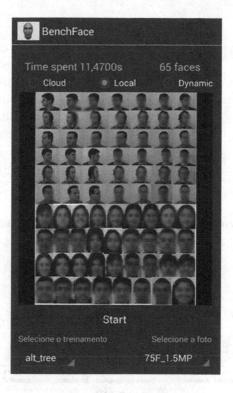

Fig. 3. BenchFace application screen.

5 Experiment and Analysis of Results

This section presents three experiments and analysis of the results obtained with the objective of validating the proposed Decision System. In all, different scenarios were used for the state of network and cloud resources. While the first two experiments demonstrate, respectively, the selection of APs and VMs in the isolated mode cloudlets, the third presents the results of the joint selection of these resources. All tests had 95% confidence interval. More details are presented in the following subsections.

5.1 Experiment 1 - Network Selection

This experiment inserts the mobile device into scenarios with different levels of RSSI and wireless network throughput. The Decision System performs network selection through the fuzzy system, which contains specific profiles for the evaluated application, according to the data size supported. The scenarios were defined through three locations in the test environment, according to Table 1. It is important to note that, unlike the values in dBm that are RSSIs captured by the device, the throughput in Mbps refers to the current traffic in the respective AP.

Table 1. Network selection scenarios.

Size	Scenario	OF-AP 1		OF-AP 2		OF-AP 3	
		RSSI (dBm)	Traffic (Mbps)	RSSI (dBm)	Traffic (Mbps)	RSSI (dBm)	Traffic (Mbps)
3 MP	1	−75,37	9,12	−44,03	17,56	−34,20	26,40
	2	−82,27	41,99	−42,37	30,19	−33,33	9,91
	3	−73,77	9,76	−32,19	13,52	−47,63	30,73
8.5 MP	1	−62,53	8,89	−49,12	9,14	−42,31	27,32
	2	−87,36	39,27	−31,85	15,09	−44,25	5,03
	3	−73,83	8,47	−32,19	8,72	−46,12	29,32

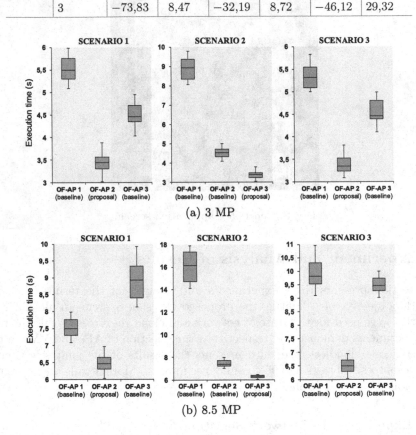

Fig. 4. Results of network selection.

Figure 4 displays the results in the boxplot after the experiments are performed. The proposal labels represent the OF-APs selected by the Decision System, and "baseline" results of the executions in the other OF-APs for comparison. The values obtained through the network selection with the BenchFace application, demonstrate that the calibration of the fuzzy system allowed to obtain considerable gains in the elapsed time. In all scenarios for image sizes of 3 MP and 8.5 MP, the choice of OF-APs was made based on the ones that had the compatible RSSI and offloading values, as defined in the pertinence functions. The gains become more evident when the fuzzy rules were driven mainly by the APs' throughput in larger images, as is verified in scenarios 2 and 3 in 8.5 MP. Finally, it is also observed how a low level of RSSI caused a great impact on the application, as can be seen in the performance of OF-AP 1 in scenario 2 to 8.5 MP. The highest percentage gains obtained for the second best performance were 25.74% to 3 MP and 31.58% to 8.5 MP, both in the third scenario.

5.2   Experiment 2 - Selection of VM in the Cloudlet

The second experiment evaluates, in an isolated way, the behavior of the VM selection in the cloudlet. Scenarios with varying CPU processing levels and memory usage of each of these available resources are used. The Decision System makes the selection of VMs using the offloading cost calculation (Eq. 1). As in the previous evaluation, three scenarios have been defined, as shown in Table 2. It is noteworthy that in this selection step, three VMs were used, where the first two contain 2 vCPUs and the third only 1 vCPU, both with 2 GB of memory.

Table 2. Selection of VM in the cloudlet scenarios.

Size	Scenario	VM 1		VM 2		VM 3	
		CPU (%)	Mem (%)	CPU (%)	Mem (%)	CPU (%)	Mem (%)
3 MP	1	4,82	41,96	72,93	42,23	50,63	78,66
	2	48,27	79,37	78,02	80,71	3,07	41,15
	3	47,14	49,73	3,72	81,64	3,73	43,14
8.5 MP	1	1,87	41,67	73,77	41,98	51,53	81,37
	2	47,40	83,14	77,31	81,27	2,07	41,62
	3	48,93	43,57	2,05	81,23	2,23	42,21

The results for 3 MP and 8.5 MP images are presented in Fig. 5. In both image sizes, the benefits of the decisions made by the proposed system through cost calculation are evident. Through this strategy, the ability to select distinct VMs, through the use of the processing time criterion (P), stands out. In this way, it was possible to verify situations in which virtual machines with a lower amount of vCPUs than the others, present better offloading results, as verified in scenarios 2 for both image sizes. In addition, it was possible to obtain effective decisions through the weights assigned to each of the criteria, where it is verified in scenarios 3 for VMs 1 and 2 that the CPU was, in fact, more determinant than the memory for these two virtual machines, allowing offloading executions with less average time. Regarding the highest percentage gains when compared to the second best performance, we obtained 44.36% for 3 MP and 48.33% for 8.5 MP, both in the scenario 1.

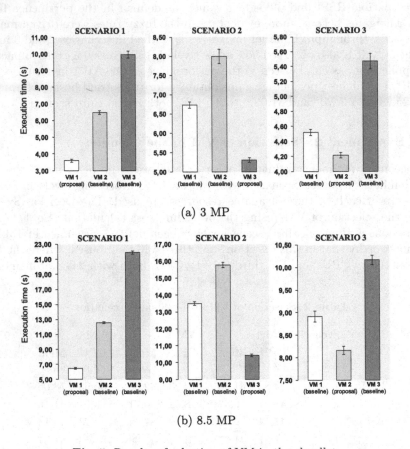

(a) 3 MP

(b) 8.5 MP

Fig. 5. Results of selection of VM in the cloudlet.

5.3   Experiment 3 - Joint Network and VM Selection in Cloudlet

Different from the strategy adopted in the previous experiments, the behavior of the Decision System in the joint selection of resources (wireless networks and VMs) is verified. The scenarios were defined in the same way as the previous evaluations, where they are detailed in Table 3.

Figure 6 presents the results of the evaluation, demonstrating the combination of 'OF-AP'-'VM' selected by the Decision System, and other offloading results for comparison. It is verified in all the scenarios that the shortest average execution time was obtained with the proposed System, verifying the full functioning of the fuzzy decisions in conjunction with the cost calculation. To further illustrate the impact of RSSI variations and network throughput, and the CPU

Table 3. Evaluation scenarios.

3 MP	OF-AP 1		OF-AP 2		OF-AP 3	
	−72,52 dBm	8,16 Mbps	−33,18 dBm	26,62 Mbps	−43,25 dBm	16,28 Mbps
	VM 1		VM 2		VM 3	
	48,32% CPU	78,47% Mem	4,58% CPU	42,54% Mem	3,75% CPU	42,82% Mem
8.5 MP	OF-AP 1		OF-AP 2		OF-AP 3	
	−62,42 dBm	9,15 Mbps	−43,17 dBm	27,48 Mbps	−48,17 dBm	8,42 Mbps
	VM 1		VM 2		VM 3	
	48,25% CPU	78,42 Mem	77,08% CPU	85,02% Mem	3,05% CPU	42,23 Mem

and memory of the VMs in the runs, the upload, download, and offloading times differ in color in the graphics. Regarding the results, it is observed that for the size of 3 MP there was a gain of 58.58% compared to the baseline of the second best performance. In the 8.5 MP scenario, the choice of VM 3 with only 1 vCPU, obtain a gain of 30.31% when compared to the second least time.

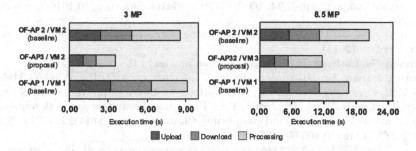

Fig. 6. Results of joint network and VM selection in cloudlet.

6 Conclusions and Future Directions

This work implemented and evaluated a framework for selecting access point and cloudlet resources, using as main selection criteria the application type running to meet its QoS requirements. Unlike other solutions, the centralization of the proposed system in the SDN controller dispensed its processing on the mobile device.

Through the results of the evaluation of the Decision System in real environment, it was possible to testify the effectiveness of the decisions making. Using different applications types and with the mobile device in different scenarios, it was demonstrated that through the fuzzy thresholds and cost formula used, offloading executions were more advantageous when handoff trigger and VM selection were made in the cloud than the executions without the use of the system presented in this work. In addition, the strategy of aligning the OpenFlow rules to the Decision System provided gains in offloading execution, routing the data to the new VM in the cloudlet.

As future work, the authors plan to extend the Decision System so that it is possible to execute the selection through heterogeneous networks, such as between WiFi and 4G, as well as different types of cloud resources besides cloudlets such as public and ad-hoc clouds. Also, we should use machine-learning techniques along with the proposed decision system to get better accuracy in the decisions, also including the mobile device state such as the battery level.

References

1. Multi-attribute decision making: a simulation comparison of select methods. Eur. J. Oper. Res. **107**(3), 507–529 (1998). https://doi.org/10.1016/S0377-2217(97)00147-1
2. A survey of vertical handover decision algorithms in fourth generation heterogeneous wireless networks. Comput. Netw. **54**(11), 1848–1863 (2010). https://doi.org/10.1016/j.comnet.2010.02.006
3. Supporting mobility-aware computational offloading in mobile cloud environment: J. Netw. Comput. Appl. **94**, 93–108 (2017). https://doi.org/10.1016/j.jnca.2017.07.008
4. Han, J., Pei, J., Kamber, M.: Data Mining: Concepts and Techniques. Elsevier, Amsterdam (2011)
5. Khalaj, A., Lutfiyya, H.: Handoff between proxies in the proxy-based mobile computing system. In: 2013 International Conference on MOBILe Wireless MiddleWARE, Operating Systems and Applications (Mobilware), pp. 10–18. IEEE (2013)
6. Lee, D., Lee, H., Park, D., Jeong, Y.S.: Proxy based seamless connection management method in mobile cloud computing. Cluster Comput. **16**(4), 733–744 (2013). https://doi.org/10.1007/s10586-013-0249-8
7. Li, J., Bu, K., Liu, X., Xiao, B.: ENDA: embracing network inconsistency for dynamic application offloading in mobile cloud computing. In: Proceedings of the Second ACM SIGCOMM Workshop on Mobile Cloud Computing, pp. 39–44. ACM (2013)
8. Li, W., Zhao, Y., Lu, S., Chen, D.: Mechanisms and challenges on mobility-augmented service provisioning for mobile cloud computing. IEEE Commun. Mag. **53**(3), 89–97 (2015). https://doi.org/10.1109/MCOM.2015.7060487
9. Mach, P., Becvar, Z.: Mobile edge computing: a survey on architecture and computation offloading. CoRR abs/1702.05309 (2017). http://arxiv.org/abs/1702.05309
10. Mitra, K., Saguna, S., Åhlund, C., Luleå, D.G.: M2c2: a mobility management system for mobile cloud computing. In: 2015 IEEE Wireless Communications and Networking Conference (WCNC), pp. 1608–1613, March 2015. https://doi.org/10.1109/WCNC.2015.7127708
11. Perera, C., Zaslavsky, A., Christen, P., Georgakopoulos, D.: Context aware computing for the internet of things: a survey. IEEE Commun. Surv. Tutor. **16**(1), 414–454 (2014). https://doi.org/10.1109/SURV.2013.042313.00197

12. Ravi, A., Peddoju, S.K.: Mobility managed energy efficient android mobile devices using cloudlet. In: 2014 IEEE Students' Technology Symposium (TechSym), pp. 402–407, February 2014. https://doi.org/10.1109/TechSym.2014.6808085
13. Ravi, A., Peddoju, S.K.: Handoff strategy for improving energy efficiency and cloud service availability for mobile devices. Wirel. Pers. Commun. **81**(1), 101–132 (2015). https://doi.org/10.1007/s11277-014-2119-y
14. Saad, H.B., Kassar, M., Sethom, K.: Always best connected and served based scheme in mobile cloud computing. In: 2016 3rd Smart Cloud Networks Systems (SCNS), pp. 1–8, December 2016. https://doi.org/10.1109/SCNS.2016.7870560
15. Viola, P., Jones, M.: Rapid object detection using a boosted cascade of simple features. In: Proceedings of the 2001 IEEE Computer Society Conference on Computer Vision and Pattern Recognition, CVPR 2001, vol. 1, pp. I-511–I-518. IEEE Computer Society (2001). https://doi.org/10.1109/CVPR.2001.990517
16. Wang, Y., Chen, R., Wang, D.C.: A survey of mobile cloud computing applications: perspectives and challenges. Wirel. Pers. Commun. **80**(4), 1607–1623 (2015)
17. Zhou, B., Dastjerdi, A.V., Calheiros, R.N., Srirama, S.N., Buyya, R.: A context sensitive offloading scheme for mobile cloud computing service. In: 2015 IEEE 8th International Conference on Cloud Computing, pp. 869–876, June 2015. https://doi.org/10.1109/CLOUD.2015.119

Cloud Computing Adoption in the Government Sector in Brazil: An Exploratory Study with Recommendations from IT Managers

Teófilo Branco Jr.[1(✉)], Isaías Bianchi[1,2(✉)],
and Filipe de Sá-Soares[1(✉)]

[1] Centro ALGORITMI, University of Minho, Braga, Portugal
teofilotb@hotmail.com, fss@dsi.uminho.pt
[2] Federal University of Santa Catarina, Florianópolis, Brazil
isaias.bianchi@ufsc.br

Abstract. Cloud Computing constitutes an alternative for organizations that want to optimize the use of computing resources and rationalize costs with IT infrastructure. However, the adoption and implementation in the government sector pose several challenges, regarding IT control, data protection in the Internet, efficient use of computing resources and cost rationalization. Within the government sector, the lack of knowledge about issues involving adoption and migration to cloud computing may negatively impact IT. This study aims to identify the factors influencing the adoption of cloud computing in the government sector in Brazil. We carried out the study interviewing IT professionals that successfully migrated to the cloud with three organizations, two large and public universities and one data processing agency. Using the approach *Value-Focused Thinking*, we analyzed the data collected from the interviews. Our Findings revealed a set of twenty-one recommendations to take into account when implementing cloud computing in the government sector, such as using a pilot project, training, and consulting, among others. These recommendations are useful to guide the IT decision makers in the process of cloud computing adoption and implementation as an efficient and reliable approach in the government sector.

Keywords: Cloud computing · Government sector ·
Recommendations for adoption · Interviews

1 Introduction

Cloud Computing (CC) has been a major technological trend in recent years, drawing the attention of both IT professionals and researchers. Although many publications concentrate on the technical aspects of CC, the focus on organizational aspects is increasingly frequent given the interest of organizations in adopting this technology [1]. The literature includes works on the process and life cycle that enable the creation of a favorable setting within organizations to implement CC solutions [1].

Cloud computing may be valuable to private and public organizations [2]. However, Mallmann and Maçada [2] argue that there are relatively few studies investigating

© Springer Nature Switzerland AG 2019
R. Miani et al. (Eds.): GPC 2019, LNCS 11484, pp. 162–175, 2019.
https://doi.org/10.1007/978-3-030-19223-5_12

CC adoption in the context of public sectors compared to a large number of studies in the private sector. In particular, in a developing country such as Brazil, in the government sector, the number of studies is limited.

Most studies attempt to identify technological issues in CC [3]. On the other hand, few studies are investigating the organizational aspects of cloud computing and concerns about recommendations. Regarding the government sector, usually, the studies did not have the concern to discuss the issues related to having successful implementation. The review of those works led us to compile a list of recommendations that may prove useful to IT managers when they consider the organizational requirements needed to adopt CC in a secure and efficient manner.

Motivated by the context above, the purpose of this study is to investigate the factors and to identify a set of recommendations for the successful adoption of CC in the government sector in Brazil.

2   Cloud Computing in Public Govern Area (G-Cloud)

G-Cloud (Government Cloud) in the public service domain is a pay-per-use model that allows public agencies and citizens access to a network. This network provides configurable and reliable computing resources that are provisioned and released with minimal management effort for the consumer. The government can use the power of the G-Cloud to provide essential public services. In the future, online public service providers can use all G-Cloud models to provide services that are more complex. G-Cloud can be considered a new paradigm shift for online public services [4].

Nowadays, cloud computing in the Government area can solve problems in e-Government (e-Gov) and further optimize the capacity of governance. Additionally, in the cloud, it is possible to specify metrics and compile statistics for cost savings and better planning, such as datacenter usage, peak loads, power consumption, and time. Cloud databases offer an unprecedented scale without compromising performance. This capability should be considered if the target system demands high-level, on-demand scalability, that is, large scale scalability [5].

The adoption of cloud computing in the government (G-Cloud) promotes the improvement of public services for the citizens and the transparency of government processes. Cloud architectures help the implementation of e-governance by enabling government policies directed for the citizens. Several services can be offered by enabling government policies that are directed towards the citizens, for instance: Government for Government (G2G), Government for Business (G2E), and Government for Consumer (G2C) [4].

2.1   Cloud Computing Deployment

Hybrid clouds involve the composition of two or more types of clouds (private, community, or public). In the private cloud deployment model, the cloud infrastructure only focuses on the internal workings of the organization [6]. The goal of a private cloud is to use the services within the organization, taking advantage of the cloud's technological advantages. Usually, the private cloud offers a higher degree of security than public clouds, since the data is under the control of the organization. The private cloud has the vantage over the public cloud in terms of security and privacy. A private cloud also has the potential to give the organization greater control over infrastructure and computing resources [1]. For instance, if there is inefficiency of computing resources capacity in the organization's own data center, a private cloud can provide cost savings. These non-utilized capabilities can be managed through a self-service interface, automated management of computing resources, and can even allow the commercialization of idle capabilities to other partner companies [6]. The organization with a private cloud can create a partnership with a public cloud provider to form a cloud hybrid. Another benefit of the hybrid cloud is that the cloud can enable the organization to take advantage of the scalability and cost-effectiveness that a public cloud offers without exposing applications and data considered critical to third parties [1, 6].

Table 1. Factors to consider with cloud computing implementation

Item	Reference
Planning the cloud deployment process in well-defined phases and steps	[7]
Assessing the benefits of cloud computing in general and for the government sector	[5, 8–10]
Aligning the cloud project with strategic planning	[11]
Survey of stakeholder expectations and needs	[8]
Verification of the factors of influence in the organizational, technological and environmental context	[9, 10, 12]
Assessment of the organization's maturity level for cloud adoption	[9, 10, 13]
Assessment of the organization's readiness to adopt the cloud	[14]
Prospective suppliers to support and provide services and equipment	[8]
Estimating cloud costs	[2, 8]
Return on investment analysis	[8]
Definition of the implementation model	[15]
Selection of service models	[16, 17]
Assessment of the impacts of the cloud	[16]
Adequating cloud computing for the area of e-Gov (G-Cloud)	[5, 8, 17]
Detailing project and implementation approach	[7]
Development of the migration plan for the cloud	[8]
Adequacy for compliance with current legislation	[2, 18, 19]
Cloud security planning	[20–24]
Assignment of roles and responsibilities of the actors in the cloud environment	[25]
Assembling the service portfolio to the cloud	[7]
Selection of cloud solution providers	[24, 26, 27]
Definition of the Service Level Agreements (SLAs)	[28]

Based on the literature review process, we identified remarkable points to take into account in order to deploy cloud computing. Table 1 presents a brief description of each item.

Section 3 presents the method used in this research. As our purpose is to identify recommendations for a successful cloud computing deployment in the government sector, we carried out an exploratory study.

3   Research Methodology

Few studies have attempted to identify a set of recommendations to adopt cloud computing in a developing country such as Brazil. Our study intends to contribute to this research objective. The study adopts and inductive strategy using qualitative data from semi-structured interviews to collect data from different points of view [29], building upon the practical experiences from key members of the government sector that have adopted cloud computing [30].

3.1   Data Collection and Analysis

In order to learn about these individuals' recommendations for cloud computing adoption, we conducted interviews with experts in IT Cloud in the government sector that successfully migrated to the cloud. In order to reduce contextual bias, we adopted a convenience sampling method to select a variety of organizations in the government sector from different contexts with a variation in institutional size, strategy, structure, and processes [31].

Interviews were conducted with the organizations' IT decision-makers at the top management level and middle management levels (IT Director, Manager, and IT Coordinator) that are usually responsible for cloud computing [32]. The interviews aimed to learn about the practical experiences of IT managers in the process of cloud computing implementation in the government sector. Table 2 provides information about the organizations.

Table 2. Information about organizations

ID	State	Organization type	Size
A	Southeast	University	Extra Large, over 100 IT employees and more than four thousand students
B	Southeast	Data Processing agency	Extra Large, over 100 IT employees and more than eight units.
C	South	University	Extra Large, over 100 IT employees and more than four thousand students

Table 3 provides information regarding the interviewees.

Table 3. Profile of Interviewees

ID	People interviewed	Position	Education	Experience in IT (years)
A	3	Division director	Ph.D.	20
		Manager	Master	18
		IT coordinator	Master	8
B	6	Division director		
		Marketing manager	Master	19
		Support manager	Master	10
		Software development	Master	9
		Manager	Specialist	12
		Cloud computing	Specialist	7
		Coordinator	Specialist	5
		IT coordinator		
C	3	IT director	Ph.D.	4
		IT coordinator	Master	16
		Security coordinator	Specialist	10

The interview script structured had three parts: the first part, included general questions about the organization; the second part included personal questions about the interviewee, and the last part included questions about their experiences with cloud computing adoption. We developed a guide based on the initial items identified in the literature review (Table 1). By using a guide and pinpointing key aspects of cloud computing, we were able to more easily conduct interview. The following type of question was asked to each interviewee: "What are the expectations and goals of cloud computing in your organization?" Additionally, there were questions concerning the advantages of CC; limitations in accordance with current legislation; service migration process to the cloud; impacts on IT, preparation of the internal environment; selection of the implementation model and services; prospective suppliers; level of maturity of the organization; investment and operational costs; criteria for selection of suppliers; service agreements; application development; cloud management; conformities and auditing; risk management and security.

The final question was intended to complement issues that have not been adequately covered in the literature, in particular, in the government sector. This question aimed to enrich the practical experiences of cloud computing implementation. Between August and September of 2018, we conducted face-to-face interviews. All of the interviews were recorded. We followed recommendations by Myers and Newman [33] to make the interview process more effective. We performed a verbatim transcription of all the interviews and used the application "Atlas TI" to assist in data analysis.

To analyze the interviews, we adopted the approach proposed by Keeney [34]. Based on the assumption that the adoption of CC can be configured as a decision-making problem, we applied Keeney's [35] Value-Focused Thinking (VFT) approach, taking into account the list of important values to the context of decision-making. The next section presents the findings of this study.

4   Results of the Study

This research aimed to identify recommendations for the adoption of CC in the government sector, particularly in public organizations in Brazil. In three organizations, twelve experienced IT professionals in cloud computing were interviewed.

Table 4. Recommendations proposed by interviewees

Category	Description
Alignment with customers	Be in consonance with customers, identifying business needs and expectations
IT governance	Define an IT policy with roles and responsibilities, transparency with agreements the board of directors in the organization
Costs of investments	Evaluate the costs of cloud computing and return on investment
Cloud sustainability	Contribution of necessary financial resources obtained from financing and optimization of IT resources
Studies of prospection	Carry out studies on technological solutions in order to increase the knowledge required to take better decisions regarding the choice of the CC solution to be adopted
Consulting	Specialized support to guide the deployment process
Training	Training of the team to operate the cloud and guide the customers
Pilot project	Start the cloud implementation with a small project to get know-how and expertise to further expand.
Challenges to overcome	Predict and mitigate the difficulties and challenges in the cloud deployment
Cloud management	Efficient management of the cloud
Cloud operational support	Define a strategy to the support and maintenance of all users
Marketing in the cloud	Disseminate cloud services catalog for merchandising
Migration to the cloud	Define the criteria to migrate to the cloud easily
Decentralize systems	Assign the responsibility for developing applications and systems to smaller units within the cloud system
Decentralize data centers	Centralize the infrastructure management and distribution of operational environment management to customers
Shift to public cloud	Support of public clouds to relieve traffic peaks and as an efficient and versatile customer service strategy, preserving cloud and data security
Infrastructure requirements	Establishment of technical parameters for the choice of cloud solutions
Service standard	Establishment of an operational standard for the offered services
Customer benefits	Provide the customer functionalities that can make the cloud membership more attractive
Cloud security	Development of a risk and security plan for cloud operation
Legislation	Legal background for the protection of personal data, privacy, confidentiality, and confidentiality of information

Remarkable insights were collected from the interviews. Twenty-one categories resulted from the data analysis coding of the interviews, on issues considered important in the process of implementing cloud computing in public governmental organizations. Table 4 presents a list of recommendations to the public government in order to successfully adopt cloud computing. In addition, a description for each category was also developed.

Based on the categories and recommendations presented in Table 4, the next subsections detail these recommendations. It is important to note that all of these recommendations came from the practitioner's experience in cloud computing projects in the government sector in Brazil.

4.1 Alignment with Customers

In order to have a cloud project aligned with customers' expectations, it is important to provide good services and to have a high customer retention rate. To ensure this alignment, the following recommendations are suggested: create a survey to identify customer needs and the requirements; provide personalized service to the clients.

4.2 IT Governance

IT governance plays an important role in cloud computing, assuming that the cloud environment is organized to support IT activities and to maintain the infrastructure required for cloud services.

In this sense, deliberations involving IT with political backing in the organization are necessary, so that these are duly respected and fulfilled. The following recommendations were suggested by the respondents: regulate IT through an IT board, develop standards for cloud use, and implement its own structure for cloud management.

4.3 Costs of Investments

In order to deploy a cloud in the government sector or in any public institution, it's essential to have a well-defined plan with expected costs and a budget for investments. A financial support and administrative function in the institution becomes critical to business success. In this sense, the following recommendations were listed by the interviewees: make an accurate estimation of implementation costs; evaluate the human resources costs involved, even if they are being paid by central administration, as is the case in general public administrations; estimate costs required for cloud support; raise the costs to be spent with software licenses; and evaluate the costs to be allocated in the process of renting public clouds to provide support to the private cloud of organization.

4.4 Cloud Sustainability

The cloud computing environment requires constant investment, whether in training, maintenance, or upgrading of new equipment. It is desirable that these costs can be sustained by the sale of cloud services. One way to promote self-sustainability is following some of these recommendations: draw up an annual budget for costs in the cloud; prepare a price list of cloud services; receive IT resources from client units; and develop an annual investment plan for cloud modernization.

4.5 Prospective Studies

It is important to conduct prospective studies on cloud technologies to define cloud models and promote the expansion and extension of the use of their resources. These studies can be carried out through the following actions: participation in events about CC; visits to other institutions that use the cloud; requesting proof of concept from technology companies that use the cloud; researching the literature on innovations in the cloud environment; consulting with statistical and trend publications such as Gartner magazine; promoting presentations by specialists; and promoting meetings with clients in order to learn about their expectations.

4.6 Consulting

A consulting service from a company that specializes in nontechnical computing and is supported by the manufacturer can provide important support for the development of the cloud environment. For this reason, the following recommendations should be considered: hire a consulting company to implement the cloud; train staff regularly; and rely on cloud solution vendor support.

4.7 Training

Training is important so that the CC environment works appropriately. The following recommendations can promote training: search specialized journals and magazines to acquire expertise and knowledge about cloud computing; implement ISO certification for the cloud; perform spot audits of the cloud environment; hire specialized training; share knowledge through wiki knowledge platforms; publish and disseminate operation manuals; participate in specialized forums on the subject; develop root-analysis diagrams to detect sources of problems; seek to keep the team cohesive and perennial; produce regular documentation such as news and periodicals; and promote workshops.

4.8 Pilot Project

An efficient way to deploy the cloud is through a pilot project. A well-designed and well-managed initial project is desirable for the team to acquire knowledge of the technology, should be flexible and open to change. To do this, the following recommendations are important: initially deploy a pilot cloud project in an evolving way; seek to use free open source software initially; acquire technology maturity in a practical and evolutionary way; progressively expand the pilot project; rely on specialized company consulting from the start; and maintain the initial cloud environment away from the traditional enterprise environment.

4.9   Challenges to Overcome

Respondents reported some difficulties during the cloud deployment process. The lack of knowledge on the client's behalf was cited as a serious difficulty, and in some cases led to erroneous assumptions and improper operations. Another difficulty is that legacy occur in relation to the use policy's implementation, where excessive rules may hamper or greatly restrict user freedom. Users with a complicated structure where the internal processes are not well defined hinder the implementation of the cloud. Also, another difficulty is that legacy systems are often not compatible with the new cloud environment, and the systems migration is impaired. Another difficulty is related to systems that require authentication of users, especially in cases of authentication with Microsoft Active Directory (AD) functionality. Lastly, according to the interviews, there were many cases where the customer had a strong sense of ownership over the data center and many customers were resistance to join the cloud environment because they did not trust in it.

4.10   Cloud Management

The interviewees emphasized the importance of efficiently managing customers' cloud projects and of implementing a system of timely communication of events to customers, demonstrating transparency and partnership in cloud management.

4.11   Cloud Operational Support

Regarding operational support of the cloud, the interviewees felt that a level 1 of local support service should be implemented for immediate customer service and an additional two levels should be implemented in order to handle more complicated occurrences that can not be resolved at previous levels. The cloud manager should only be involved at the highest level of occurrences delegating levels 1 and 2 to local cloud support at the customer site. However, some steps need to be taken by the cloud management body, such as link monitoring, implementation of event control systems, and the establishment of rules for firewall release.

4.12   Marketing in the Cloud

The importance of encouraging the use of cloud through the dissemination of services through marketing was reported. Some examples of possible measures include the implementation of a commercial management, the development of events for the dissemination of cloud services, the production of printed and media catalogs of services, the promotion of the cloud on internal sites and the development of campaigns for use of the services and provide a cloud usage simulator on the corporate site of the managing body for experimental use by the client. Establish metrics for the sale of cloud services and make efforts to join the cloud.

4.13 Migration to Cloud

The process of migration to the cloud environment must be done through design and requires a lot of care and attention. The following recommendations can be useful to assist the process of migrating services to the cloud: set up a separate network for the legacy systems of the company to be migrated; stimulate customers' spontaneous adherence to the cloud; initially migrate web services; carefully evaluate what will be migrated to the cloud; assess the technical feasibility of each migration project; and elaborate a model of migration containing requirements, model of solution and points to consider positive and negative for this decision making.

4.14 Decentralize Systems

In the cloud environment, system production must be stimulated. While managing the cloud core, it is important that the administration of systems be decentralized to the units responsible for each. The interviewees made the following recommendations on this subject: outsource software factory to produce cloud systems; stimulate the production of customized sites for customers; and delegate application development to client units; against third-party applications.

4.15 Decentralize Datacenters

The datacenter management should also be decentralized, with a sufficient support structure being set up for the client units. In this sense, it is desirable to implement the following actions: assign unique URL for each client; deliver customer portals that can be customized by clients; provide a management environment so that each client can manage it; and allocate an IT administrator on each client unit to provide environmental management and technical support services.

4.16 Shift to Public Cloud

The ability to extend processing and storage resources through public clouds is of great value. To this end, interviewees made the following recommendations: when contracting public clouds, request the management of the data; establish criteria for contracting public clouds; establish key points for transshipment in public clouds; perform tests with external providers; evaluate the contracting of a financial broker to cover immediate and emergency costs with public clouds; and adopt preventive measures against inefficiencies and breaches of contract of companies that provide public clouds.

4.17 Infrastructure Requirements

The cloud infrastructure must be well planned for in order for the business environment to have operational support. To ensure these infrastructure requirements, important recommendations have been suggested: develop the technical specification of infrastructure requirements of the cloud environment; choose to work with the cloud orchestrator who has hyper convergent infrastructure; choose an orchestrator that has developed free software; request assistance and terms of references from specialized companies; and hire an integrated cloud solution.

4.18 Service Standard

The definition of service standards is important for preserving the security of the cloud environment. In this sense, observing the following recommendations may be convenient: virtualize all cloud projects; implement centralized access authentication; give customers agility and autonomy to manage resources in a standardized way; and foster innovation and service development by observing basic rules and standards for security and systems development.

4.19 Customer Benefits

The identification of customer benefits is the most efficient way to ensure the success of cloud deployment in the organization, building loyalty and winning allies. In this sense, the advantages to customers can be perceived by emphasizing and demonstrating the following resources: saving resources by clients; adopting administrative transparency of the cloud environment; providing operational performance; offering and reinforcing the importance of automatic scalability; giving self-administration of the environment to the client; offering an environment-friendly operation; providing statistics on resource use; demonstrating the savings in electricity received by the customer; demonstrating the savings obtained in software licensing costs; offering attractive price in relation to the market for customer's adhesion; providing a reduced cost to the customer; and allowing customization of the environment by the customer.

4.20 Cloud Security

Information security in the cloud environment requires great attention from organizations, as several critical aspects of clouds are related to this topic. Therefore, there were many recommendations to fulfill this goal: establish local security rules; encrypt data communications; implement auditing and notifications to users in case of non-compliance with security rules; implement firewall management; implement manual connectivity control; invest in the training of the security team; perform security tests regularly; guide users in the use of cloud resources; deploy security team; and keep innovation projects confidential.

4.21 Legislation

Compliance with legislation is one of the important precepts in public administration. Greater care with citizens is necessary for the preservation of their personal data and compliance with the various laws that govern regulate the protection of personal data. Therefore, the interviewees pointed out important recommendations: protect users' personal data, guide public administration users and employees about current legislation; and users from public clouds.

5   Conclusions

Regarding the characteristics of this study, all of the clouds adopted by the organizations are private and were implemented in less than five years. In addition, he clouds implemented in these organizations do not allow for migration to public clouds. One of the reasons for adopting only private clouds within these organizations is that the IT is focused only on the internal user and operations, without a commercial purpose.

The recommendations recorded were the result of the cooperation of the interviewees, based on their experience and the concordant points between them. All the users and the managers are satisfied with the return on investments in this type of technology. Additionally, various improvements were perceived in terms of IT resources and data processing, among other issues, suggesting that the deployment of this technology is feasible.

To summarize, this research found twenty-one recommendations for the successful adoption of CC in the government sector that are based on a set of interviews performed in three organizations in Brazil. The aim was to have a list of cloud computing recommendations not only from a literature review perspective but also from the view of practitioners. In the case of this research, these recommendations emerged from the experiences of the interviewees that had success in the implementation of cloud computing in the government sector. Therefore, the recommendations from this study can aid managers in making better decisions regarding cloud computing implementation in the public sector.

This research has some limitations. The collected data was limited to three public organizations in Brazil. Nevertheless, these organizations are important and relevant in the context of the country, due to the IT infrastructure and the knowledge and expertise of the interviewees on the domain of cloud computing.

Due to the length of this article, we did not discuss and compare the findings with other studies from the literature review. We intend to continue investigating this topic to improve the results of these recommendations with other studies. For instance, to classify the order of importance of each recommendation.

The validation of the recommendations in other contexts and countries as well as the comparison of concerns between private and public organizations regarding implementation of cloud environments will improve our understanding of the adoption of this technology. We also intend to identify the impact of each recommendation in the process of deploying CC, in order to create a roadmap to assist decision-makers in the process of maximizing the benefits of this technology.

Acknowledgments. This work has been supported by FCT – Fundação para a Ciência e Tecnologia within the Project Scope: UID/CEC/00319/2019.

References

1. Branco, T., Sá Soares, F., Rivero, A.L.: Key issues for the successful adoption of cloud computing. Procedia Comput. Sci. **121**, 115–122 (2017)
2. Mallmann, G., Maçada, A.C.: Adoption of cloud computing: a study with public and private hospitals in a developing country. Int. J. Innov. Technol. Manag. **15**(05), 1850044 (2018)

3. Senyo, P., Addae, E., Boateng, R.: Cloud computing research: a review of research themes, frameworks, methods and future research directions. Int. J. Inf. Manag. **38**(1), 128–139 (2018)
4. Bhisikar, A.: G-Cloud: new paradigm shift for online public services IaaS PaaS SaaS. Int. J. Comput. Appl. **22**(8), 24–29 (2011)
5. Tripathi, A., Parihar, B.: E-Governance challenges and cloud benefits. In: Proceedings - 2011 IEEE International Conference on Computer Science and Automation Engineering, CSAE 2011, vol. 1, pp. 351–354 (2011)
6. Goyal, S.: Public vs private vs hybrid vs community - cloud computing: a critical review. Int. J. Comput. Netw. Inf. Secur. **6**(3), 20–29 (2014)
7. Conway, G., Curry, E.: Managing cloud computing: a life cycle approach. In: 2nd International Conference on Cloud Computing and Services Science CLOSER 2012, no. January, pp. 198–207 (2010)
8. Isaca, Controls and Assurance in the Cloud: Using COBIT-5 (2014)
9. Alshamaila, Y., Papagiannidis, S., Li, F.: Cloud computing adoption by SMEs in the north east of England: a multi-perspective framework. J. Enterp. Inf. Manag. **26**(3), 250–275 (2013)
10. Date, H., Ramaswamy, R., Gangwar, H.: Understanding determinants of cloud computing adoption using an integrated TAM-TOE model. J. Enterp. Inf. Manag. **28**(1), 107–130 (2015)
11. Qian, R., Palvia, P.: Towards an understanding of cloud computing's impact on organizational IT strategy. J. Inf. Technol. Case Appl. Res. **15**(4), 34–54 (2013)
12. Low, C., Chen, Y., Wu, M.: Understanding of determinants of cloud computing adoption. Ind. Manag. Data Syst. **111**(7), 1006–1023 (2011)
13. Mattoon, S., Hensle, B., Baty, J.: Cloud computing maturity model guiding success with cloud capabilities. Computing, no. December, p. 13 (2011)
14. Trivedi, H.: Cloud Adoption Model for Governments and Large Enterprises (2013)
15. Weinhardt, C., et al.: Cloud computing – a classification, business models, and research directions. Bus. Inf. Syst. Eng. **1**(5), 391–399 (2009)
16. Dekker, D.L.: Cloud Security Guide for SMEs. ENISA, 710 01 Heraklion, Greece (2015)
17. Velte, A.T., Velte, T.J., Elsenpeter, R.: Cloud Computing: A pratical Aproach. McGraw-Hill, New York (2010)
18. Poullet, Y.: Data protection legislation: what is at stake for our society and democracy? Comput. Law Secur. Rev. **25**(3), 211–226 (2009)
19. Morais, N.S.D.: Proposta de Modelo de Migração de Sistemas de Ambiente Tradicional para Nuvem Privada para o Polo de Tecnologia da Informação do Exército Brasileiro, p. 101 (2015)
20. Ross, R., Oren, J.C., McEvilley, M.: Systems security engineering an integrated approach to building trustworthy resilient systems, NIST Special Publication (800-160), p. 121 (2014)
21. CSA: Security Guidance for Critical Areas of Focus in Cloud Computing V3.0, Cloud Security Alliance, vol. 3, p. 155 (2011)
22. NIST: Guide for Applying the Risk Management Framework to Federal Information Systems, NIST Special Publication 800-37, vol. Rev 1, no. February, p. 93 (2010)
23. Jansen, W., Grance, T.: Guidelines on Security and Privacy in Public Cloud Computing, p. 80 (2011)
24. Dempsey, K., et al.: Information Security Continuous Monitoring for Federal Information Systems and Organizations, NIST Special Publication 800-137, vol. Special Pu, p. 80 (2011)
25. Lui, F.: NIST Cloud Computing Reference Architecture Recommendations of the National Institute of Standards and Technology, Nist Special Publication, vol. 500, no. 292, p. 28 (2011)

26. Johnson, D., Grayson, K.: Cognitive and affective trust in service relationships. J. Bus. Res. **58**(4), 500–507 (2005)
27. Repschlaeger, J., et al.: Decision model for selecting a cloud provider: a study of service model decision priorities. In: 19th Americas Conference on Information Systems, AMCIS 2013 - Hyperconnected World: Anything, Anywhere, Anytime, vol. 2, pp. 1031–1041 (2013)
28. Stankov, I., Datsenka, R., Kurbel, K.: Service level agreement as an instrument to enhance trust in cloud computing - an analysis of infrastructureas-a-service providers. In: 18th Americas Conference on Information Systems 2012, AMCIS 2012, vol. 5, pp. 3813–3822 (2012)
29. Myers, M.D.: Qualitative Research in Business and Management, 2nd edn. Sage Publication, London (2013)
30. Benbasat, I., Goldstein, D.K., Mead, M.: The case research strategy in studies of information systems. MIS Q. **11**(3), 369–386 (1987)
31. Dubé, L., Paré, G.: Rigor in information systems positivist case research: current practices, trends, and recommendations. MIS Q. **27**(4), 597–636 (2003)
32. Bianchi, I., et al.: Baseline mechanisms for IT governance at universities. In: 25th European Conference on Information Systems (ECIS), Guimarães, Portugal, 5–10 June 2017, pp. 1551–1567 (2017)
33. Myers, M.D., Newman, M.: The qualitative interview in IS research: examining the craft. Inf. Organ. **17**(1), 2–26 (2007)
34. Keeney, R.L.: Value Focused Thinking - A Path to Creative Decisionmaking. Harvard un ed., Cambridge, London (1992)
35. Keeney, R.L.: Modeling values for telecommunications management. IEEE Trans. Eng. Manag. **48**(3), 370–379 (2001)

Dynamic Resource Allocation in Hybrid Mobile Cloud Computing for Data-Intensive Applications

Mohammad Alkhalaileh$^{(\boxtimes)}$, Rodrigo N. Calheiros, Quang Vinh Nguyen, and Bahman Javadi

School of Computing, Engineering and Mathematics, Western Sydney University, Sydney, Australia
{mohammad.nour,r.calheiros,q.nguyen,b.javadi}@westernsydney.edu.au

Abstract. Mobile cloud computing is a platform that has been used to overcome the challenges of mobile computing. However, emerging data-intensive applications, such as face recognition and natural language processing, imposes more challenges on mobile cloud computing platforms because of high bandwidth cost and data location issues. To overcome these challenges, this paper proposes a dynamic resource allocation model to schedule data-intensive applications on integrated computation resource environment composed of mobile devices, cloudlets and public cloud which we refer as hybrid mobile cloud computing (hybrid-MCC). The allocation process is based on a system model taking into account different parameters related to the application structure, data size and network configuration. We conducted real experiments on the implemented system to evaluate the performance of the proposed technique. Results demonstrate the ability of the proposed technique to generate an adaptive resource allocation in response to the variation on application data size and network bandwidth. Results reveal that the proposed technique improves the execution time for data-intensive applications by an average of 78% and saves the mobile energy consumption by an average of 87% in compared to using only a mobile device while the monetary cost increased only 11% due to using cloud resources and mobile communication.

Keywords: Hybrid mobile cloud computing ·
Data-intensive mobile applications · Offloading technique ·
Mobile application scheduling · Resource allocation ·
Application execution modelling

1 Introduction

The use of mobile devices such as smartphones and tablets underwent a tremendous increase due to the advancement in functionalities supported by enhanced features such as high connectivity, faster CPU, large memory, and sophisticated

© Springer Nature Switzerland AG 2019
R. Miani et al. (Eds.): GPC 2019, LNCS 11484, pp. 176–191, 2019.
https://doi.org/10.1007/978-3-030-19223-5_13

sensors. In 2019, it is estimated that 46% of the internet traffic will be generated by mobile devices with an estimated 30.6 Exabyte generated monthly [7]. Although mobile devices are now equipped with considerable high-performance computation resources, they still face major challenges in meeting the requirements of computation-intensive and data-intensive mobile applications.

Cloud Computing has been extensively proposed to overcome the shortcomings of mobile computing. Cloud computing provides computation and storage as services in a highly scalable and secure manner. Satyanarayanan et al. [19] argue that cloud computing model is potentially the best solution to solve the deficiencies in mobile device resources. The integration of mobile computing and cloud computing is known as Mobile Cloud Computing (MCC) [5]. MCC aims to augment mobile devices by improving and optimizing their computing capabilities while performing compute-intensive tasks in cloud-based resources [22]. Migrating resource-intensive computations from smartphone devices to the cloud via wireless communication technologies are refer to the concept of computation offloading. Computation offloading has been studied intensively in the literature and different techniques have been proposed for optimizing energy consumption and meeting user Quality of Service (QoS) metrics such as response time and monetary cost. These techniques include computation augmentation [1], device cloning [6], nearby-resource computation [19], provisioning middleware [10,12,17] and context-aware and profiling [13,22]. While there are some works about computation offloading, most of them are limited to computation-intensive applications which confined on simple MCC environment.

In this work, we propose a dynamic resource allocation model to schedule data-intensive applications on integrated computation resource environment composed of mobile devices, cloudlets and public cloud which we refer as hybrid mobile cloud computing (hybrid-MCC). We consider hybrid-MCC to construct new efficient MCC resource models. Moreover, we model a *data-intensive* mobile application scheduling and allocation as a multi-objective optimization problem for hybrid-MCC. Data-intensive mobile applications could be face recognition, data analytics and natural language processing [2]. The work contribution can be listed as:

- Multi-objective optimization of device energy and monetary cost on the hybrid-MCC environment under the constraints of mobile device energy and task deadline.
- Propose a data-aware offloading technique for data-intensive applications on hybrid-MCC environment.
- Performance evaluation of the proposed technique using real experiment and simulation under various working conditions.

The rest of the paper is structured as follows. In Sect. 2, we investigate the related work on task scheduling and allocation optimization on MCC. Section 3 presents an overview of the system architecture as a hybrid-MCC environment. Application execution models and problem formulation are described in Sect. 4, while the proposed data-aware offloading technique explained in Sect. 5. The model performance evaluation and experimental results are discussed in Sect. 6. Section 7 provides conclusions and future work.

2 Related Work

In this section, we review the existing works on task scheduling and allocation optimization on MCC from different perspectives based on different optimization objectives.

It is critical for mobile applications to deliver complex high-performance functionalities at a lower energy level. Mobile device I/O processing and network communications are energy-hungry components [1]. Offloading heavy tasks to the cloud can reduce energy consumption in an efficient way. Abolfazlia et al. [1] showed that mobile computation augmentation can deliver intensive computation to mobile users, save device energy use and prolong battery life. Different energy-based models have been proposed in literature such as: mobile device cloning in remote resources [6], code offloading and migration [8], application and network profiling [11], and application decomposition and reusability [10,15].

However, the aforementioned energy-based MCC solutions focus on application code complexity migration for device energy optimization and do not consider the variation of context parameters such as input data size, network bandwidth, and corresponding data communication cost. Mobile network performance has a significant contribution to improving application responsiveness and thus optimizing the energy consumption [4]. Offloading to nearby resources such as cloudlets [19] can enhance application responsiveness and availability. The decision to run an application locally or remotely is complicated and requires steady monitoring of network conditions and application profiling [10].

Data-intensive applications such as customized data analytics services, natural language processing, and face recognition are resource-intensive applications that require machines with powerful CPUs and huge memory space to load dynamic application code and data. These applications bring additional challenges for energy and cost optimization [20]. Processing large data files on mobile devices has direct overhead on device energy, whereas transferring large data files over mobile networks can increase the device idle time, as well the total computation cost and time. The literature shows high attention to resource elasticity and scalability. Resource-based MCC optimization models focus on cloud resource scaling and VM parallelism [12], elastic applications segmentation and deployment on hybrid-MCC and workflow-aware execution partitioning [17]. Sanaei et al. [18] highlighted the significance of having intelligent and scalable context-aware systems for mobile cloud applications that are capable of handling dynamic mobile environment.

For cost optimization, Nan et al. [16] studied the challenges of data-intensive mobile applications. The study uses monetary cost optimization as a significant factor to enhance user QoS. Minimizing monetary cost and enhancing customers QoS require an efficient cost optimization model. Zhou et al. [21] proposed a three-tier MCC middleware that empowers programmers with computation alternatives based on the application cost model and the offloading decision maker. Even though the proposed model includes the task data size in generating an optimized execution application tasks plan, the data size is marginally small and cannot reflect the scenario of data-intensive application scheduling on MCC.

The main common issue among the researches above is the lack of consideration the contribution of data size and MCC application complexity in building MCC architectures. To overcome this shortcoming, we propose an optimization technique for execution data-intensive MCC applications on the hybrid-MCC environment.

3   System Architecture

In this paper we propose a data-intensive mobile application offloading optimization framework on hybrid-MCC environment. The environment leverages three types of resources, namely, public cloud, cloudlet and mobile device. The public cloud provides high powerful and scalable resource. Cloudlet provides computation service to the mobile clients for sensitive requests. These resources can be

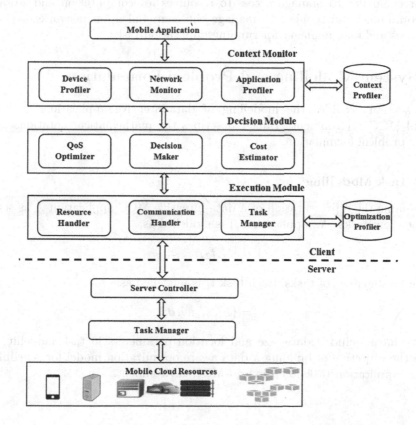

Fig. 1. Proposed hybrid-MCC offloading decision optimization framework.

accessed via Wi-Fi or cellular network. For a mobile device, we assume its ability to perform local computation and storage under the constraints of energy and wireless interface.

The proposed offloading optimization framework consists of components that provides services of context monitoring, decision making and application execution. Figure 1 illustrates the proposed framework.

The context monitor module is responsible for profiling context parameters at run time and supports the decision maker with the energy and monetary cost estimations. The framework offers three profilers, namely, device profiler for energy usage, network monitor for available mobile network information and application profiler to record the heuristic data about application execution with awareness to context information of network bandwidth.

The decision-making module is a QoS optimizer which aims to find the best application execution plan on a solution space where each solution is estimated by the cost estimator. The decision is based on user QoS and estimated execution time, total device energy and monetary cost.

The execution module is responsible for running the received application execution plan from the decision maker. It has three main components: The resource handler to manage access to resources for computation and storage, the communication handler to manage the communication networks between resources and task manager for running application tasks.

4   System Modelling and Problem Formulation

This section provides the modelling of data-intensive applications and the hybrid-MCC environment. Table 1 describes the mathematical notations used in the problem formulation.

4.1   Task Modelling

We assume the representation of a data-intensive MCC application A as set of independent tasks. An application A is modelled as:

$$A = \{t_1, t_2, \ldots, t_n\} \tag{1}$$

where n is number of tasks. Each task t_i is modelled as:

$$t_i = \{L_i, s_i, w_i, \partial_i\} \tag{2}$$

We have included data size and location parameters in task modelling to serve the objective of building a data-aware optimization model for scheduling mobile application tasks on a hybrid-MCC environment.

4.2   Resource Modelling

The system assumes three computation resources, namely, public cloud, cloudlets and mobile devices. A mobile device P_m is modelled as:

$$P_m = \{\alpha, \beta_{down}, \beta_{up}, \beta_{cost}, d, e, w_m\} \tag{3}$$

A mobile device is connected to a cloudlet and the public cloud via Wi-Fi or cellular networks. A cloudlet or public cloud virtual machine P_{cloud} is modelled as:

$$P_{cloud} = \{\beta_{down}, \beta_{cost}, p_{cost}, w_{cloud}\} \tag{4}$$

4.3   Application Execution Models

This section describes the cost estimation models involved in formulating the mobile application scheduled to run the application tasks in the hybrid-MCC

Table 1. Problem formulation notations

Symbol	Definition
t_i	Application Task i
L_i	Task input file location, either locally or remotely
s_i	Task input size
w_i	The number of task execution instructions
∂_i	Task deadline
β_{down}, β_{up}	Available network download and upload bandwidth
β_{cost}	The monetary cost of data communication using mobile network
d	Mobile device storage
e	Available device energy (Joule)
α	Available device memory
w_m	The device processing power
p_{cost}	Cost of processing in a cloud machine
w_{cloud}	Processing power of a cloud machine
C	Estimated total monetary cost of the application
E	Estimated total energy consumption in the mobile device
D_{t_i}	Estimated execution time for task t_i
$\varnothing_i$	Task t_i data size sensitivity factor
β_s, β_r	Network bandwidth between data location and computation target
l	The network latency
$D_{t_i}^W$	The task waiting time in a remote server
λ	The mean rate of arrival task execution request to a remote server
L_q	The mean number of task requests in the queue
M^W	Application waiting time

environment. In order to find the application execution plan, three estimation values need to be calculated, namely, task execution time, total mobile energy consumption and total monetary cost.

Task Execution Time Model. The task execution time for task t_i is the sum of task processing time $D_{t_i}^P$ in the target computation environment P_{target}, data communication time $D_{t_i}^C$ and task average waiting time D^W for remote execution which can be calculated by using Little's rule [14].

$$D_{t_i} = D_{t_i}^P + D_{t_i}^C + D^W \tag{5}$$

$$D_{t_i}^P = w_{i,target} + (s_i * \emptyset_i) \tag{6}$$

$$D_{t_i}^C = \frac{s_i}{min(\beta_s, \beta_r)} + l \tag{7}$$

$$D^W = \frac{L_q}{\lambda} \tag{8}$$

Mobile Device Energy Model. The energy consumption in the mobile device E is estimated by calculating E^P the total processing energy consumed by the mobile device, E^W the waiting energy particularly when the local execution time is less than the remote execution time, since the system assumes parallel tasks execution among the computation environment and E^C which is mobile energy consumption for data transfer communication.

$$E = E^C + E^P + E^W \tag{9}$$

$$E_i^P = D_{t_i}^P * \epsilon_i^P \tag{10}$$

$$E^P = \sum_{i=1}^{m} E_i^P \tag{11}$$

$$M^W = max(0, \sum_{i=1}^{m} D_{t_i}^P - max(\sum_{i=1}^{c} D_{t_i}^P, \sum_{i=1}^{cl} D_{t_i}^P)) \tag{12}$$

$$E^W = M^W * \epsilon^W \tag{13}$$

$$E^C = \sum_{i=1}^{m} D_{t_i}^C * \epsilon^C \tag{14}$$

where:

- $\sum_{i=1}^{m} D_{t_i}^P, \sum_{i=1}^{c} D_{t_i}^P, \sum_{i=1}^{cl} D_{t_i}^P$: are the total processing time for all tasks executed locally (mobile device) and remotely (the public cloud and cloudlet), respectively. We consider the waiting energy consumption only if the waiting time M^W has non-negative value.
- $\epsilon_i^P, \epsilon^W, \epsilon^C$: the estimated energy consumption in the mobile device for task t_i, remote execution waiting and data communication, respectively.
- m, c, cl: the number of tasks to be executed in mobile device, the public cloud and cloudlet, respectively.

Monetary Cost Model. The monetary cost represents the amount of money to run the mobile application on the proposed hybrid-MCC environment. This includes two parts: total remote task processing cost C^P in cloudlet and the public cloud and total data communication cost C^C.

$$C = C^P + C^C \tag{15}$$

$$C^P = \sum_i^c C_i^P \tag{16}$$

$$C_i^P = D_{t_i}^P * p_{cost} \tag{17}$$

$$C^C = \sum_i^n (s_i * \beta_{cost}) \tag{18}$$

4.4   Problem Formulation

The main objective is to find the best mobile application offloading plan in which the total energy consumption on the mobile device and the total monetary cost are reduced in respect to individual task deadline and available mobile battery energy. The offloading plan represents tuple for each task t_i and the selected computation environment among local execution on the mobile device P_m, the cloudlet or the public cloud P_{cloud}. Precisely, the optimization problem is formulated as a monetary cost (C) multiplied by mobile energy consumption (E) due to the assumption of equal contribution on the optimization and the difference on both measurement units:

$$min(C * E) \tag{19}$$

Subject to:

$$D_{t_i} < \partial_i, \forall t_i \in A$$
$$E < e$$

5   Proposed Data-Aware Offloading Technique

Mobile application offloading aims to augment mobile device capabilities by migrating computation to more powerful resources. In this work, we propose a data-aware offloading technique to study the contribution of data size for mobile application offloading decision in hybrid-MCC environment. To accomplish this objective, we adopted Particle swarm optimization (PSO) [9] as evolutionary search optimization technique to find the best offloading plan based on optimization objective in (Eq. 19). This section discuses the proposed offloading technique in which an optimized tasks allocation and scheduling plan is generated.

PSO is an evolutionary computational technique that optimizes a problem by iteratively trying to improve a candidature solution with respect to quality cost measurement. It simulates the behaviour of movement organisms in a bird flock or fish schools. In our approach, a particle represents randomized application execution plan on available resources. Figure 2 provides an example of a particle position. There are ten tasks to schedule. In such case, a particle is ten-dimensional and its position has ten coordinates. The coordinate index (coordinate 1 through coordinate 10) maps into tasks (t_1 through t_{10}). The value of each coordinate is a real number in range (0..3]. Coordinate value in range (0..1] correspondent task is allocated to mobile device and Coordinate value in range (1..2] correspondent task is allocated to cloudlet while Coordinate value in range (2..3] correspondent task is allocated to the public cloud.

Particle's Position

Crd.1	Crd.2	Crd.3	Crd.4	Crd.5	Crd.6	Crd.7	Crd.8	Crd.9	Crd.10
0.38	1.28	1.86	2.90	2.73	2.63	0.91	2.59	0.47	1.78

Task to Resource Mapping

t_1	t_2	t_3	t_4	t_5	t_6	t_7	t_8	t_9	t_{10}
M	CL	CL	C	C	C	M	C	M	CL

Fig. 2. Example of the encoding of a particle's position.

To reflect the objective of scheduling tasks on the defined computation environment, the fitness function is used to determine the goodness of a particle position by estimating the optimization value for a given solution according to the total monetary cost C (Eq. 15) and the total energy E (Eq. 9) consumed by the mobile device. The fitness function accepts a PSO particle in which the position represents an application tasks scheduling solution. Energy estimation and cost calculation are based on task execution time D (Eq. 5) including processing, communication and waiting time. The data communication time D^C for task t_i depends on task data location. D^C is only considered if data storage and computation environment are in different locations. The fitness function considers the impact of D^C time on mobile device energy and monetary cost. Algorithm 1 shows the main steps of finding the optimal offloading scheduling plan for data-aware mobile applications.

The task processing time D^P is calculated based on task t_i computation requirement and task data size. The impact of data size is measured by experimenting task processing with different data sizes. The processing time D^P is used to estimate task processing energy for local task execution, and task processing monetary cost C^P for remote execution. However, the system assumes extra energy consumption when the mobile device is in idle state, this occurs when total local execution is less than the maximum remote execution in cloudlet or public cloud.

Algorithm 1. Task scheduling for data-aware offloading

1: Inputs : set of application tasks T, computation resources R
2: Output : application tasks schedule S
3: Update resources' metadata
4: Setting up PSO Environment P
5: Initialize PSO Particles $P[NumP]$ $NumP$: number of particles
6: $P.gbest = $ inf Initialize global best $gbest$
7: **for** $i = 1$ to $NumP$ **do**
8:     Randomize $P[i].POS$
9:     $FitCost = PSOFitFun(P[i].POS, T)$
10:     UpdateBestPos $(P, P[i], FitCost)$
11: **end for**
12: Run PSO Iterations // $NumL$: number of iterations
13: **for** $i = 1$ to $NumL$ **do**
14:     **for** $j = 1$ to $NumP$ **do**
15:         Calculate $P[j].VELOCITY$
16:         Update $P[j].POS$
17:         $FitCost = PSOFitFun(P[j].POS, T)$
18:         UpdateBestPos $(P, P[j], FitCost)$
19:     **end for**
20: **end for**
21: $MinCost = PSOFitFun(P.gbest.POS, T)$
22: $S = (P.gbest.POS, MinCost)$
23: **return** S

---

6   Performance Evaluation

Performance evaluation for the proposed data-aware offloading technique has been conducted using two sets of experiments. The first set is a real experiment, to validate the model by comparing the result of the proposed execution model and offloading technique against real execution. For this experiment, we have implemented a real MCC environment as illustrated in Fig. 1. In the second experiment set, we used synthetic application data to evaluate the proposed offloading technique.

6.1   Experimental Setup

The configuration of the hybrid-MCC resources includes a mobile devices, cloudlets and public cloud which are listed in Table 2. We considered a single machine for task processing in the public cloud and cloudlet. For mobile network bandwidth, we conducted the experiment with three communication networks (3G, 4G, and Wi-Fi). Table 3 presents details about bandwidth values for used networks. We have recorded and used minimum and maximum bandwidth in real application execution for each network type. Recorded values are used to build a uniform distribution model for the experimental work. We initialized the application tasks structure with 30 tasks. Each task has the following properties:

Table 2. Computation resources configuration

Resource type	No. cores	Memory (GB)
EC2 Linux t2.2xlarge Intel Xeon	8	32
Cloudlet Intel Xeon	4	8
LG Nexus 5 Qualcomm	2	2

Table 3. Communication networks bandwidth

Network type	Min. bandwidth (MB/s)	Max. bandwidth (MB/s)
3G	1.5	2.6
4G	3.9	9.5
Wi-Fi	10.8	20.5
Network latency	**Min. latency (s)**	**Max. latency (s)**
Latency	0.6	11.5

- Computation requirement (task workload) D^P: we used the workload model proposed by Anglano and Canonico [3]. The model used to determine the task deadline with 1000 s granularity. Task deadline values have been uniformly distributed with 205 s and 590 s for minimum and maximum time, respectively.
- The task data file locations (L) are distributed randomly between the public cloud server, the mobile device, and other cloud storage (i.e. AWS S3).
- Task data size (s) model: we assume three different scenarios for the application data model to create each task, namely, small (20–200 MB), medium (200–500 MB) and large (500–20000 MB).
- Task data sensitivity factor ($\emptyset$): the factor has the value between [0..1] which measures the task execution response to the change of data size.

6.2   Model Validation

In this section, we provide the validation for the proposed execution model using a real-time execution scenario. We run an application with 30-task of small data model using both proposed model and real implementation for three different communication networks.

Figure 3 shows the comparison between the proposed model and real execution results in three different communication networks and three performance metrics including execution time, mobile energy and monetary cost. The result shows some discrepancies between the proposed model and real execution scenario because of the difference in available bandwidth and network latency in real execution scenario and the proposed model. We observed the major error in 3G network. As you can see in Table 3, the bandwidth for 3G network is between

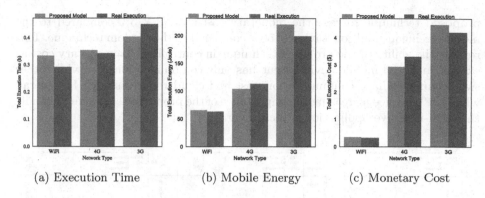

(a) Execution Time   (b) Mobile Energy   (c) Monetary Cost

Fig. 3. Application execution model validation using real experiments for three different communication networks

1.5 and 2.6 but in real execution, the bandwidth is unstable because of bandwidth fluctuation. The average errors for execution model are 8% for execution time, 11% for energy consumption and 15% for the monetary cost. Based on the observations, the proposed execution model is accurate enough to use for offloading in the hybrid-MCC system.

6.3 System Evaluation and Experimental Results

After validation of the execution model, we used the similar setup to evaluate the proposed offloading technique under different working conditions. We compared the proposed technique with two other techniques including mobile only and random offloading. The application tasks were demonstrated based on the aforementioned data size scenarios. In addition, the performance measurements that we used are execution time, mobile energy and monitory cost. Figures 4, 5 and 6 show the results of running the mobile application on three techniques for three different communication networks.

Figure 4 shows experimental results when using the 3G network. Figure 4(a) illustrates that the proposed technique has significant execution time reduction in comparison to the other two techniques for the three data size models. In comparison to the random technique, execution time reduction increased from 25% in small data size to 56% in medium data size and 63% in large data size. For the same experiment, the result of the proposed technique compared to the mobile technique reduced the execution time by average 73% for three data size models. Moreover, Fig. 4(b) shows high mobile energy consumption saving with increasing of the data size. For example, the proposed technique can save mobile energy consumption around 57% in small data size, 74% in medium data size and 78% in large data size in compared with the random technique. For the same experiment, the result of the proposed technique compared to the mobile technique can save the mobile energy consumption by average 78% for the three data size models. Moreover, Fig. 4(c) highlights the ability of the proposed technique to save the monetary cost around 2–3% compared to the mobile technique and cost saving of 50% compared to the random technique. This reveals the ability of the proposed technique in controlling the monetary cost as execution in the mobile environment has only communication cost while other two techniques have communication cost and cloud resources cost. In general, while the data size increasing the importance of the proposed technique to handle the data-intensive application is increasing.

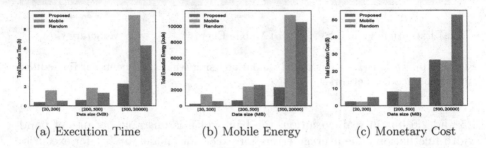

(a) Execution Time   (b) Mobile Energy   (c) Monetary Cost

Fig. 4. System performance measurements with 3G network for different data sizes

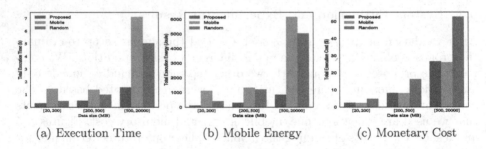

(a) Execution Time   (b) Mobile Energy   (c) Monetary Cost

Fig. 5. System performance measurements with 4G network for different data sizes

Similar results can be observed in case of 4G network as shown in Fig. 5. Figure 5(b) result shows energy consumption saving of the proposed technique compared with the mobile technique with 89% for large data size compared to 80% using 3G network due to higher energy consumption of 4G network. Also Fig. 6(b) shows average 90% and 84% in saving mobile energy consumption of the proposed technique compared with the mobile technique and the random technique, respectively for three data size model using Wi-Fi network. This again confirms the significance of the proposed model to save energy while using different communication networks.

Based on the results, the proposed technique improves execution time for data-intensive application for large data size sets compared to the random technique by average of 51% and saving mobile energy consumption by average of

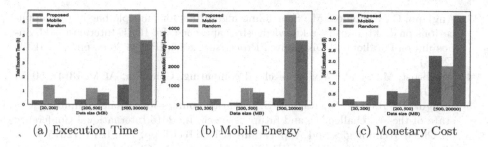

(a) Execution Time   (b) Mobile Energy   (c) Monetary Cost

Fig. 6. System performance measurements with Wi-Fi network for different data sizes

77% while the average monetary cost saving improvement is 48%. Moreover, the proposed technique improves execution time for data-intensive application for large data size sets compared to the mobile technique by average of 78% and saving mobile energy consumption by average of 87% while the average of monetary cost is only 11% higher due to using cloud resources and mobile communication.

In summary, the proposed technique shows high capability in handling data-intensive applications in compared with the mobile and the random techniques through reducing mobile energy consumption and monetary cost. It can be stated that for data-intensive applications, it is critical to use the proposed technique since the execution time and mobile energy consumption will be very high, but for small data size applications we could possibly use the mobile technique or the random technique.

7   Conclusions and Future Work

We proposed a QoS-aware resource allocation model to schedule data-intensive mobile applications on hybrid-MCC environment. The model generates an application execution plan with consideration to different aspects according to application complexity, input data size, available network bandwidth, and available mobile device energy. Results indicated sufficient behaviour particularly with execution time and energy. As a future work, we will study the integration of edge computing as improvement to the hybrid-MCC environment to handle data-intensive MCC application requirements. Moreover, we are planning to study task queuing behaviour on remote servers. Furthermore, we are planning to build a prediction framework for generalizing offloading decision according to most significant parameters.

References

1. Abolfazli, S., Sanaei, Z., Gani, A., Xia, F., Yang, L.T.: Rich mobile applications: genesis, taxonomy, and open issues. J. Netw. Comput. Appl. **40**, 345–362 (2014)
2. Ahnn, J.H.J.: Data-Intensive Mobile Cloud Computing. Ph.D. thesis, UCLA (2015)

3. Anglano, C., Canonico, M.: Scheduling algorithms for multiple bag-of-task applications on desktop grids: a knowledge-free approach. In: IEEE International Symposium on Parallel and Distributed Processing, 2008. IPDPS 2008, pp. 1–8. IEEE (2008)
4. Armbrust, M., et al.: A view of cloud computing. Commun. ACM **53**(4), 50–58 (2010)
5. Bangui, H., Rakrak, S., Raghay, S.: External sources for mobile computing: the state-of-the-art, challenges, and future research. In: 2015 International Conference on Cloud Technologies and Applications (CloudTech), pp. 1–8. IEEE (2015)
6. Chun, B.G., Ihm, S., Maniatis, P., Naik, M., Patti, A.: Clonecloud: elastic execution between mobile device and cloud. In: Proceedings of the Sixth Conference on Computer Systems, pp. 301–314. ACM (2011)
7. Cisco Visual Networking Index: Global mobile data traffic forecast update, 2013–2018. White paper (2014)
8. Cuervo, E., et al.: MAUI: making smartphones last longer with code offload. In: Proceedings of the 8th International Conference on Mobile Systems, Applications, and Services, pp. 49–62. ACM (2010)
9. Eberhart, R., Kennedy, J.: A new optimizer using particle swarm theory. In: Proceedings of the Sixth International Symposium on Micro Machine and Human Science, 1995. MHS 1995, pp. 39–43. IEEE (1995)
10. Giurgiu, I., Riva, O., Juric, D., Krivulev, I., Alonso, G.: Calling the cloud: enabling mobile phones as interfaces to cloud applications. In: Bacon, J.M., Cooper, B.F. (eds.) Middleware 2009. LNCS, vol. 5896, pp. 83–102. Springer, Heidelberg (2009). https://doi.org/10.1007/978-3-642-10445-9_5
11. Kemp, R., Palmer, N., Kielmann, T., Bal, H.: Cuckoo: a computation offloading framework for smartphones. In: Gris, M., Yang, G. (eds.) MobiCASE 2010. LNICST, vol. 76, pp. 59–79. Springer, Heidelberg (2012). https://doi.org/10.1007/978-3-642-29336-8_4
12. Kosta, S., Aucinas, A., Hui, P., Mortier, R., Zhang, X.: ThinkAir: dynamic resource allocation and parallel execution in the cloud for mobile code offloading. In: Infocom, 2012 Proceedings IEEE, pp. 945–953. IEEE (2012)
13. Lin, T.Y., Lin, T.A., Hsu, C.H., King, C.T.: Context-aware decision engine for mobile cloud offloading. In: Wireless Communications and Networking Conference Workshops (WCNCW), 2013 IEEE, pp. 111–116. IEEE (2013)
14. Little, J.D.: A proof for the queuing formula: L= λ w. Oper. Res. **9**(3), 383–387 (1961)
15. March, V., Gu, Y., Leonardi, E., Goh, G., Kirchberg, M., Lee, B.S.: μcloud: towards a new paradigm of rich mobile applications. Procedia Comput. Sci. **5**, 618–624 (2011)
16. Nan, X., He, Y., Guan, L.: Optimal resource allocation for multimedia cloud based on queuing model. In: 2011 IEEE 13th International Workshop on Multimedia Signal Processing (MMSP), pp. 1–6. IEEE (2011)
17. Rahimi, M.R., Venkatasubramanian, N., Mehrotra, S., Vasilakos, A.V.: MAPCloud: mobile applications on an elastic and scalable 2-tier cloud architecture. In: Proceedings of the 2012 IEEE/ACM Fifth International Conference on Utility and Cloud Computing, pp. 83–90. IEEE Computer Society (2012)
18. Sanaei, Z., Abolfazli, S., Gani, A., Shiraz, M.: Sami: Service-based arbitrated multi-tier infrastructure for mobile cloud computing. In: 2012 1st IEEE International Conference on Communications in China Workshops (ICCC), pp. 14–19. IEEE (2012)

19. Satyanarayanan, M., Bahl, V., Caceres, R., Davies, N.: The case for VM-based cloudlets in mobile computing. IEEE Pervasive Comput. **8**, 14–23 (2009)
20. Wang, Y., Chen, R., Wang, D.C.: A survey of mobile cloud computing applications: perspectives and challenges. Wireless Pers. Commun. **80**(4), 1607–1623 (2015)
21. Zhou, B., Dastjerdi, A.V., Calheiros, R., Srirama, S., Buyya, R.: mCloud: A context-aware offloading framework for heterogeneous mobile cloud. IEEE Trans. Serv. Comput. **10**, 797–810 (2015)
22. Zhou, B., Dastjerdi, A.V., Calheiros, R.N., Srirama, S.N., Buyya, R.: A context sensitive offloading scheme for mobile cloud computing service. In: 2015 IEEE 8th International Conference on Cloud Computing (CLOUD), pp. 869–876. IEEE (2015)

A Multi-device Cloud-Based Personal Event Management System

Rita Francese[✉], Michele Risi, and Genoveffa Tortora

University of Salerno, 84084 Fisciano, SA, Italy
{francese,mrisi,tortora}@unisa.it

Abstract. Personal Information Management Systems (PIMSs) enable the individuals to be the holders of their own personal information and provide them support to retrieve and organize it in a secure way. LifeBook is a PIMS running on the mobile device which manages in secure way information concerning events captured by all the user's devices. To this aim, we present the LifeBook Security Model to protect user data stored on the cloud. Events are classified considering both the user's context and their similarity w.r.t. other user events. Similarity is computed by considering content, location, time, and the type of the given event. LifeBook offers a re-find feature for searching and visualizing content already seen in the past, content of which the user remembers aspects such as the time and/or the place she was when the event occurred. The relationships among the user events are adaptively created by a process to extract characteristic information on the user habits based on the Principal Component Analysis (PCA).

Keywords: Personal Information Management System ·
Mobile application · Event management · Information refinding

1 Introduction

Nowadays people are subject to information overloading: data come from an increasing number of sources, such as emails, messages (Facebook, Twitter, SMS, Whatsapp), SMS and phone calls. These data are collected by different devices (e.g., PCs, smartphones, tablets, smart TVs) and are stored on them with different representation and/or format. As an example, iOS and Android offer features for sharing data among different devices. Also Google apps, such as Gmail and Google Drive, enables to share emails, documents and many kinds of data among the user devices, but data are handled by the cloud providers.

Personal Information Management Systems (PIMS) enables the individuals to be the holders of their own personal information and offer methods and techniques to handle user's personal and professional information in various formats, including emails, files, multimedia content, SMSs and phone call data. The PIMS main aim is to let people get their personal information at the right time and

R. Miani et al. (Eds.): GPC 2019, LNCS 11484, pp. 192–207, 2019.
https://doi.org/10.1007/978-3-030-19223-5_14

place, and with proper form and good quality [31]. A smartphone may be considered a PIMS, but the user contents are managed locally in each device or fragmented and handled by the various cloud providers.

The amount of personal information is exponentially increasing, while the storage capacity of the human memory is always the same. Often the user may need to refind [6] information concerning an event, such as refind the calling number of a phone call received two days ago in a specific place, or refind a message received on Facebook yesterday morning, or refind a web search performed in his office. The various strategies adopted by the users when re-retrieving an object from their personal stores may be based on the following elements [11]: the recollection of a property that object has, a previous experience with the object, a temporal reference to that object, such as when it was previously accessed, etc. Indeed, people may know some items useful to refind the needed information, such as a telephone number of a call she did not answered when she was at the University, etc. In the above example if the user has two smartphones she has to search the list of the calls on the two different devices and perform repetitive searches for obtaining the required answers [21]. A PIMS should be able to simplify this kind of task by capturing all the information related to a user and model them as events [29].

In this paper, we enhance LifeBook, a PIMS running on different smart devices (smartphone, tablet and PC) proposed in [15]. LifeBook stores the user's events involving his devices, such as phone calls, SMS, email, Notes, Facebook messages, posts and events, Internet searches, calendar, tagged data, and Dropbox notifications. The event search uses an information retrieval approach to retrieve all the events which better satisfy a set of conditions. In the preliminary version of LifeBook [15] aspects related to data security where demanded to Google cloud and information refinding was based on a similarity map whose weights were manually set by the user. An initial prototype was also evaluated; from this experimentation, we studied the real impact of such a PIMS and the need of improving security to let the user own her information and enhancing the adaptivity of Lifebook [14].

The paper is structured as follows. Section 2 discusses related work. In Sect. 3, we describe the event-based approach adopted by LifeBook, its architecture, including the proposed information retrieval technique for adaptively navigating among correlated events and the adopted security model. In Sect. 4, final remarks conclude the paper.

2   Related Work

Personal Information Management has a long history, starting from Vannevar Bush's Memex [5], a device envisioned in 1940s which would compress and store all of the user books, records, and communications. Many web applications have been developed for storing and retrieving personal data, such as: Lifestreams [12], Stuff-I've-Seen [10], Haystack [3], MyLifeBits [16], Seetrieve [18] and Personal Dataspaces [4]. In particular, Microsoft research proposed MyLifeBits [16], an application having as heart a SQL Server database that can store content and metadata for a variety of types, including contacts, documents, emails, events, photos, songs, and video. An ad-hoc developed camera, SenseCam, takes pictures of the user's everyday-life, also monitoring the brightness and temperature of his environment. Another system proposed by Microsoft Research is Stuff I've Seen [10]. Similarly to LifeBook, it facilitates information re-use by providing a unified index of information (email, Web page, document, appointment) that a user has seen. It also exploits rich contextual cues can be used in the search interface. LifeBook securely manages information on different devices and exploits an event-based approach, providing also location-based interfaces.

Emerging PIMS may adopt a technical architecture based on local storage or cloud-based storage [1]. In a cloud-based model, service providers (social networks, online office suites, healthcare providers etc.) or specialized cloud-based PIMS providers take in charge the data management. In the former model personal data are stored in user devices (e.g., laptops, smartphones, tablets). Many recent projects are based on personal clouds, aiming at preserving user data from "curious" cloud service providers [2], such as Mailpile[1], a client mailer running on the user computer which enables to have control over own data and privacy; personal cloud features are offered by Lima[2], hosting personal files in the user home. In this way they are accessible only by the user devices which talk to each other in peer-to-peer modality and are not mined by third parties.

Personal cloud may be managed by Network-attached storage (NAS) devices, such as Synology[3] or LenovoEMC[4], which are devices with high capacity, reliable home network storage to easily share and access files, photos, videos and music between all the user devices and with other users, such as familiar or friends. Samsung proposes SAMI [30], a cloud-based software platform that will ingest data from wearables and other inputs and manage that data in the cloud. Many applications enable the user to perform self-hosting, having a server at home in order to host personal data and services on it. Thanks to them users may organize and deliver their digital contents on his own network, sharing them locally or safely around the world. Examples are Cozy Cloud[5], OwnCloud [26] and YounoHost[6]. The use of these applications implies administrator responsibilities: to host a website, emails and have an instant messaging system running, the server needs to stay online all 24/7.

Facebook may be considered one of the most used PIMS. It enables to manage the user personal information basing on the time line, but it is possible to search the user content. It does not provide refinding features and the user data suffer of the privacy concern of cloud providers.

---

[1] https://www.mailpile.is.
[2] https://meetlima.com/index.php?lang=en.
[3] https://www.synology.com/en-global.
[4] https://lenovo-na-en.custhelp.com.
[5] https://cozy.io/en/.
[6] https://yunohost.org/.

Recently Google proposed My Activity[7], a Google application which shows everything the user does in his Google account. It is possible to filter results based on time, which Google products has been used, or specify search keywords. But the user does not put all its information on the cloud, thus in many cases there is the need of remembering the interested device, such as in case of a phone call.

Hwang and Cho developed a Web application named Mobile Life Browser [20] aiming at collecting log information from a mobile device and at visualizing the personal everyday-life on a map. Their approach exploits a Bayesian network model for understanding the user's life and extracting meaningful information useful for searching the log database. The search interface is appropriate for the PC.

Le-Phuoc *et al.* [22] proposed an Android app for integrating user's data on a single user's mobile device, without any external server. It uses Semantic Web technologies for creating a unified integration view to query personal information from different sources. A consolidated graph created in RDF contains the aggregated personal information from different data spaces. The provenance information of the data acquired from difference data spaces is also stores as a graph.

Techniques for refinding files and web pages have been proposed in [9]. This PC-based system is based on a query-by-context model over a context memory snapshot, draws inspirations from human memory mechanism. Hailpern et al. [19] proposed a contextual history-based search tool, allowing users to search on the base of temporal relationships (before, during, and after) between data items. SpotLite enables MAC users to search apps, documents, images and other files stored on the various user devices. Also additional results like Wikipedia, news sites, Maps, iTunes and movie listings are offered.

3   The Proposed Approach

The life of a user can be seen as a collection of personal events. LifeBook keeps track of all the events that can be caught by his various electronic devices and enables the user to refind and retrieve them. LifeBook stores personal events in an Event Database on the cloud.

3.1   The Event Model

A personal event (PE) is an observable occurrence of a phenomenon that involves the user and is collected by one of his devices. A PE is either explicitly stored by the user (e.g., the meeting scheduled at 3 pm in Lab 2 on April 23th using the Calendar app), or can be implicitly gathered by the sensor device (John went home at 10 as resulting by his position detected by his smartphone's GPS).

A PE is characterized by the following attributes:

- *id*, a unique identifier of the event;

---

[7] https://myactivity.google.com/myactivity.

- *device*, the device that collected the event;
- *type*, the type of the personal event, with reference to the generating application, (e.g., phone call, SMS);
- *s_time*, starting time of the event;
- *e_time*, ending time of the event;
- *location*, coordinates in the form of latitude, longitude and address of the site where the event started;
- *uri*, uniform resource identifier that contains the link of the resource on the cloud. It contains all data related to the resource, e.g. for a contact the resource contains all the contact data (e.g., name, surname, telephone number(s), email address(es)).

Each event can be related to one or more other events. This relationship enables the user to navigate among memory objects (events) which are correlated, as better described in Sect. 3.3. The event model is deeply detailed in [15].

3.2   System Architecture

The client of LifeBook collects the local events and send them to the back-end on the server, which collects all the events involving the various user's LifeBook devices and synchronize them in such a way that each device can access to all the events, independently from the device where the event was originated. The main LifeBook server and client data exchange features are the following:

- *Client Data Collection.* The client collects all the events involving itself (local store command).
- *Server Updating.* The collected events are periodically transferred by the client on the server which, updates the event database. All the information related to an event are uploaded, including pictures and videos.
- *Event Map Updating.* The LifeBook server hosts an event map which collects all the user events generated in the various device. The map has to be updated when new events are collected.
- *Client Updating.* periodically the client send to the server the id of the last event it has stored in its local map. The server send to it all the events that has not been recorded yet by the client.
- *Search Content.* When the user requires a content indexed by the mobile device, but available on the server, such as a picture produced by another device, the server search it and send it back to the client.

Synchronization occurs by default every minute, if the device is not in use. To reduce the battery consumption the user can manually configure the time interval according to his needs.

The client application is composed of two parts, as shown in Fig. 1:

- *Interaction sub-system (foreground).* It supports the user in the retrieval of the information;

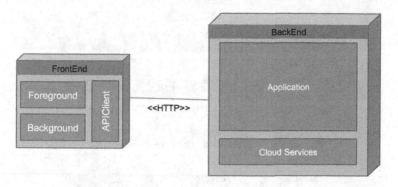

Fig. 1. The LifeBook system.

- *Background sub-system.* It is implemented as a background service, which collects events related to the device. The user can suspend/resume or stop the execution of this service from the option menu on his device. It communicates with the back-end trough API REST.

The access to the native client feature (i.e., Camera, SMS, phone call, GPS) has been performed by using the Cordova hybrid technology, while the interface has been developed with the multi-platform framework Ionic and Angular. The LifeBook back-end has been performed by using a cloud technology offering REST services accessible by the user client for searching and storing the events of interest. The events are captured by the device and stored on the cloud and successively analyzed by using an Information Retrieval technique which produces for each user an event map, useful for retrieving similar events. In case the device is off-line the collected events are stored into a local Database.

The LifeBook back-end has in charge the event management consists in two components: the application, i.e., the presentation and the business layer of LifeBook, and Cloud Service, which represents the external cloud services used by the application. Concerning the latter, the current version of LifeBook moved from Parse[8] to Google cloud. One of the first reason of this change is privacy of data, one of the main Google cloud platform benefits[9]. The Google security model takes advantage of the same security model offered by Gmail, Search and other Apps. It exploits the authentication service offered by Firebase. Another reason is scalability, the LifeBook back-end may use the scalability features offered by Google App Engine (PaaS) and satisfy the user request also when the user traffic varies. In the current version of LifeBook we also enhance the privacy of the user data by following the security approach described in Sect. 3.5.

LifeBook is composed of the following subsystems, as depicted in Fig. 2:

---

[8] http://www.parse.com.
[9] https://cloud.google.com/security/.

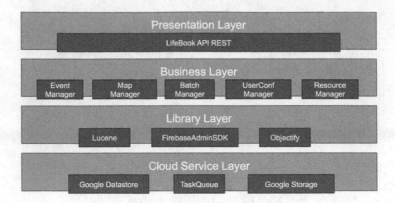

Fig. 2. The LifeBook layers.

- the Presentation Layer exposes the API REST endpoints accessible by the front-end; In particular API handling the user information, background operation on data, event and resource management;
- the Business Layer contains the subsystems handling the various entities (e.g, EventManager, ResourceManager);
- the Library Layer contains the supporting libraries, such as the IR features offered by Lucene, the SDK of the Firebase authentication subsystem, and the object-relational mapping library Objectify;
- the Cloud Service Layer contains the Google Cloud services, such as App Engine, Datastore and Google maps, adopted for reverse-geolocation.

The LifeBook database and files have been stored by using NoSql Google Datastore and the file system Google Storage, respectively [13]. The REST services offered to the client application have been implemented by using Google App Engine (PaaS) con Jersey, following the JAX-RS specification. The REST services are documented following the OpenAPI specifications. The project has been imported in Firebase, which has offered the authentication service, adopted by the LifeBook API.

3.3 Event Searching Interfaces and Navigation

If a user remembers all the relevant details, he could directly access the desired data. There is the need of helping the user in information re-finding when he recalls partial information on the context the user was when the event happened. Users might remember a place, a time interval, a contact of the context he was when that event happened.

Often re-finding information is based on the marking of relevant information. But this approach often fails because it is difficult for the user identify the information he probably will reuse. Thus, it is relevant to consider what people can remember, what strategies are successful for remembering and how we can design and implement tools that better support them in information re-finding.

(a)   (b)   (c)

Fig. 3. The search interface (a), correlated events (b), and the spatio-temporal search map view (c).

The re-finding feature of LifeBook enables to search user data by filtering them filter with standard criteria or by surfing events which are correlated to a selected event. The filtering options enables to set the event attributes on which perform the search: free text, user device, textual content taken from the URI attribute (e.g., contact name, email, body, subject), Date (start and end), Location and Event Type. As an example, by appropriately setting the filter option it is possible to answer the following queries:

- Search all the calls without answer I received last week when I was at the GPC 2019 conference in Brazil.
- John sent me three days a go a document by email or by Whatsapp. Please find it.
- Find an SMS I received two or three days ago from John on my Samsung S4 or on my HUAWEI Y6.

The *refind process* is composed of the following steps:

1. filter definition - selects the appropriate filters by using the apposite tab of the client GUI, shown in Fig. 3(a). In particular, this figure depicts the definition of the event type search criteria. As an example, it is possible to search events related to incoming, out-coming, missed or unknown calls. It is also possible to combine search criteria. The selected combination is shown by the tab color: when an element has been selected for the search its tab in the GUI shows the number of selected elements. When the user selects the event position (i.e., the Place tab) he can access to a map and circle the spatial area to be searched for events.

2. event selection - After having received search results, the user selects one of them (shown on the top of Fig. 3(b)) and navigates a conceptual map displaying correlated events. Relationships between events are stored on the cloud according to a conceptual map. This map is updated each time a new event is detected by applying a similarity function between the given event and the each other on the cloud. When a correlation exists, i.e., the similarity function is greater than a given threshold, the relation between two events is stored into the conceptual map. All these operations are performed in background exploiting a queue data structure to handle multiple events. The similarity function applied on two events returns a value between 0 and 1. This value ranks the relation existing between the two events on the basis of the information provided by the client of LifeBook when the event is captured, as better detailed in the next section.
3. event cofinding - When the user selects an event in the search results and press the Correlated Event button, LifeBook shows all the events related to the selected one ordered in a decreasing way with respect to similarity rank.
4. spatio-temporal PEs representation - LifeBook also offers specific interface for space-based queries and for spatio-temporal queries. The latter is shown in Fig. 3(c). It enables to show the user's event on a map and the events related to it delimited by a circular spatial area, which radius is determined by the user directly on the map. These events are identified by colored pins and icons related to the event type. In particular, the color represents the temporal information on a gradient, where white color is recent and black color represents a remote event. The time range is selected by using a touch-based slider, shown in the top of this figure. Each event type has associated a different icon. On the top of each icon the similarity rank with respect to the given event is shown in terms of starred score.
5. PE visualization - the selected event is highlighted in the ranked list and a preview of its content is shown. If the user click on the PE its whole content (such as file, video, image, web page) is provided by the server and visualized.

3.4 Event Correlation

Event similarity is calculated starting from the event attributes Location, Content, Time, and EventType and by applying an information retrieval technique based on a distance matrix between the pair of events. In particular, the matrix represents the *aggregate multivariate distance*, computed by first determining the distance matrix for each attribute, then normalizing the distance matrices into the range $[0, 1]$; finally, aggregating the obtained distance matrices [15].

Location, Content and Time are quantitative measures. *Location* is represented by the Longitude and Latitude measures, detected when the event happens. *Content* represents the textual information associated to the event. *Time* is the temporal time when the event occurs. The associated distance matrices are LocationDist, ContentDist and TimeDist, respectively.

Given two events e_i and e_j that occurred in the points p_i and p_j, respectively, *LocationDist* is computed in terms of the *Haversine distance* h that computes the distance between p_i and p_j on a sphere when their longitude and latitude are known [27]. In particular, we computed:

$$LocationDist_{i,j} = \min(1, \log(\frac{h(p_i, p_j)}{R_{1000}} + 1)),$$

where R_{1000} is radius of the Earth divided by the constant 1000. Moreover, the user can assign a label to a specific location, e.g., "home" or "at work".

ContentDist is computed by using the Latent Semantic Indexing (LSI) technique [17]. This information retrieval technique has been used to compare the event content (used as a query) with another set of events and to rank the similarity of all possible pairs of event contents. See [15] for further details.

Let $t_{i,j}$ be the distance value (measured in minutes) between time ranges of two events e_i and e_j, which is 0 when ranges overlap, the TimeDist matrix distance is computed as follows:

$$TimeDist_{i,j} = 1 - \frac{1}{1 + \log(t_{i,j} + 1)},$$

whilst EventType matrix distance is computed:

$$EventDist_{i,j} = \begin{cases} 0 & if\ EventType_i = EventType_j; \\ 1 & otherwise. \end{cases}$$

Finally, the Rank between events e_i and e_j is:

$$Rank_{i,j} = 1 - (LW \cdot LocationDist_{i,j} + CW \cdot ContentDist_{i,j} + DW \cdot TimeDist_{i,j} + EW \cdot EventDist_{i,j}),$$

where $LW + CW + DW + EW = 1$. In particular, LW, CW, DW, and EW are scaling constants (weights) that reflect the importance of the attribute within the user context. The relation between two events e_i and e_j is reported in the event map if $Rank_{i,j}$ is greater than a given threshold t.

The weights of $Rank_{i,j}$ are computed in such a way to be adapted to the user behavior by adopting dynamic principal component analysis (DPCA). Principal component analysis (PCA) is useful to identify linearly related variables that describe most of the variability in the data. Application of static PCA on a data with time-dependent structure is unreliable, since the procedure attempts to linearly approximate the complex non-linear relations between variables [22]. Instead, dynamic PCA (DPCA), a simple extension of PCA, can reveal the dynamics of the underlying data structure.

Many study of time series data in event detection problems suggests that a feature extraction method should be applied to understand the complex structures of the data and differences among them. The dependence of measurements suggests that additional time-dependent variables should be introduced to data analysis. Extraction of time-dependent variables was originally accomplished by introducing dynamic principal component analysis.

This method applied to one dimensional time series data considers a collection of observations, $y(1), y(2), ..., y(N) \subseteq Rp$ from a biomedical signal y(k), where N is the number of observations. The data matrix Y for further PCA is arranged as follows:

$$Y = [y(k - I + 1), y(k - I + 2), \ldots, y(k)]$$

where l is a time lag. We set l as four weeks, from Monday to Sunday.

3.5   Security

Ideal PIMS should transform the current provider centric system into a system centered on individuals able to manage and control their online identity [1]. Individuals should be able to decide whether and with whom to share their personal information, for what purposes, for how long, and to keep track of them and decide to take them back when so wished.

PIMS may run by a professional operator offering cloud services on secure hardware. Thus, security is handled by the PIMS formerly. If the PIMS a properly designed, each user data is strongly isolated from that of others. Thus, if the data of a user are compromised, this does not hold for the others [2].

In the following we describe how LifeBook has been carefully designed with the goal to provide security as well as privacy to users.

System and Threat Model. We consider the high-level architecture for cloud data utilization services illustrated in Fig. 4. At its core, the architecture consists of three entity types: the user device collecting the event, in the left-hand side of the figure, the user device searching the systems for event similarity, in the right-hand, and the LifeBook server. Several devices belong to the same user. Events are stored in the event map EM on the server.

To keep sensitive data confidential from unauthorized entities, including the LifeBook server, cryptographic methods have to be applied to each event by the user device collecting it before outsourcing and the cloud services should offer similarity search capability over encrypted data. The followed approach assumes the cloud server acts in an "honest" fashion, e.g., it does not alter the content of the messages and correctly follows the designated protocol specification, but is "curious" to infer and analyze the user data, for example for selling them for marketing analyses. That is, the cloud would honestly store and search data as requested; however, the cloud would also have financial incentives to learn those stored user personal data, which should be protected and hidden from the cloud. The transmission between server and client occurs on a secure connection, such as the one offered by Google Cloud. The following three processes perform the main features of LifeBook.

- *Key distribution.* It is essential that the user multiple devices use a common secret key for secured communication among them. Key distribution is a problem largely investigated in literature [8, 24, 28]. One of the most recent is Quantum Key Distribution, exploiting quantum mechanics to distribute cryptographic keying material between two parties with theoretically unconditional security. Device distance has limited 200 m.

Let us assume that the user owns n devices $D_1, \ldots, D_n$. The distribution process consists of the following steps:

1. The user downloads the client LifeBook on one of his devices, said D_1.
2. He gets an asymmetric key (K).
3. Quantum Key distribution is adopted to share K with the other $D_2, \ldots, D_n$ on which LifeBook is installed.

– *Event collection.*

1. The user device D_i. captures an event e, such as an SMS.
2. D_i encrypts the event e with K.
3. D_i sends $K(e)$ to the LifeBook server.
4. The LifeBook server updates the Event Map EM with $K(e)$ without knowledge on its content.

– *Event search.*

1. The user composes a query by using the Client interface on one of his devices D_i, D_i cyphers the query and sends it to the LifeBook server.
2. The server performs the similarity search over the event map EM which returns the closest possible events based on pre-specified similarity metrics without decryption and provides the results back to the client.
3. D_i deciphers the result with K and displays it, selects an event and sends the event id to the server.
4. The server provides the ciphered URI.
5. D_i deciphers the URI and displays it.

Secure Similarity Search. The features to be designed are the following:

Create the similarity map while prevent the cloud server from learning event contents. To create the map When a new event e_z has been provided by the user client, the server has to update the event map by computing the $ContentDist_{z,j}$ between events e_z and e_j, for every event e_j in EM. The text normalization (i.e., stemming and stop-wording) is performed on the client, determining a set of terms characterizing the event content. The encrypted version of these terms is sent to the server which constructs the terms-document matrix, then apply LSI (Latent Semantic Indexing) and the cosine similarity.

We also grant that the cloud is able to compute $EventDist_{z,j}$ without knowing the event type.

$$EventDist_{z,j} = \begin{cases} 0 & if\ K(EventType_i) = K(EventType_j); \\ 1 & otherwise. \end{cases}$$

Information concerning location and time can be encrypted, as in respectively. But a curious cloud can easily get them:

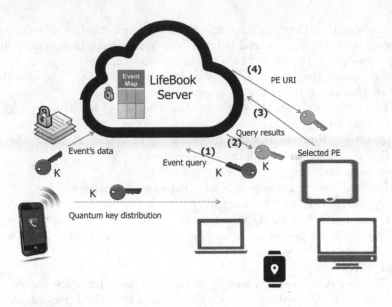

Fig. 4. Security model of event search over the cloud data.

– *time.* Events are transmitted when they are generated with an insignificant delay, so time information may be taken from the cloud log;
– *location.* The cloud can get the user position from his IP address. It is possible to hide it in several way, for example by using a personal VPN service, but this features requires the user intervention and cannot be automated by the LifeBook client.

Search the similarity map to produce a ranked list of similar events. The text normalization is performed on the client, determining a set of terms characterizing the query content. The encrypted version of these terms is sent to the server which searches the map without time overhead, since the map is already encrypted.

The whole encrypted document is sent to the server to be available to the other devices.

Security Analysis. The security of the proposed approach concerns the following aspects:

– *Authentication and access control.* LikeBook manages both the user-centric identity authentication and behavioral authentication approaches, which should be ensure to reduce the threat of fraudulent attacks. They specify if the user can access to the cloud and the level of access permission to the data, respectively.
– *Cyphering approach.* We adopted the same approach U.S. Government uses to protect classified information: the Advanced Encryption Standard (AES)

[25]. We use it also for cyphering images and videos. Other approaches may be selected, such as the one proposed in [23] and [7], respectively.

– *Key distribution.* It is based on quantum mechanics. It has the property that two communicating users are able to detect any presence who tries to gain knowledge of the key. In this case the communication is suspended.
– *Data privacy.* Each PE is encrypted using traditional symmetric encryption techniques before outsourced into the cloud, so the data privacy is well protected. The same consideration hold also for the terms associated to a given PE and its event type.
– *Event map privacy.* As the relevant terms of a PE are encrypted by the selected symmetric encryption techniques, the event map privacy can be well protected as long as the secret key K is kept confidential.

4 Conclusion

LifeBook is a Personal Information Management System supporting the user in the re-finding of information related to events occurring on his devices, in specific user context, such as place and time. Serverless and multi platform mobile technologies have been adopted and security features have been provided for let the user be the owner of her information. LifeBook uses a conceptual map created by exploiting Information Retrieval techniques for navigating the user content on the base of the event similarity and offers a location-based interface to graphically show the spatio-temporal relationships occurring among user events. We adopted a technique based on the Principal Component Analysis to automatically adapt the weights used to rank the events on the base of user's context and habits.

In the future we plan to conduct both usability and performance evaluation of LifeBook both in natural and controlled settings.

References

1. EDPS opinion on personal information management systems. Towards more user empowerment in managing and processing personal data. https://edps.europa.eu/sites/edp/files/publication/16-10-20_pims_opinion_en.pdf
2. Abiteboul, S., André, B., Kaplan, D.: Managing your digital life with a personal information management system. Commun. ACM **58**(5), 32–35 (2015)
3. Adar, E., Karger, D., Stein, L.A.: Haystack: per-user information environments. In: Proceedings of the 8th International Conference on Information and Knowledge Management, pp. 413–422. ACM (1999)
4. Blunschi, L., Dittrich, J.P., Girard, O.R., Karakashian, S.K., Salles, M.A.V.: A dataspace odyssey: the IMeMex personal dataspace management system. In: Conference on Innovative Data Systems Research (CIDR), pp. 114–119 (2007)
5. Bush, V., Wang, J.: As we may think. Atlantic Mon. **176**, 101–108 (1945)
6. Capra III, R.G., Perez-Quinones, M.A.: Using web search engines to find and refind information. Computer **38**(10), 36–42 (2005)

7. Chung, Y., Lee, S., Jeon, T., Park, D.: Fast video encryption using the H.264 error propagation property for smart mobile devices. Sensors **15**(4), 7953–7968 (2015)
8. Curtmola, R., Garay, J., Kamara, S., Ostrovsky, R.: Searchable symmetric encryption: improved definitions and efficient constructions. In: Proceedings of the 13th ACM Conference on Computer and Communications Security (CCS), pp. 79–88. ACM (2006)
9. Deng, T., Zhao, L., Wang, H., Liu, Q., Feng, L.: Refinder: a context-based information refinding system. IEEE Trans. Knowl. Data Eng. **25**(9), 2119–2132 (2013)
10. Dumais, S., Cutrell, E., Cadiz, J., Jancke, G., Sarin, R., Robbins, D.C.: Stuff i've seen: a system for personal information retrieval and re-use. In: Proceedings of the 26th Annual International ACM SIGIR Conference on Research and Development in Information Retrieval (SIGIR), pp. 72–79. ACM (2003)
11. Elsweiler, D., Ruthven, I., Jones, C.: Towards memory supporting personal information management tools. J. Am. Soc. Inform. Sci. Technol. **58**(7), 924–946 (2007)
12. Fertig, S., Freeman, E., Gelernter, D.: Lifestreams: an alternative to the desktop metaphor. In: Conference Companion on Human Factors in Computing Systems, pp. 410–411. ACM (1996)
13. Francese, R., Gravino, C., Risi, M., Scanniello, G., Tortora, G.: On the use of requirements measures to predict software project and product measures in the context of Android mobile apps: a preliminary study. In: 41st Euromicro Conference on Software Engineering and Advanced Applications, pp. 357–364. August 2015
14. Francese, R., Gravino, C., Risi, M., Scanniello, G., Tortora, G.: Mobile app development and management: results from a qualitative investigation. In: IEEE/ACM 4th International Conference on Mobile Software Engineering and Systems (MOBILE-Soft), pp. 133–143, May 2017
15. Francese, R., Risi, M., Scanniello, G., Tortora, G.: Lifebook: a mobile personal information management system on the cloud. In: Proceedings of the International Working Conference on Advanced Visual Interfaces (AVI), pp. 184–191 (2016)
16. Gemmell, J., Bell, G., Lueder, R.: MyLifeBits: a personal database for everything. Commun. ACM **49**(1), 88–95 (2006)
17. Gusfield, D.: Algorithms on Strings, Trees, and Sequences: Computer Science and Computational Biology. Cambridge University Press, New York (1997)
18. Gyllstrom, K., Soules, C.: Seeing is retrieving: building information context from what the user sees. In: Proceedings of the 13th International Conference on Intelligent User Interfaces, pp. 189–198. ACM (2008)
19. Hailpern, J., Jitkoff, N., Warr, A., Karahalios, K., Sesek, R., Shkrob, N.: YouPivot: improving recall with contextual search. In: Proceedings of the SIGCHI Conference on Human Factors in Computing Systems, pp. 1521–1530. ACM (2011)
20. Hwang, K.S., Cho, S.B.: A lifelog browser for visualization and search of mobile everyday-life. Mob. Inf. Syst. **10**(3), 243–258 (2014)
21. Karger, D.R., Jones, W.: Data unification in personal information management. Commun. ACM **49**(1), 77–82 (2006)
22. Le-Phuoc, D., Le-Tuan, A., Schiele, G., Hauswirth, M.: Querying heterogeneous personal information on the go. In: Mika, P., et al. (eds.) ISWC 2014. LNCS, vol. 8797, pp. 454–469. Springer, Cham (2014). https://doi.org/10.1007/978-3-319-11915-1_29
23. Liu, W., Sun, K., Zhu, C.: A fast image encryption algorithm based on chaotic map. Opt. Lasers Eng. **84**, 26–36 (2016)

24. Mailloux, L.O., Sargeant, B.N., Hodson, D.D., Grimaila, M.R.: System-level considerations for modeling space-based quantum key distribution architectures. In: Annual IEEE International Systems Conference (SysCon), pp. 1–6 (2017)
25. Miller, F.P., Vandome, A.F., McBrewster, J.: Advanced Encryption Standard. Alpha Press, Orlando (2009)
26. Patawari, A.: Getting Started with ownCloud. Packt Publishing Ltd., Birmingham (2013)
27. Robusto, C.: The Cosine-Haversine formula. Am. Math. Mon. **64**, 38–40 (1957)
28. Wang, W., Xu, P., Yang, L.T., Chen, J.: Cloud-assisted key distribution in batch for secure real-time mobile services. IEEE Trans. Serv. Comput. **11**(5), 850–863 (2018)
29. Westermann, U., Jain, R.: Toward a common event model for multimedia applications. IEEE MultiMed. **14**(1), 19–29 (2007)
30. Wootton, C.: Integrating with SAMI, pp. 273–299. Apress, Berkeley (2016)
31. Zhong, C.: Research on Personal Information Management. In: Proceedings of the 5th International Conference on Computational and Information Sciences, pp. 371–374 (2013)

CNTC: A Container Aware Network Traffic Control Framework

Lin Gu[1], Junjian Guan[1], Song Wu[1(✉)], Hai Jin[1], Jia Rao[2], Kun Suo[2], and Deze Zeng[3]

[1] National Engineering Research Center for Big Data Technology and System, Services Computing Technology and System Lab, Cluster and Grid Computing Lab, School of Computer Science and Technology, Huazhong University of Science and Technology, Wuhan 430074, China
{lingu,junjianguan,wusong,hjin}@hust.edu.cn
[2] The University of Texas at Arlington, Arlington, USA
{jia.rao,kun.suo}@uta.edu
[3] University of Geosciences, Beijing, China
dazzae@gmail.com

Abstract. As a lightweight virtualization technology, containers are attracting much attention and widely deployed in the cloud data centers. To provide consistent and reliable performance, cloud providers should ensure resource isolation since each host consists of multiple containers sharing the host kernel. As a mainstream container system, Docker uses CGroup to provide CPU, memory, and disk resource isolation. Unfortunately, all present solutions ignore the network resource, leading to the resource competition and violating the performance of networked hosts. Although several researches discuss the possibility of leveraging *Linux Traffic Control* (TC) module to guarantee network bandwidth, they fail to capture the diversity and dynamics of container network resource demands and therefore cannot be applied to container-level network traffic control. In this paper, we propose a *Container Network Traffic Control* (CNTC) framework which can provide strong isolation and container-level management for network resource with joint consideration of container characteristics and quality of service. To simplify the traffic control, we also design a series of APIs which allow inexpert programmers to perform complicated traffic control on each container. Through experiment results, we show that CNTC works well in all network modes of containers.

Keywords: Container network · Traffic control · Network isolation

1 Introduction

Recently, container, as lightweight virtualization technology, has been widely deployed in cloud data centers and shows its great significance in performance improvement and cost reduction [8]. Many companies, such as Amazon and Google, have implemented their own container-based virtualization environment

© Springer Nature Switzerland AG 2019
R. Miani et al. (Eds.): GPC 2019, LNCS 11484, pp. 208–222, 2019.
https://doi.org/10.1007/978-3-030-19223-5_15

and provided an effective development pipeline for both service providers and end users. Compared with traditional VM technology, container guarantees better efficiency with fewer resources by sharing the host's OS system kernel using namespace [4,17] rather than requiring an OS per application. However, as a light-weighted version of VM, containers can only give an application level of abstraction, therefore fail to provide strong hardware isolation and complicated resource management. Note that the resource demands of different containers vary on both type and amount, i.e. FTP server as a typical bandwidth-sensitive application while Redis as a latency-sensitive one. When multiple containers run on one host machine and share the OS kernel with each other, resource competition can never be avoided and seriously hinders the system performance [11].

To tackle this issue, Docker uses CGroup [3] to enable CPU, memory, and disk resource allocation for containers. Sadly, network resource, required by thousands of containers within one host to perform intra and inter host communication, is totally ignored in present container framework. Therefore, it is critical to provide a network traffic control framework for container network.

To provide a lightweight network traffic control, *Traffic Control* (TC) [2] provided by Linux system is considered as an ideal candidate. It consists of three components: class, filter, and Qdisc. When a network packet from container arrives at TC module, it is first categorized into a class by the filter, and then lined up at the Qdisc which belongs to the corresponding class. According to the network packet source and type, TC can create a large number of classes with different network resource allocation. These queueing packets will be further scheduled and sent to the destination according to the embedded control algorithms in Qdisc. Due to its lightweight and strong scalability, TC now is widely used in virtualized environment and scenarios for network traffic control. For example, Barker et al. [7] use TC to reduce service latency by balancing the tradeoff between sharing and dedicating network bandwidth for latency-sensitive applications running on VMs. While Ma et al. [12] propose a cluster management framework that leveraging TC to provide bandwidth limitation and network resource isolation for bandwidth-consuming applications.

Some researches also show the possibility and advantages of introducing TC into container systems [9]. Yet, we argue that TC cannot be directly applied to container network traffic control due to the following three factors. First, containers are running under multiple network modes to adapt to different workloads [20], e.g., overlay mode for allowing more flexibility and security in network management and non-overlay mode for achieving good performance but undermines security. TC, on the other hand, can only be functional in non-overlay mode which does not require packet encapsulation. While for containers in overlay mode, TC is invalid due to the failure of TC filters. TC has two filters: IP filter and Classid filter. IP filter fails in the packet encapsulation of overlay which will hide the container IP. Classid filter fails in the going across network namespaces of container packets because Classid is private information which only belongs to one namespace. That is, TC cannot provide a one-size-fits-all solution and fails to manage containers under multiple modes. Second, raw TC operation and configuration are relatively complicated and require a full understanding of the traffic control details. Some tools like tcng [5] are proposed to simplify the configuration. Yet they are designed for VM and cannot be applied to container management for the reason that tcng only simplifies the TC command into a script, the calculation process is still complicated and can only be operated by experts. Finally, TC only focuses on static network traffic control. That is, once a TC command is carried out, its organization and resource configuration cannot be changed. As a result, when a new container is activated, we are not able to adjust resource allocation of the existing containers with a global consideration of the resource requirements and quality of service. Similarly, if a launched container is deactivated, the freed resource cannot be reallocated to other containers to improve resource utilization. Note that containers are short-lived and varied. In other words, each server can host hundreds or thousands of launched containers which are frequently activated and deactivated. The original TC resource allocation algorithm cannot deal with the high dynamic in the container environment and will lead to a performance degradation [20].

To overcome these three challenges, we propose a *Container Network Traffic Control* (CNTC) framework to ensure network resource isolation with careful consideration of container characteristics. Compared to TC, CNTC is a simple and easy-to-use container network traffic control framework, which provides the container with the bandwidth, priority, and latency control with a dynamic scheduling algorithm to achieve resource reallocation for higher utilization. The main contributions of this paper are summarized as follows:

1. We provide a detailed analysis of resource competition in container network. Through extensive experiments, we show that TC cannot even balance the network resource allocation between different containers. We then reveal the reason for the invalidity of TC under overlay mode by taking a close look at the design of TC.
2. Based on the above findings, we propose CNTC to provide network resource isolation and traffic control for containers by providing a container level resource scheduling strategies under overlay mode through *Container Network ID* (CNid). We further design a set of easy understanding APIs to simplify the configuration of the network resource in a what you see is what you get way. To deal with the dynamic of the container, a dynamic online resource allocation algorithm is also proposed to meet the variability of containers.
3. Finally, we implement a prototype of CNTC and provide extensive experiments on various use cases. The results show that the framework can guarantee bandwidth and latency constraints for the container in all network modes with relatively low overhead.

The rest of this paper is organized as follows: Sect. 2 explains the background and motivation, including network modes of the container and the architecture of TC which give an important guideline on designing CNTC. Then Sect. 3 describes the detailed design of CNTC. In Sect. 4, we evaluate the usability of the framework by use cases. Section 5 discusses some related works and Sect. 6 concludes this work.

2   Background and Motivation

This section introduces network modes and characteristics of the container. We also analyze the design of TC, which helps us better understand the incompatibility between TC and the container. There are two reasons for the incompatibility between TC and the container as follows.

(1) Incompatibility caused by Modes. The design of container network modes falls into two categories: overlay and non-overlay. Overlay runs on top of another network to build virtual links between nodes. Many network modes leverage overlay, e.g., *Docker's native overlay network*. A container packet using overlay is encapsulated by VXLAN and host's UDP header as shown in Fig. 5 where we can see that the encapsulation hides the container IP. Another design is non-overlay, e.g., *NAT* which maps container IP to host to achieve connectivity. Overlay and non-overlay have their advantages and disadvantages to suit different workloads. The non-overlay does not need encapsulation, so it is simple but lacks security and flexibility. The overlay is the complement of non-overlay whose goal is to provide more security and flexibility for the network. It is noticeable that TC is invalid under the overlay. The reason is that TC has two filters to achieve packet identify, i.e. Classid filter and IP filter, which both fail to trace the container packet under multiple network modes. For Classid filter, it is not designed for container and the Classid of any container packet cannot be kept when it goes across network namespace. As for the IP filter, it needs the container IP to trace packet. Sadly, overlay mode hides the container IP which means IP filter only works well under non-overlay mode.

(2) Incompatibility caused by Characteristics. The container has the characteristics of short live and variability. For example, a survey of 8 million container usage reveals that 27% of containers have a lifetime no more than 5 minutes and 11% shorter than 1 minute [6] and Google Search launches about 7,000 containers every second [1]. However, TC is complicated and static which cannot meet the characteristics of containers. First, TC is implemented with various scheduling algorithms based on mathematical principles, which is not friendly to inexpert programmers. Second, TC is static at its organization and resource configuration. When programmers try to use different restrictions on data streams, TC builds a hierarchical tree. Once the TC command is carried out, the tree cannot be changed. Moreover, the resource configuration of TC is also static. TC algorithms only support to guarantee a static bandwidth, it does not support allocation by weight dynamically. Variability is one of the most important characteristics of containers. So when the number of containers decreases, the freed resource cannot be allocated by TC to other containers for better resource utilization.

To validate the invalidity of TC on container network traffic control, we perform two experiments on both bandwidth and latency with two containers, i.e. *Container 1* (CN1) and *Container 2* (CN2), on the same host under *Docker's native overlay* mode. The benchmark is *Iperf*. CN1 is a bandwidth consuming container, which runs 6 TCP connections (tcp 1 - tcp 6) in parallel and CN2

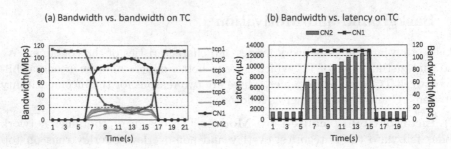

Fig. 1. Experiments on bandwidth and latency under overlay network using TC

runs 1 TCP connection. Figure 1(a) shows the result of bandwidth. From time slots 1–6, only CN2 is launched. From time slot 7, CN1 is activated and CN2 suffers a severe performance degradation. It can be observed that CN1 gets 6/7 of the total bandwidth while CN2 gets only the rest 1/7 because following the principle of link-fairness, the network resource will be allocated to the container according to the number of connections. Next, we evaluate the latency control of TC to guarantee a maximum 2 ms latency. CN1 uses the same setting and runs an unrestricted TCP while CN2 runs *ping* under a guarantee. The results in Fig. 1(b) show that the activation of CN1 causes an increase in latency of CN2 and hinders the latency constraint.

The above analysis and experiments reveal that TC is invalid, complicated, and static. These incompatibilities also give us the guideline on designing a traffic control framework for the container network.

3   System Design

Through the above analysis and discussion, we can conclude that TC cannot meet the needs of the container network traffic control. To tackle this issue, we introduce CNTC, a *Container Network Traffic Control* framework shown in Fig. 2, targeting the following three goals.

1. **One size fits all:** The container has multiple network modes to suit different workloads, but container network traffic control is required in all cases. Therefore, CNTC should work well under all network modes.
2. **Easy to use:** The configuration of the TC is complicated. A series of easy-to-use APIs should be provided to enable container network traffic control with simple commands.
3. **Dynamic adjustment:** Containers are short-lived and varied. It means that CNTC must be able to automatically adjust the resources of containers when the status of containers changes.

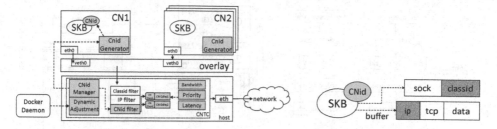

Fig. 2. Overview of CNTC   **Fig. 3.** Difference between CNid, Classid, and IP

3.1 CNid and CNid Filter

As we mentioned above, TC is invalid under the overlay mode. To achieve a valid traffic control framework under different network modes for containers, we propose a new module as CNid and CNid filter to enable container-level packet tracing and resource allocation. To achieve this goal, two problems have to be solved: (1) How can we identify the source and destination container of each network packet after overlay encapsulation? (2) How to keep the identification of packets across network namespaces?

By analyzing the design of raw TC shown in Fig. 3, we can obtain that Classid and IP are only part of SKB (a structure keeping all control information of network packet) reference which will be lost when across network namespaces or will be encapsulated under overlay mode. So they cannot be used to trace and identify container packets. To solve this problem, we propose CNid to identify each container packet and a CNid Manager consisting of a bitmap to keep a record of CNid status, i.e. 0 for available and 1 for occupied. When a container is activated, CNid Manager looks for an available ID from the low bit of the bitmap. If a container is deactivated, it can quickly release the CNid by setting its status as 0. Then, to ensure the traceability of the CNid, we also propose a CNid Generator which is in charge of inserting CNid into SKB structure as a member which leads to CNid not be encapsulated under overlay mode. By integrating CNid into the SKB structure, our CNid will not be released and re-created even when across network namespaces.

With the above design, Fig. 5 shows the procedure of a network packet from its source container to host. When a container is activated, the CNid Generator requests for an available CNid from CNid Manager. The Manager looks up for an available CNid and returns it to the Generator. Then a network stack call is made to send a packet from the container namespace to the host namespace as shown in Fig. 4(a). The packet is sent via eth0 where veth_xmit is called in which the CNid Generator marks the CNid for SKB of the packet. Then, the packet goes across network namespace and joins the receive queue of the host CPU. Finally, it is received by the host network stack. After the packet arrives at overlay, its SKB buffer will be encapsulated and sent the CNid filter for further process as shown in Fig. 4(b). CNid filter identifies the packet using cnid_classify which gets

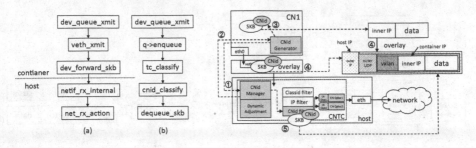

Fig. 4. Networking call stack   **Fig. 5.** Path of container packets

the CNid from the SKB to generator the CN class ID. Then, cnid_classify uses the ID to find the CN class corresponding to the packet. Finally, the packet is added to the CN Qdisc of this class and will be sent by dequeue_skb in turns.

3.2 Simple APIs

TC is complicated, which has many traffic control algorithms falling into two categories: (1) Classless algorithms, which are used for constant types of data streams. (2) Classful algorithms, whose role is to use different restrictions on multiple types of data streams. We believe that classful algorithms are more suitable for the container which produce and process various types of data streams. However, to use classful algorithms, inexpert programmers need to understand the traffic control details and the mathematical formulas of the algorithms which are complicated just like what we mentioned in Sect. 2. Therefore, we propose these APIs in the form of container startup parameters shown in Table 1 to allocate network resources in a simple and easy style.

Take the latency as an example to show how we simplify the calculations. Generally, we use HFSC to guarantee latency which is one of the classful algorithms. To guarantee 100 kbps bandwidth and 20 ms latency for a container, the TC algorithm needs a command like *m1 250* kbit *d 8* ms *m2 100* kbit which has not a description of 20 ms leading to confusing and complication. This command indicates a container has a normal bandwidth of 100 kbit and TC can send 250 kbit in 8 ms during burst.

We simplify this command by a startup parameter in the style of container (*–rate 100* kbit *–latency 20* ms). We convert this parameter to TC command using the following two formulas. *8* ms can be calculated by Formula (1) where $Latency_I$ indicates the value of *–latency* and $Bandwidth_I$ indicates *–rate*. Following the principle of HFSC, when the latency of container C is guaranteed, other containers share this host are also allowed to send a *Maximum Transmission Unit* (MTU) size packet. That is to say, even the bandwidth-consuming container cannot occupy the network resource and some bandwidth needs to be reserved for the rest containers. Therefore, considering the reserved bandwidth, the actual process time of packets from container C as L_C can be calculated as

Table 1. Startup parameters for container traffic control

Parameter	Description
Rate	Static bandwidth for the container
Weight	Dynamic bandwidth and dynamic priority for the container
Priority	The order in which containers obtain idle bandwidth
Latency	Maximum latency for the container

$$L_C = Latency_I - \frac{MTU}{Bandwidth_I} = 20\,\text{ms} - \frac{1500\,\text{byte}}{100\,\text{kbit}} = 8\,\text{ms} \tag{1}$$

and the guaranteed bandwidth of container C as B_C should be

$$B_C = \frac{Bandwidth_I * Latency_I}{L_C} = \frac{100\,\text{kbit} * 20\,\text{ms}}{8\,\text{ms}} = 250\,\text{kbit} \tag{2}$$

which provides the same latency and bandwidth guarantee as the raw TC commend.

3.3 Dynamic Adjustment

As we mentioned above, containers are short-lived and varied. Now, with the help of CNid, we enable the identification of container packets. Yet, how to deal with the online adjustment of traffic control and resource allocation is still an issue to be addressed. So we propose the *Dynamic Adjustment module* to overcome the following two challenges: (1) How to adjust the TC organization? (2) How to adjust network resource?

Firstly, to adjust TC organization, Dynamic Adjustment needs to communicate with the Docker Daemon for monitoring the status of containers. When a container is activated, it requests an available CNid from the Manager and creates a new CN class and CN Qdisc. Secondly, Dynamic Adjustment should adjust the resources obtained by containers to achieve a higher utilization considering two factors: bandwidth and priority. Without loss of generality, we provide two adjustment ways taking into consideration of both rate and weight to allocate bandwidth for containers called rate-style and weight-style containers, respectively. Rate-style is a static allocation that guarantees the container to obtain a certain bandwidth while weight-style is a dynamic one which allocates bandwidth in proportion. Therefore, the static and dynamic containers are mixed on the same host. Changes in container status result in changes in rate and weight, ultimately affecting bandwidth allocation. In addition, weight also indicates dynamic priority, so changes in weight lead to changes in priority. Therefore, we propose a dynamic adjustment algorithm in Algorithm 1 to reallocate the bandwidth and reconfigure priority.

Algorithm 1. DYNAMICADJUSTMENT

1: **function** INITIAL
2:     $B_s \leftarrow 0, W_s \leftarrow 0, W_d \leftarrow 0$
3:     $B_d \leftarrow B_{max}$
4:     $\{C_i\} \leftarrow \varnothing$
5: **end function**
6:
7: **function** CONTAINERSACTIVATIONHANDLE(C_n)
8:     $\{C_i\} \leftarrow \{C_i\} \bigcup C_n$
9:     $D\{d_r, d_w, d_p, d_l\} \leftarrow GetDemand(C_n)$
10:     **if** $d_w = NULL$ **then**
11:         $B_d \leftarrow B_d - d_r$
12:         $B_s \leftarrow B_s + d_r$
13:     **else**
14:         $W_d \leftarrow W_d + d_w$
15:     **end if**
16:     $UpdateResource(\{C_i\})$
17:     $PriorityHandle(\{C_i\})$
18: **end function**
19:
20: **function** UPDATERESOURCE($\{C_i\}$)
21:     **for** $\{C_i\}$ **do**
22:         $D\{d_r, d_w, d_p, d_l\} \leftarrow GetDemand(C_i)$
23:         $W_s \leftarrow 0$
24:         **if** C_i is rate-style **then**
25:             $d_w \leftarrow \frac{W_d}{B_d} * d_r$
26:             $W_s \leftarrow W_s + d_w$
27:         **else**
28:             $d_r \leftarrow \frac{B_d}{W_d} * d_w$
29:         **end if**
30:     **end for**
31: **end function**

Lines 1–5 are the initialization. The bandwidth is divided into two parts: static bandwidth and dynamic bandwidth which are represented by B_s and B_d. They are the bandwidth obtained by rate-style and weight-style containers. Similarly, the weight is also composed of two parts: W_s and W_d representing static weight and dynamic weight for rate-style and weight-style. $\{Ci\}$ indicates a network resource configuration for all containers.

The adjustment on bandwidth is handled by lines 10–15 and lines 20–31. When a static rate-style container is activated, static bandwidth increases while dynamic bandwidth decreases that means weight-style containers must reduce their bandwidth to satisfy the new rate-style container (lines 11–12). When a dynamic weight-style container is activated, dynamic weight increases while static bandwidth remains unchanged that means the new weight-style container does not affect the bandwidth of the rate-style containers, but the bandwidth of other weight-style containers is reduced due to the increase in dynamic weight leading to less bandwidth for each weight (line 14). After that, Dynamic Adjustment calls $UpdateResource$ to update the resources of all containers. Rate-style container needs to update its weight because the change of weight sum leading to different weight per bandwidth (lines 25–26) and weight-style container adjusts its rate according to the change of dynamic bandwidth (line 28).

To achieve adjustment on priority, $PriorityHandle$ (line 17) is called. However, the priority way of TC is invalid for the container because TC has only eight priority levels. When containers' types of weight are more than eight, it is

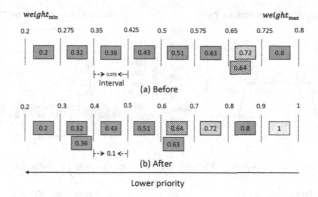

Fig. 6. Priority interval

not possible to set priority for containers. So we propose a new way to set priority called *priority interval* where each interval represents a priority level which is shown in Fig. 6(a). When the type of weight is less than eight, Dynamic Adjustment sets the priority in the positive order of weight. If the type of weight is more than eight, the priority levels are not enough. Therefore Dynamic Adjustment leverages the *priority interval*. When the weight of a new activated container is out of range, the *priority interval* adjustment is triggered. Figure 6(b) shows the *priority interval* after the activation of the container with weight 1 where we can see that the priorities of some containers have changed.

4 Evaluation

This section presents an evaluation of CNTC. The default experiment settings are listed as follows: (1) Hardware: experiments are performed on two servers connected by Gigabit Ethernet. Each server contains an Intel Core i5-7200 2.50 GHz CPU (2 cores) with 16 GB of DDR4 RAM and 256 GB HDD. (2) Software: we use Ubuntu 16.04.5 and Linux kernel 4.14.5. The Docker version is 17.09.0-ce. The overlay network is *Docker's native overlay* and the non-overlay network is *NAT*. (3) Benchmark: bandwidth benchmark is *Iperf* and latency benchmark is *ping*. We first evaluate the validity of the framework under the overlay network. Next, we observe the dynamic adjustment when the status of containers changes. Finally, we measure the overhead of the framework to see if it fits into a lightweight containerized environment.

4.1 Validity

Multiple network modes of the container are suitable for different application scenarios. But no matter what the scenario, it needs network traffic control. In this subsection, we evaluate the validity of CNTC under the overlay network of three aspects: bandwidth, latency, and priority.

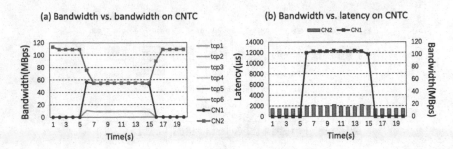

Fig. 7. Experiments on bandwidth and latency under overlay network using CNTC

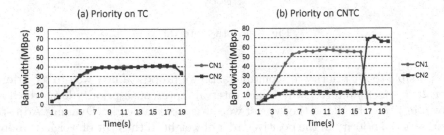

Fig. 8. Experiments on priority under overlay network using TC and CNTC

We repeat the experiments on Sect. 2 to confirm the valid control of bandwidth and latency in our framework. Figure 7(a) is the result of bandwidth which shows that when *container1* (CN1) is activated, the bandwidth of *container2* (CN2) drops, but it guarantees both containers get equal bandwidth which means CN1 cannot steal bandwidth by increasing the number of its connections. Next, Fig. 7(b) shows the latency experiment. When the unrestricted CN1 is activated, the latency of CN2 has a small fluctuation increase. But it hardly exceeds 2 ms latency guarantee which means the framework meets the performance requirement set by CN2. Finally, we evaluate the valid control of the priority. The priority indicates the order in which containers obtain idle bandwidth. For better representing the competition for idle bandwidth, we set a minimum bandwidth for both containers leading to more idle bandwidth and set CN1 has a higher priority. Figure 8(a) is the result on TC where two different priority containers are not treated differently. And Fig. 8(b) shows the result on CNTC where CN1 gets about 5 times the bandwidth of CN2, which embodies their priorities.

From the results of these experiments, we can conclude that CNid solves the problem of TC invalidity under overlay network mode.

4.2 Dynamic Adjustment

When the status of containers changes, CNTC should adjust the resources according to the change. We observe the dynamic adjustment of our framework by changing bandwidth and priority.

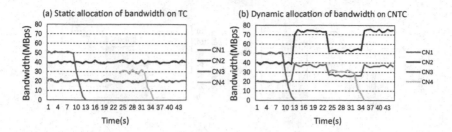

Fig. 9. Experiments on bandwidth adjustment

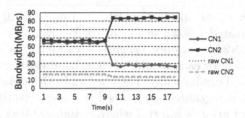

Fig. 10. Experiment on priority adjustment

First, we observe the adjustment of the bandwidth. We use 4 containers. *Container1* (CN1) and *container2* (CN2) are weight-style and their weight ratio is 1:2. *Container3* (CN3) and *container4* (CN4) are rate-style which are guaranteed 50 MBps and 30 MBps static bandwidth, and they are deactivated or activated during the experiment. We use TC and CNTC under *NAT* which is a type of non-overlay networks that make the TC valid. Since TC does not support allocation by weight, CN1 and CN2 can only be allocated in static by manual in TC experiment. For better observing the dynamic adjustment of bandwidth, we disable the idle bandwidth competition by priority which is shown in Sect. 4.1. From Fig. 9(a), we can observe that CN1 and CN2 do not adjust the bandwidth allocation on TC which means the change of container status leads to a waste of bandwidth. Figure 9(b) is the result of CNTC which achieves dynamic adjustment. When CN3 is deactivated at time slot 13, CN1 and CN2 obtain this 50 MBps of idle bandwidth by a ratio of 1:2. When the CN4 is activated at time slot 24, they shrink bandwidth to meet the requirement of CN4. Finally, they obtain this bandwidth again because of the deactivation of CN4. These experiments show that CNTC has higher utilization than TC.

Next, we evaluate the dynamic adjustment of priority. Take containers of Fig. 6(a) as an example. We select containers with weights of 0.64 and 0.72 (denoted as *container1* and *container2*) to observe change in priority. The other containers are still running on the host, but they do not send any data. Figure 10 is the process of the experiment. Raw CN1 and raw CN2 are estimated by us which represent the bandwidth they should have obtained by weight. CN1 and CN2 represent the bandwidth actually obtained after their competition on idle bandwidth. Before time slot 10, *container1* and *container2* have the same

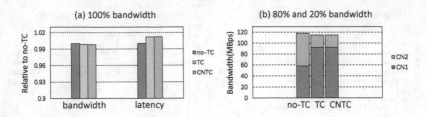

Fig. 11. Overhead of CNTC

priority, so they get equal idle bandwidth. At time slot 10, a container with a weight of 1 is activated (shown in Fig. 6(b)). We can observe two trends: (1) Raw CN1 and raw CN2 have dropped slightly because the increase of weight sum leads to less bandwidth for each weight. (2) The bandwidth actually obtained by containers has changed dramatically. The idle bandwidth obtained by *container2* is almost 5 times that of *container1* caused by new activated container which leads to the change of *priority interval* where *container2* becomes a priority over *container1*.

These experiments exemplify the advantages of CNTC by the factor that it significantly improves the resource utilization and satisfies the service quality of all containers at the same time.

4.3   Overhead

Container is lightweight virtualization technology, so any traffic control framework with a high overhead is not appropriate. In this section, we measure the overhead of CNTC.

First, we measure the case of allocating 100% bandwidth to a container to observe the overhead of bandwidth and latency under *NAT* using without resource control (no-TC), TC with IP filter, and CNTC. Figure 11(a) shows the result which uses no-TC as the baseline, and the result of the other two cases are a relative value of the baseline. We can see that TC and CNTC have almost the same performance and a bandwidth degradation of only 0.16% relative to no-TC. The latency overhead is relatively high. The increase in latency of TC and CNTC are 1.19% and 1.24%, respectively. But their absolute value does not exceed 0.006 ms. Therefore, in the absence of competition, our framework provides almost the same performance as TC with very low overhead compared to no-TC. Next, we investigate the situation of competition. We use two containers that are allocated with 80% and 20% of bandwidth. Figure 11(b) shows that the bandwidth degradations of TC and CNTC are 2.7% and 2.8%, respectively. Note that CNTC shows a similar result to TC which reveals the fact that CNTC dos not cause extra overhead rather than packet scheduling itself. So, it can be learned from the above experiments that CNTC framework does not cause much overhead and is suitable for the lightweight container network traffic control.

5   Related Work

Recently, many cloud resource management researches, especially network resource, have been proposed. Therefore, providing management for the network resource is important to both cloud providers and customers [13]. Current network resource management and traffic control researches can be divided into two categories: (1) third-party frameworks designed by the researcher and programmers, and (2) raw frameworks integrated into OSs and developing platforms like Linux TC.

(1) Third-party Frameworks. Shieh et al. [18,19] consider the fairness of congested links in VM. However, link granularity control is too complex for hundreds of containers. In addition, they cannot guarantee a specific bandwidth which is used to estimate worst completion time that the applications really care about. Rodrigues et al. [10,16] use a self-designed speed limiter for ingress and egress traffic. The limit of ingress needs congestion information between hosts, which makes the congested network worse. Popa et al. [14,15] offer guaranteed allocations for network resources in switches which require hardware support. These approaches use a third-party framework in which they take into account too many factors that complicate the situation which leads to high overhead. These are not what the container wants since the container is designed for high performance.

(2) Raw Frameworks. TC is built into the Linux kernel and focuses on single host egress network traffic control. Many researches which require lightweight network traffic control leverage TC. Ma et al. [12] consider container placement as a variable. Therefore, they achieve isolation and fairness through container scheduling. But they use TC to guarantee specific bandwidth to the container, which is only suitable for container clusters deployed under non-overlay networks. Herbein et al. [9] present mechanisms to allocate, throttle, and prioritize CPU, network bandwidth, and I/O bandwidth resources in containerized HPC environments. Their mechanisms use TC to achieve network traffic control. Barker et al. [7] use TC to manage the latency impact and to provide a choice between sharing and dedicated bandwidth for latency-sensitive applications. In summary, these works only use TC as a tool. They neither find the incompatibility between TC and the container, not customize the TC to better serve the container.

6   Conclusion

In this paper, we present CNTC, a framework to provide network resource management for containers by leveraging lightweight network traffic control module TC. The proposed CNTC framework can provide container-level network resource allocation and network traffic control with a very low overhead. Based on this framework, we further provide a series of APIs to simplify the complicated container network traffic control commend, such as bandwidth allocation and latency control, on each container. An online resource management algorithm is also proposed to adjust the resource allocation when the number and type of containers change. The evaluation results validate the efficiency and correctness of our CNTC framework.

Acknowledgements. This work is supported by National Key Research and Development Program under grant 2016YFB1000501, National Science Foundation of China under grant No.61732010, and Pre-research Project of Beifang under grant FFZ-1601.

References

1. Containers: The future of virtualization & sddc. https://goo.gl/Mb3yFq
2. Linux advanced routing & traffic control. https://www.lartc.org/
3. Linux control groups. https://www.kernel.org/doc/Documentation/cgroup-v1/cgroups.txt
4. Linux namespace. https://www.kernel.org/doc/Documentation/namespaces/
5. Linux traffic control next generation. http://tcng.sourceforge.net/
6. The truth about docker container lifecycles. https://goo.gl/Wcj894
7. Barker, S., Shenoy, P.: Empirical evaluation of latency-sensitive application performance in the cloud. In: Proceedings of ICMR, pp. 35–46. ACM (2010)
8. Dua, R., Raja, A.R., Kakadia, D.: Virtualization vs containerization to support PaaS. In: Proceedings of IC2E, pp. 610–614. IEEE (2014)
9. Herbein, S., et al.: Resource management for running HPC applications in container clouds. In: Kunkel, J.M., Balaji, P., Dongarra, J. (eds.) ISC High Performance 2016. LNCS, vol. 9697, pp. 261–278. Springer, Cham (2016). https://doi.org/10.1007/978-3-319-41321-1_14
10. Jeyakumar, V., Alizadeh, M., Mazières, D., Prabhakar, B., Kim, C., Greenberg, A.: Eyeq: practical network performance isolation at the edge. In: Proceedings of NSDI, pp. 297–312. USENIX (2013)
11. Khalid, J., Rozner, E., Felter, W., Xu, C.: Iron: isolating network-based CPU in container environments. In: Proceedings of NSDI, pp. 1–17. USENIX (2018)
12. Ma, S., Jiang, J., Li, B., Li, B.: Maximizing container-based network isolation in parallel computing clusters. In: Proceedings of ICNP, pp. 1–10. IEEE (2016)
13. Mogul, J.C., Popa, L.: What we talk about when we talk about cloud network performance. In: Proceedings of SIGCOMM, pp. 44–48. ACM (2012)
14. Popa, L., Kumar, G., Chowdhury, M., Krishnamurthy, A., Ratnasamy, S., Stoica, I.: Faircloud: sharing the network in cloud computing. In: Proceedings of SIGCOMM, pp. 187–198. ACM (2012)
15. Popa, L., Yalagandula, P., Banerjee, S., Mogul, J.C., Turner, Y., Santos, J.R.: Elasticswitch: practical work-conserving bandwidth guarantees for cloud computing. In: Proceedings of SIGCOMM, pp. 351–362. ACM (2013)
16. Rodrigues, H., Santos, J.R., Turner, Y., Soares, P., Guedes, D.: Gatekeeper: supporting bandwidth guarantees for multi-tenant datacenter networks. In: Proceedings of WIOV, pp. 784–789. USENIX (2011)
17. Sharma, P., Sharma, L., Shenoy, P.: Containers and virtual machines at scale: a comparative study. In: Proceedings of Middleware, pp. 1–13. ACM (2016)
18. Shieh, A., Kandula, S., Greenberg, A., Kim, C., Saha, B.: Sharing the data center network. In: Proceedings of NSDI, pp. 309–322. USENIX (2011)
19. Stoica, S., Pan, R., Vahdat, A., Varghese, G.: Netshare and stochastic netshare: predictable bandwidth allocation for data centers. In: Proceedings of SIGCOMM, pp. 5–11. ACM (2012)
20. Suo, K., Zhao, Y., Chen, W., Rao, J.: An analysis and empirical study of container networks. In: Proceedings of INFOCOM, pp. 1–9. IEEE (2018)

BlockP2P: Enabling Fast Blockchain Broadcast with Scalable Peer-to-Peer Network Topology

Weifeng Hao[1], Jiajie Zeng[1], Xiaohai Dai[1], Jiang Xiao[1(✉)], Qiangsheng Hua[1],
Hanhua Chen[1], Kuan-Ching Li[2], and Hai Jin[1]

[1] National Engineering Research Center for Big Data Technology and System,
Services Computing Technology and System Lab, Cluster and Grid Computing Lab,
School of Computer Science and Technology,
Huazhong University of Scinece and Technology, Wuhan 430074, China
`jiangxiao@hust.edu.cn`
[2] Department of Computer Science and Information Engineering,
Providence University, Taichung, Taiwan

Abstract. Blockchain technology offers an intelligent amalgamation of distributed ledger, *Peer-to-Peer* (P2P), cryptography, and smart contracts to enable trustworthy applications without any third parties. Existing blockchain systems have successfully either resolved the scalability issue by advancing the distributed consensus protocols from the control plane, or complemented the security issue by updating the block structure and encryption algorithms from the data plane. Yet, we argue that the underlying P2P network plane remains as an important but unaddressed barrier for accelerating the overall blockchain system performance. Our key insights from comparative assessments reveal the fact that P2P topology highly affects the broadcast speed of blockchain data, leading to poor performance and vulnerable to double spending attacks. In this paper, we introduce BlockP2P, a novel optimization design to accelerate broadcast efficiency and meanwhile retain the security. BlockP2P first operates the geographical proximity sensing clustering, which leverages K-Means algorithm for gathering proximity peer nodes into clusters. It follows by the hierarchical topological structure that ensures strong connectivity and small diameter based on node attribute classification. We finally propose the parallel spanning tree broadcast algorithm to enable fast data broadcast among nodes both in the intra- and inter- clusters. To clarify the influence of each tier, we carefully design and implement a blockchain network simulator. Evaluation results show that BlockP2P can exhibit promising performance compared to Bitcoin and Ethereum.

Keywords: Blockchain Peer-to-Peer network · Network clustering ·
Network topology · Broadcast algorithm

© Springer Nature Switzerland AG 2019
R. Miani et al. (Eds.): GPC 2019, LNCS 11484, pp. 223–237, 2019.
https://doi.org/10.1007/978-3-030-19223-5_16

1   Introduction

Today blockchain technology has attracted increasing attention as the cornerstone of trust across a wide realm of society sectors from finance, industrial logistics to healthcare. Its beneficial characteristics including traceability, decentralization, and transparency spout out the massive proposals of blockchain systems and projects. Unfortunately, the real-world blockchain adoption experiences serious technical challenges that impede its further development, especially from the aspect of the overall system performance. State-of-the-art researches mainly focus on advancing the consensus algorithms in the consensus layer [11], as well optimizing the data storage in the data layer [25]. However, few studies have been conducted from the network layer (i.e., lying between the two layers) that can update the topology under consensus guarantee, while adapting the dynamic on-chain blockchain data traffic.

In particular, the lack of consideration in the blockchain network layer can not only lead to poor performance, meanwhile bring about high risks of double spending attacks. As shown in Table 1, it normally takes on average 6 s to ensure a block received by 50% of the total nodes in the Ethereum network, and up to 10 s, on average, for 90% of the nodes [2]. Since the generation time of a new block is only 15 s in Ethereum, this network-level latency becomes a major barrier that limits the blockchain performance (i.e., *Transactions Per Second* (TPS)), leading to high potential of forks. Therefore, it is urgent to reduce blockchain network latency, so as to improve the overall performance of blockchain systems with stronger security.

Table 1. Broadcast time per block

Ratio of nodes	50%	90%
Time (s)	6	10

Existing trials related to optimize the network latency can be divided into two categories, according to the different topologies they are concerned about. On one hand, the fully distributed unstructured topology of Bitcoin network is optimized by shortening the network diameter. However, it will bring in huge computation overheads because each node needs to repeatedly calculate the network distance between it and all the rest ones [21,22]. On the other hand, Ethereum employs the fully distributed structured topology that increases the connectivity of the entire network, but the growth of Ethereum nodes will introduce high maintenance cost of such structured topology.

To compromise the above limitations, in this paper, we propose an optimized network protocol namely *BlockP2P* to minimize the total blockchain network latency. First, BlockP2P gathers the proximity peer nodes into clusters based on the K-Means algorithm. We then optimize the inter-cluster topology by organizing the nodes into a Harary-like graph with high connectivity and small diameter. Finally, a parallel spanning tree broadcast algorithm is designed to speed up the data broadcast, by eliminating the multiple rounds of message in a single communication process. To facilitate the evaluation of performance in the large-scale network, we design and implement *BlockSim*, a simulator to simulate the running of blockchain network without affecting the accuracy of the evaluation results. With the help of BlockSim, we conduct several experiments to compare BlockP2P protocol with the counterpart protocols in Bitcoin and Ethereum. The experimental results show that BlockP2P protocol can effectively reduce blockchain network latency.

In summary, this paper makes the following novel contributions:

- To the best of our knowledge, this is the first in-depth analysis of influential factors of blockchain performance in the network layer, by uncovering the two sequential phases of the underlying P2P network.
- We introduce an optimized blockchain network protocol *BlockP2P* to reduce blockchain network latency.
- To verify the feasibility and efficiency of BlockP2P protocol, we design and implement *BlockSim*, a blockchain simulator for large-scale network simulation.
- Experimental results demonstrate that BlockP2P can effectively reduce network latency from three different aspects compared to Bitcoin and Ethereum.

The rest of the paper is organized as follows. Section 2 presents the background knowledge about the network protocol of current blockchain systems. Related work on network optimization is stated in Sect. 3. Section 4 elaborates the design of BlockP2P in three steps. Extensive experiments are conducted in Sect. 5 to evaluate the system performance in terms of reducing network latency. Finally, we conclude the paper in Sect. 6.

2   Background

P2P network enables direct information interaction between different nodes in the blockchain network. As shown in Fig. 1, the process of information interaction between two nodes can be divided into two phases: connection establishment marked by gray circles, and data transmission marked by red circles. Since the connection status among nodes is relatively stable and the time taken to establish connection is usually very short, the most important component of the total network latency is the broadcast latency in the phase of data transmission. However, configurations of both phases can have effects on the broadcast latency.

In the phase of connection establishment, different network topologies may be formed among the nodes. Different network topologies will have different effects on the broadcast latency, which can be measured by network connectivity and network diameter [5]. The network connectivity refers to the number of neighbor nodes connected to each node in the network. The larger the network connectivity is, the more neighbors a node can broadcast the data each time. In this way, the overall time spent on the network broadcasting can be reduced. The network diameter refers to the maximum network delay between any two nodes in the

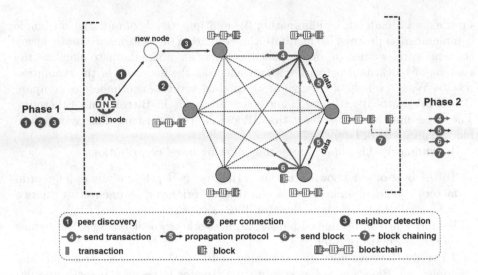

Fig. 1. Workflow of blockchain P2P network

network. The smaller the network diameter, the shorter the average broadcast time between any two nodes, thus accelerating the overall broadcast time across the network. As a result, optimizing the network topologies of nodes including the network connectivity and diameter can effectively reduce the broadcast latency.

In the phase of data transmission, Gossip algorithm is used to broadcast the data from a node to its neighbors [16]. During the process of broadcast, a node firstly selects the nodes from its neighbors to disseminate the data using the propagation protocol. The node which receives the data repeats the process above until all the nodes in the network have received the data. More specifically, the propagation protocol [8,15] used by Gossip algorithm further includes three steps. First, a node (i.e., sender) sends an *INV* message to its neighbor node before sending one piece of data (namely a transaction or a block in the context of blockchain). Second, the neighbor node determines whether it has received the data before. If not, it returns a *getdata* message back to the sender; otherwise, it ignores the *INV* message. Finally, before the end of timeout set by the sender, if the sender receives the *getdata* message, it sends the piece of data to the neighbor. It should be noted that a node only broadcasts data to its directly connected neighbors. The broadcast process will run in many rounds by each node, until each node in the network has received the data. As a result, Gossip protocol may lead to large data broadcast latency due to many rounds of broadcast. Besides, three steps of the propagation protocol bring extra communication rounds, which exacerbate the problem of large broadcast latency.

3   Related Work

The information propagation delay reveals the performance of blockchain systems [11], since the high latency increases the time for all the nodes to reach a consensus. The high network latency makes the system more vulnerable to malicious attacks [23]. Network latency is related to the interaction of information between nodes as mentioned in Sect. 2. The interaction consists of two phases: the connection establishment and the data transmission. We will present the existing optimization works in these two phases.

Connection Establishment. The topological structure of the mainstream blockchain systems can be divided into two categories: one is the unstructured topology in Bitcoin [20], the other is the structured topology in Ethereum [2] (i.e., Kademlia) and NKN [4] (i.e., Chord). To measure the quality of network topology, two metrics including network diameter and connectivity are adopted. Nodes in unstructured topology are randomly connected, which results in a large network diameter. In order to minimize the network diameter, BCBPT protocol utilizes the proximity clustering algorithm based on the number of network hops between nodes, and then connects the nodes that are physically proximal [12]. However, BCBPT brings in high algorithm complexity, as each node needs to calculate the network hops to all other nodes. Croman et al. reveal that Bitcoin cannot fully utilize the bandwidth in the network, which has serious impact on transactions processing, then they proposed to reduce the network latency of blockchain starting with optimizing the network topology [6]. Compared with the unstructured topology, the structured topology has a good network connectivity. But its network diameter is also very large, since the network latency between nodes is not taken into consideration when they try to establish a connection. Moreover, creating the structured network topology brings in huge computation cost, because of the large size of blockchain network (e.g., the size of nodes in Ethereum has almost reached to $10k$). The cost will increase significantly as the network size further increases, the same with the network latency.

Data Transmission. The blockchain network is the broadcast channel for data. Some efficient broadcast protocols [13,14] are proposed to speed up the progress of broadcast. Bitcoin employs the flood-based [10] algorithm to broadcast the data, while Ethereum adopts the gossip-based [24] broadcast algorithm. Both of these two algorithms bring huge redundant data in broadcast, because the data will be sent multiple rounds before it meets the terminational conditions of the broadcast. Besides, the multi-message transfer in the propagation protocol greatly lowers the speed of data broadcast [9,15]. An attempt to solve the problem above is conducted by Decker et al. [8], which tries to optimize the Bitcoin network by removing the process of verification and pipelining the process of block propagation. However, their ideas are only at the conceptual stage and further experiments are needed to prove it.

4   Design

Figure 2 gives an overview of how the BlockP2P protocol operates, which is composed of three parts: node clustering, topology construction, and broadcast optimization. First, to reduce the complexity of building the network topology for the whole network and ensure parallel broadcast between clusters, a *Geographical Proximity Sensing Clustering* (GPSC) method based on the K-Means algorithm [7] is devised. Second, a *Structured Hierarchical Network Topology* (SHNT) approach is proposed to construct the topology of node connection with a high network connectivity and a small diameter. Third, we design a *Parallel Spanning Tree Broadcast* (PSTB) mechanism to parallelize the broadcast processes in both intra-cluster and inter-cluster nodes.

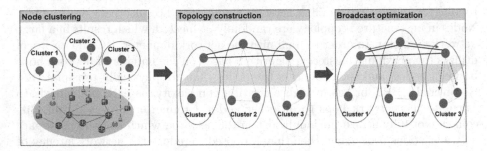

Fig. 2. Overview of the BlockP2P

4.1   Node Clustering

To guarantee proximal and coequal clustering, BlockP2P implements the GPSC method to organize the nodes across the network into several clusters, based on the well-known K-Means algorithm. The average number of nodes in a cluster is the key parameter in the K-Means algorithm that requires careful design. On one hand, such number can not be set too large, otherwise, it will bring in high communication latency between two intra-cluster nodes. On the other hand, a small value may increase the communication cost between two inter-cluster nodes, since it enlarges the number of clusters. According to the previous studies in [5] and [17], the optimal setting of the number of nodes in a cluster should be $logN$. After the number of nodes in a cluster is set, GPSC organizes all the nodes into several clusters in three stages as depicted in Fig. 3(a).

Selection of Cluster Centers. First, we describe how GPSC selects the nodes as cluster centers. One simple way is to perform iterative computation of K-Means algorithm continuously. However, it brings in huge computation costs since it requires each node to measure the network latency between it and all the other nodes, whose computation costs are too high. To reduce the computational complexity, GPSC creates a candidate subset for selecting cluster centers in advance. In particular, with network latency as the Euclidean distance between two nodes, GPSC selects the cluster centers in three steps as follows:

- **Step 1:** Calculate the Euclidean distance $T(n_i, n_j)(i \neq j)$ between any two nodes in the candidate subset. Find the nodes pair with the furthest distance to form a new set $S_m(1 \leq m \leq K)$, where K represents the number of network clusters, and then delete the two nodes from the candidate subset;
- **Step 2:** Add the node which is furthest from the new set to update S_m, and then remove the node from the original candidate set;
- **Step 3:** If the number of nodes in S_m is smaller than K, repeat Step 2; otherwise, the nodes in the set S_m are taken as the cluster centers.

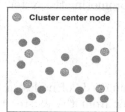 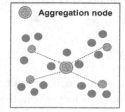 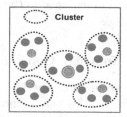

(a) Selection of cluster centers   (b) Choice of aggregation nodes   (c) Network clustering

Fig. 3. Three stages of node clustering

Choice of Aggregation Nodes. To ensure all the cluster centers are evenly distributed, assistant nodes named *aggregation nodes* C_{aggre} are chosen, each of which is located at the geometric center of a cluster. It is difficult to calculate C_{aggre} only according to the network latency between two nodes. Therefore, GPSC adopts the method of *network coordinate system* (NCS) to figure out C_{aggre} [19]. First, GPSC sets a network coordinate for each cluster center node according to Eq. (1).

$$F(H_{S_1}, ..., H_{S_k}) = \sum_{S_i, S_j \in \{S_1, ..., S_k\}, i > j} \varepsilon(d_{S_i S_j}, \bar{d}_{S_i S_j}) \tag{1}$$

where S_i and H represent the cluster centers and the network coordinates of the cluster centers respectively, d and $\bar{d}$ represent the network distances between two nodes in the actual system and network coordinate system separately, and ε represents the error function. After getting the geometric center coordinates $\bar{C}_{aggre}$, GPSC chooses the cluster aggregation node according to Eq. (2).

$$\varphi(C_{aggre}) = D_{min}^-(H_{S_i}, \bar{C}_{aggre}), \qquad S_i \in \{S_1, ..., S_k\} \tag{2}$$

where φ represents the matching function of the cluster aggregation node, $\bar{D}_{min}$ represents the minimum network distance between two nodes in NCS, and $\bar{C}_{aggre}$ represents the geometric center coordinates.

Network Clustering. Relying on the above prerequisites, GPSC finally clusters all the nodes according to an objective function $D(X_i, S_j)$ in Eq. (3).

$$D(X_i, S_j) = \omega_1 \times d_1(X_i, S_j) + \omega_2 \times d_2(S_j, C_{aggre}), \qquad \omega_1 + \omega_2 = 1 \qquad (3)$$

where X_i and S_j represent the general node and the center node respectively, d_1 represents the distance between a node and a center while d_2 represents the distance between a center and an aggregation node. Besides, ω_1 and ω_2 are two weight factors. Compared to the $O(N^2)$ complexity of BCBPT [12], GPSC can decrease algorithm complexity to $O(K \cdot N)$, which enables the fast re-clustering of nodes in response to the possible network change, thus promoting the system's robustness.

4.2   Topology Construction

The execution of the GPSC algorithm could result in hundreds of nodes in a cluster. In this way, a node has to select a small subset from the cluster to constitute its neighbors, thus constructing the network topology. As previously mentioned in Sect. 2, network connectivity and cluster diameter can have significant effects on the blockchain broadcast performance. To enable each cluster to have an optimal network connectivity and diameter, we introduce the SHNT approach to construct the network topology as shown in Fig. 4. More precisely, SHNT consists of network initialization and maintenance processes.

Network Initialization. The nodes can be divided into SPV nodes and full nodes according to their roles in the blockchain network. Compared to the full nodes, the data broadcasted by SPV nodes is much less and lighter. Due to their different behaviours in the network, SHNT regards the SPV nodes and full nodes as leaf nodes and core nodes respectively. Besides, SHNT selects one core node from each cluster as the routing node, according to the node ID randomly, which ensures the security and randomness. Routing nodes allow the data transmitted from one cluster to another. Once a piece of data is transmitted from one routing node to another, the data can concurrently broadcast in these two clusters, thus speeding up the data transmission across the whole network. The detailed description of different nodes are listed as follows.

- **Leaf node:** consisting of SPV nodes, periodically sending node information to the core node and initiating a transaction.
- **Core node:** consisting of mining nodes, maintaining and managing leaf nodes of the cluster which they are located at, and forwarding transactions or blocks among nodes in the cluster.

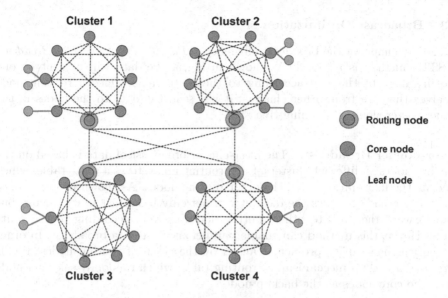

Fig. 4. Structured hierarchical network topology

- **Routing node:** selected from core nodes, storing routing node information about other clusters, and forwarding transactions or blocks among nodes in the cluster.

Based on the classification of blockchain network nodes, the construction process of blockchain network topology by SHNT can be divided into three steps. First, a leaf node is connected directly to a core node that is closest to it. Second, we construct the topology among the core nodes as a Harary-like graph, which has high connectivity and small diameter [5]. Third, a node from the core nodes is selected randomly as the routing node. Once being selected as the routing node, it will contain all the network information of other clusters. If the routing node breaks down, one of the other core nodes will replace it.

Network Maintenance. After initializing the network topology in Sect. 4.2, a natural and important concern is how to maintain the stability of network topology, especially when facing the dynamic changes, i.e., the join of new nodes and leave of old nodes. Recall that the average number of nodes in a cluster is of great importance. It will incur huge communication overhead, no matter the number of nodes is set too large or too small. To overcome the challenges brought by dynamic network, we adopt an automatic adjustment mechanism that can keep the size of each cluster stable within $O(\log N)$. In particular, the mechanism merges small clusters when many nodes churn to leave, and splits large clusters if a large number of nodes join in the same clusters. The minimal threshold to trigger *cluster merge* and maximal threshold to trigger *cluster split* are set to $\frac{\log N}{l}$ and $l \times \log N$, respectively.

4.3   Broadcast Optimization

In order to improve the broadcast efficiency, a *Parallel Spanning Tree Broadcast* (PSTB) method is adopted. As shown in Fig. 5, the data will be sent by one routing node to the rest according to the route table. Once a routing node receives the data from other clusters, it will send the data to the nodes in the same cluster along a spanning tree.

Inter-cluster Broadcast. The inter-cluster broadcast of data is based on the routing nodes of different clusters. Each routing node stores a route table, which records the information of all the other routing nodes. As shown in Fig. 5, once the routing node receives the data, it will not only broadcast in its cluster, but also forward the data to other routing nodes as well, according to the route table. Hence, this method can enable parallel and fast data broadcast. In order to reduce the security problems caused by the crash of routing nodes, PSTB proposes a backup mechanism for routing table, which randomly selects a node from the core nodes as the backup node.

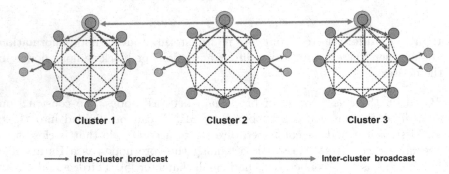

Fig. 5. Parallel spanning tree broadcast

Intra-cluster Broadcast. Only the routing node in a cluster will broadcast the data, which effectively avoids the huge network overheads brought by Gossip protocol [24]. If the broadcast source in the cluster is not a routing node, the source node will firstly send the data to the routing node. Once the routing node receives the data, it will broadcast the data in the cluster along the spanning tree. As for a spanning tree table, PSTB adopts the center-based approach to build it. First, the protocol selects a central node, and then all other nodes unicast the *INV* message to the central node to join the tree directly. In order to deal with the interference caused by the dynamic network changes, each routing node will update the spanning tree table periodically to enable the timeliness of the algorithm.

5   Evaluation

In this section, we conduct several experiments to evaluate BlockP2P. First of all, we introduce the experimental setup, including the platform configuration, implementation, and the evaluation metrics. Then, we analyze the experimental results from comprehensive perspectives, and compare BlockP2P with Bitcoin and Ethereum.

5.1   Experimental Setup

Platform Configuration. We conduct our experiments on two machines, each of which has two eight-core Intel Xeon E5-2670 2.60 Hz CPUs, 64 GB DRAM, 300 GB HDD, and InfiniBand network card, with CentOS 7.0 as the operating system.

Implementation. Without sacrificing the accuracy of experimental results, the simulation methods are adopted. In this paper, we design a generic blockchain network simulator named BlockSim based on peersim [18]. BlockSim is consisted of three core parts: *simulation-network*, *simulation-consensus*, and *simulation-data*. To simulate different network environments in the blockchain, developers can implement the interfaces provided by BlockSim as needed, which include topological connection, latency setting, network broadcast algorithm and so on. As for simulation-consensus, diverse consensus protocols can be implemented. In terms of simulation-data, common blockchain data structures can be customized, such as transactions and blocks. In particular, we implement three blockchain network protocols based on BlockSim, including Bitcoin, Ethereum, and BlockP2P, and compare their performance.

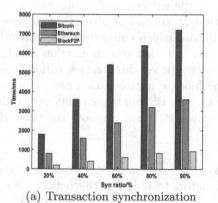

(a) Transaction synchronization

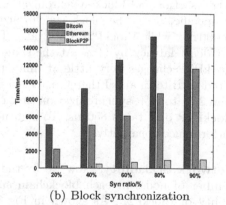

(b) Block synchronization

Fig. 6. Time taken to broadcast the transaction/block

Evaluation Metrics. In order to observe the network optimization effect of BlockP2P compared to Bitcoin and Ethereum, we establish the evaluation metrics about blockchain network performance from three aspects: (1) static performance with the number of nodes fixed (general performance); (2) dynamic performance with the number of nodes changing (network scalability); (3) stable performance with the number of nodes joining and leaving (network stability). First, general performance means how much the broadcast time of transactions and blocks consumes with the fixed nodes, when different synchronization ratios are reached. Here we consider the blockchain network scale in reality to find a reasonable maximum network size. In the real blockchain network, Bitcoin has 10,561 nodes [1], and Ethereum currently has 8,485 nodes [3]. Therefore, the maximum blockchain network size is fixed as 10,000 to fit in with the actual blockchain network size. Second, network scalability means how the broadcast time changes when the number of network nodes increase from 2,000 to 10,000, with the fixed synchronization ratio. In the case of increasing network size, different speed of the synchronization time change can reflect the blockchain system scalability. In the end, we evaluate the robustness of BlockP2P, by investigating the fluctuation of the time when lots of nodes join or leave in one data synchronization process for the evaluation of network stability. In more detail, we evaluate the network stability by measuring broadcast time of blocks fluctuates when 100 nodes join in or leave from the network every 2 s.

5.2 Experimental Results

General Performance. We first measure the time used to broadcast the data to different synchronization ratios of nodes. With the total number of nodes fixed as 10,000, two group of experiments for transactions and blocks are conducted respectively. As shown in Fig. 6, the experimental results demonstrate that the broadcast time of BlockP2P is less than Bitcoin and Ethereum both in terms of transaction and block synchronization at different synchronization ratios. To be specific, when the block synchronization ratio reaches 90%, Bitcoin takes 15,000 ms, while BlockP2P only takes 1,100 ms, which can reduce the network broadcast latency by 90%. At the same time, network synchronization time of BlockP2P changes very little at different network synchronization ratios compared to Bitcoin and Ethereum. When the block synchronization ratio changes from 20% to 90%, synchronization time change for Bitcoin takes 11,000 ms, while BlockP2P only takes 850 ms. To sum up, BlockP2P can promote the network performance apparently.

Network Scalability. Now we fix the synchronization ratio and increase the number of nodes in each blockchain simulator, to evaluate the network scalability of BlockP2P. As shown in Fig. 7, as the number of the network node increases, the data synchronization time required also gradually increases, both in terms of transaction and block synchronization. However, as for the same size of network, the synchronization time taken by BlockP2P is smaller than Bitcoin and Ethereum. Specifically, when the number of nodes is 10,000, it takes

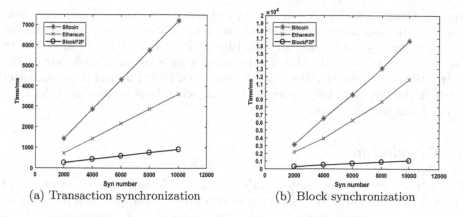

(a) Transaction synchronization   (b) Block synchronization

Fig. 7. Influence of the number of nodes on the broadcast time

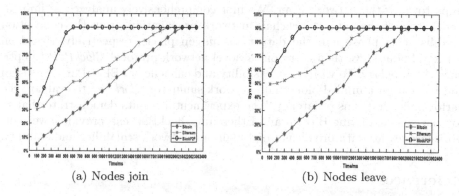

(a) Nodes join   (b) Nodes leave

Fig. 8. Influence of the join or leave of nodes on the broadcast time

7,200 ms for a transaction to propagate to 90% of the total nodes. By contrast, it only takes 920 ms for BlockP2P. The similar phenomenon takes place in terms of block synchronization. In the meanwhile, network synchronization time of BlockP2P changes very little at different network synchronization numbers compared to Bitcoin and Ethereum. When the network synchronization number changes from 2,000 to 10,000, synchronization time change for Bitcoin takes 14,000 ms, while BlockP2P only takes 720 ms. As a result, we can conclude that BlockP2P protocol can provide a higher system scalability.

Network Stability. In this section, we try to verify if BlockP2P can maintain stability of latency when the number of nodes changes dynamically. With total number of nodes initialized as 10,000 and the synchronization ratio fixed as 90%, in one process of network synchronization, we increase or decrease 100 nodes every 100 ms to observe the time and fluctuation of the network. From Fig. 8, we can find that it only takes 400 ms, and the synchronization time fluctuates slightly. Compared with the original network scale, network synchronization time has basically not changed, and fluctuation of time is weak. While Bitcoin reaches the final synchronization ratio of 90%, BlockP2P takes 2,200 ms. Compared with the original network scale, the synchronization time increases obviously, so the fluctuations are dramatic. Therefore, it shows that BlockP2P can maintain better network stability than Bitcoin and Ethereum, when large number of nodes leave from or join in the network.

6   Conclusion

The performance is the major challenge that influences the development of blockchain technology. Most of the researches draw their attention on the optimization of consensus layer or data layer, while lacking consideration of the underlying P2P network optimization. To complement these limitations, we take steps towards the network layer. We first comprehensively analyze the influential factors of the entire blockchain network propagation, from the connection establishment phase and the data transmission phase, respectively. Based on our key findings, we then carry out a novel network protocol *BlockP2P* to optimize the topology. To verify the feasibility and efficiency of BlockP2P, we design and implement a unified blockchain network simulator *BlockSim* to evaluate the performance in terms of latency. The experimental results demonstrate that in comparison to existing Bitcoin and Ethereum, BlockP2P can provide lower network latency for data broadcast, and maintain network scalability and stability.

References

1. Bitnodes. https://bitnodes.earn.com/nodes/
2. Ethereum. https://www.ethereum.org/
3. Ethernodes. https://www.ethernodes.org/network/
4. NKN. https://www.nkn.org/
5. Bhabak, P., Harutyunyan, H., Kropf, P.: Efficient broadcasting algorithm in Harary-like networks. In: Proceedings of the 46th International Conference on Parallel Processing Workshops, pp. 162–170. IEEE (2017)
6. Croman, K., et al.: On scaling decentralized blockchains. In: Clark, J., Meiklejohn, S., Ryan, P.Y.A., Wallach, D., Brenner, M., Rohloff, K. (eds.) FC 2016. LNCS, vol. 9604, pp. 106–125. Springer, Heidelberg (2016). https://doi.org/10.1007/978-3-662-53357-4_8
7. Datta, S., Giannella, C., Kargupta, H.: K-means clustering over a large, dynamic network. In: Proceedings of the 2006 SIAM International Conference on Data Mining, pp. 153–164. SIAM (2006)
8. Decker, C., Wattenhofer, R.: Information propagation in the Bitcoin network. In: Proceedings of the IEEE Thirteenth International Conference on Peer-to-Peer Computing, pp. 1–10. IEEE (2013)
9. Delgado-Segura, S., Pérez-Solà, C., Herrera-Joancomartí, J., Navarro-Arribas, G., Borrell, J.: Cryptocurrency networks: a new P2P paradigm. Mobile Inf. Syst. **2018**, 16 (2018)

10. Donet Donet, J.A., Pérez-Solà, C., Herrera-Joancomartí, J.: The Bitcoin P2P network. In: Böhme, R., Brenner, M., Moore, T., Smith, M. (eds.) FC 2014. LNCS, vol. 8438, pp. 87–102. Springer, Heidelberg (2014). https://doi.org/10.1007/978-3-662-44774-1_7

11. Eyal, I., Gencer, A.E., Sirer, E.G., Renesse, R.V.: Bitcoin-NG: a scalable blockchain protocol. In: Proceedings of the USENIX Conference on Networked Systems Design and Implementation, pp. 45–59. USENIX (2016)

12. Fadhil, M., Owen, G., Adda, M.: Proximity awareness approach to enhance propagation delay on the Bitcoin Peer-to-Peer network. In: Proceedings of the IEEE 37th International Conference on Distributed Computing Systems, pp. 2411–2416. IEEE (2017)

13. Georgiou, C., Gilbert, S., Guerraoui, R., Kowalski, D.R.: Asynchronous gossip. J. ACM (JACM) **60**(2), 11 (2013)

14. Karp, R., Schindelhauer, C., Shenker, S., Vocking, B.: Randomized rumor spreading. In: Proceedings 41st Annual Symposium on Foundations of Computer Science, pp. 565–574. IEEE (2000)

15. Kim, S.K., Ma, Z., Murali, S., Mason, J., Miller, A., Bailey, M.: Measuring Ethereum network peers. In: Proceedings of the Internet Measurement Conference, pp. 91–104. ACM (2018)

16. Li, X., Jiang, P., Chen, T., Luo, X., Wen, Q.: A survey on the security of blockchain systems. Future Generation Computer Systems (2017)

17. Luu, L., Narayanan, V., Zheng, C., Baweja, K., Gilbert, S., Saxena, P.: A secure sharding protocol for open blockchains. In: Proceedings of the 2016 ACM SIGSAC Conference on Computer and Communications Security, pp. 17–30. ACM (2016)

18. Montresor, A., Jelasity, M.: PeerSim: a scalable P2P simulator. In: Proceedings of the IEEE 9th International Conference on Peer-to-peer Computing, pp. 99–100. IEEE (2009)

19. Nagpal, R., Shrobe, H., Bachrach, J.: Organizing a global coordinate system from local information on an Ad Hoc sensor network. In: Zhao, F., Guibas, L. (eds.) IPSN 2003. LNCS, vol. 2634, pp. 333–348. Springer, Heidelberg (2003). https://doi.org/10.1007/3-540-36978-3_22

20. Nakamoto, S.: Bitcoin: A Peer-to-Peer Electronic Cash System (2008). https://bitcoin.org/bitcoin.pdf/

21. Nayak, K., Kumar, S., Miller, A., Shi, E.: Stubborn mining: generalizing selfish mining and combining with an eclipse attack. In: Proceedings of the 2016 IEEE European Symposium on Security and Privacy, pp. 305–320. IEEE (2016)

22. Neudecker, T., Andelfinger, P., Hartenstein, H.: Timing analysis for inferring the topology of the Bitcoin Peer-to-Peer network. In: Proceedings of the Ubiquitous Intelligence & Computing, Advanced and Trusted Computing, Scalable Computing and Communications, Cloud and Big Data Computing, Internet of People, and Smart World Congress. IEEE (2016)

23. Papadis, N., Borst, S., Walid, A., Grissa, M., Tassiulas, L.: Stochastic models and wide-area network measurements for blockchain design and analysis. In: Proceedings of the IEEE Conference on Computer Communications, pp. 2546–2554. IEEE (2018)

24. Sourav, S., Robinson, P., Gilbert, S.: Slow links, fast links, and the cost of gossip. In: Proceedings of the IEEE International Conference on Distributed Computing Systems, pp. 786–796. IEEE (2018)

25. Xu, Z., Han, S., Chen, L.: CUB, a consensus unit-based storage scheme for blockchain system. In: Proceedings of the 2018 IEEE 34th International Conference on Data Engineering (ICDE), pp. 173–184. IEEE (2018)

AutoCVSS: An Approach for Automatic Assessment of Vulnerability Severity Based on Attack Process

Deqing Zou[1,2], Ju Yang[1], Zhen Li[1,3](✉), Hai Jin[1], and Xiaojing Ma[1]

[1] National Engineering Research Center for Big Data Technology and System, Services Computing Technology and System Lab, Cluster and Grid Computing Lab, Big Data Security Engineering Research Center, Huazhong University of Science and Technology, Wuhan, China
lizhen_hust@hust.edu.cn
[2] Shenzhen Huazhong University of Science and Technology Research Institute, Shenzhen, China
[3] School of Cyber Security and Computer, Hebei University, Baoding, China

Abstract. Vulnerability severity assessment is an important research problem. *Common Vulnerability Scoring System* (CVSS) has been widely used to quantitatively assess the vulnerability severity, but its assessment process relies on human experts to determine metric values, which makes the assessment process tedious and subjective. This calls for tools that can assess the vulnerability severity *automatically* and *objectively*. In this paper, we move a step forward in this direction by proposing an approach for automatic assessment of vulnerability severity based on attack process, dubbed *Automatic Common Vulnerability Scoring System* (AutoCVSS). The key insight is to leverage characteristics and rules we define to model the CVSS base metrics, and assess the vulnerability severity more automatically and objectively by capturing the attributes related to the characteristics during the attack process. In order to evaluate AutoCVSS, we reproduce the attacks for 98 vulnerabilities from Linux kernel, FTP service, and Apache service with their exploits. The experimental results show that the vulnerability severity scores automatically obtained by AutoCVSS are basically in accordance with those assessed manually by security experts in the *National Vulnerability Database* (NVD), which verifies the effectiveness of our approach.

Keywords: CVSS · Vulnerability severity assessment · Software vulnerability · Attack process

1 Introduction

Most of security incidents are caused by vulnerabilities. A variety of security vulnerabilities have brought huge economic losses around the world each year, and the situation becomes more and more serious. Prioritizing vulnerabilities

© Springer Nature Switzerland AG 2019
R. Miani et al. (Eds.): GPC 2019, LNCS 11484, pp. 238–253, 2019.
https://doi.org/10.1007/978-3-030-19223-5_17

that are in urgent need of patching can be used to minimize the losses [21]. Therefore, many security vendors and security agencies have done researches on the vulnerability severity assessment and put forward their own vulnerability severity assessment systems and evaluation criteria [17–19]. In order to solve the inconsistency and incompatibility problems caused by various security assessment systems, *National Infrastructure Advisory Council* (NIAC) proposes an open and common vulnerability assessment system called *Common Vulnerability Scoring System* (CVSS) [1] which uses a value between 0–10 to represent the vulnerability severity. A higher score value indicates a greater vulnerability severity [17].

However, CVSS relies on human experts to determine metric values during the process of vulnerability severity assessment, which makes the assessment process tedious and subjective [15,20–22]. In principle, the subjective problem can be alleviated by asking multiple experts, and then select the majority opinion. But this imposes even more tedious work. As a matter of fact, it is desirable to reduce, or even eliminate whenever possible, the reliance on the intense labor of human experts. This calls for tools that can *automatically* and *objectively* assess the vulnerability severity to prioritize vulnerabilities that are in urgent need of patching. The research problem can be described as follows: *When a vulnerability is discovered and its exploits or Proof of Concepts (PoCs) are submitted to the security authority, how can the vulnerability severity be assessed automatically and objectively?*

In order to answer the above question, we present the first approach for automatic assessment of vulnerability severity, dubbed *A̲utomatic C̲ommon V̲ulnerability S̲coring S̲ystem* (AutoCVSS). The goal is to reduce the reliance on the intense labor of human experts and make the assessment process of CVSS more automatically and more objectively. Specifically, we propose a group of *characteristics* and *rules* to model each CVSS base metric according to its description. The characteristics reflect the features of each CVSS base metric, and the rules show its evaluation basis. The characteristics of each CVSS base metric are represented by a group of attributes, which can be captured during the attack process and used to evaluate the vulnerability severity according to the rules.

In order to evaluate AutoCVSS, we reproduce the attacks for 98 vulnerabilities of Linux kernel, FTP service, and Apache service with their exploits from *Exploit Database* (EDB) [2]. The experimental results show that the vulnerability severity scores automatically obtained by AutoCVSS are basically in accordance with those assessed manually by security experts in the *National Vulnerability Database* (NVD) [3].

2   Background

In this section, we briefly describe the background on CVSS, an open and common vulnerability severity assessment system provided by NIAC. CVSS has three groups of metrics: base metrics, temporal metrics, and environmental metrics [1].

In this paper, we mainly focus on base metrics reflecting the inherent characteristics of a vulnerability which are not influenced by time and users' environments. On one hand, the vulnerability severity assessment for CVSS must involve base metrics, while temporal metrics and environmental metrics are optional. On the other hand, for a vulnerability, the values of base metrics are fixed and available in the NVD, while the values of temporal metrics and environmental metrics vary with time or users' environments and are not available in the NVD. Therefore, the base metrics can be used as benchmarks for comparison. In addition, NVD uses the CVSS version 2 (i.e., CVSS v2) to evaluate vulnerabilities before CVSS version 3 (i.e., CVSS v3) was put forward in 2015, and uses both CVSS v2 and CVSS v3 for vulnerability assessment now. That is to say, almost all vulnerabilities in the NVD provide CVSS v2, and many of them do not provide CVSS v3 at the time of writing. In this paper, we select the version(s) of CVSS for each vulnerability as the NVD does.

Base metrics involve two sets of metrics: exploitability metrics and impact metrics [1]. In CVSS v2, *exploitability metrics* contain three metrics: Attack Vector (AV), Attack Complexity (AC), and Authentication (AU). These metrics are used to show how the vulnerability is accessed and whether extra conditions are required to exploit it. *Impact metrics* also contain three metrics: Confidentiality Impact (C), Integrity Impact (I), and Availability Impact (A). These metrics represent the impact of a successfully exploited vulnerability. In CVSS v3, exploitability metrics, different from those in CVSS v2, contain Attack Vector (AV), Attack Complexity (AC), Privileges Required (PR), User Interaction (UI), and Scope (S), and impact metrics are the same as those in CVSS v2. A vulnerability is assigned a CVSS base score ranging from 0 to 10. A higher score indicates a greater vulnerability severity.

3   Design of AutoCVSS

AutoCVSS has two phases: the monitoring program generation and the vulnerability severity assessment, as shown in Fig. 1. In the monitoring program generation phase, the characteristics and rules are defined to model the CVSS base metrics. For each characteristic, analyze the attributes that are captured during the attack, and then generate the monitoring program. In the vulnerability severity assessment phase, the probes of attributes involved in the monitoring program are used to instrument the exploits/PoCs, capture the attributes, and monitor the state of vulnerable software. After the process of hierarchical evaluation, the vulnerability severity is output.

3.1   Input and Output

The input of AutoCVSS consists of the description of CVSS base metrics, the *Common Vulnerabilities and Exposures IDentifier* (CVE ID), the exploits/PoCs, and the vulnerable software. The description of CVSS base metrics is used to

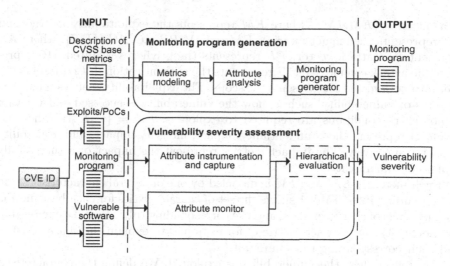

Fig. 1. Overview of AutoCVSS: the first phase generates the monitoring program and the second phase assesses the vulnerability severity. The characteristics and rules for metrics modeling in the first phase need to be defined, and the subsequent process of AutoCVSS does not involve human interaction.

model the CVSS base metrics. The CVE ID is the unique identifier of vulnerability and is used to obtain the exploits/PoCs and the vulnerable software related to the vulnerability. The exploits/PoCs for the CVE ID can be gathered from the public websites such as EDB [2]. The vulnerable software can be obtained from the relevant official websites. Besides, the monitoring program, as the output of the monitoring program generation phase, is another input of the vulnerability severity assessment phase.

The final output of AutoCVSS is the vulnerability severity, which involves the vulnerability security score and the assessment process. The vulnerability security score ranges between 0 and 10. The higher the score is, the greater the vulnerability severity is. The assessment process shows the process of hierarchical evaluation clearly, such as the level of each base metric and the evaluation basis.

It is worth noting that if the CVE ID corresponds to multiple exploits/PoCs, we use one exploit/PoC as an instance at a time to assess the vulnerability severity, and then the highest score of all instances for the CVE ID is selected as the severity of this vulnerability.

3.2 Monitoring Program Generation

In the monitoring program generation phase, there are three modules: metric modeling, attribute analysis, and monitoring program generator.

Metrics Modeling. We model the base metrics of CVSS v2 and CVSS v3 according to the description of CVSS base metrics. Base metrics are represented as a set $B = \{EM, IM\}$, where EM represents the exploitability metrics and IM represents the impact metrics. $EM = \{AV, PR, AC, AU, UI, S\}$, where AV represents the attack vector, PR represents the privileges required, AC represents the attack complexity, AU represents the authentication, UI represents the user interaction, and S represents the scope. The exploitability metrics reflect the features of vulnerability, such as how the vulnerability is accessed and whether or not extra conditions are required to exploit it. $IM = \{C, I, A\}$, where C, I, and A represent the confidentiality impact, integrity impact, and availability impact respectively. The impact metrics represent the impact of a successfully exploited vulnerability.

Each metric in EM and IM is modeled by one or several characteristics and corresponding rules. Table 1 shows the set of characteristics for each base metric, the meanings of characteristics, and the corresponding rules. We take exploitability metric AV and impact metric C for examples to explain the characteristics and their corresponding rules in detail.

AV reflects how the vulnerability is exploited. We define the characteristic $Mode$ to represent the attack mode that the attacker could choose. The value of $Mode$ involves network attack (N), adjacent attack (A), local attack (L), and physical attack (P). The rules for evaluating the level of AV are defined as follows. AV has four levels: network, adjacent, local, and physical. If $Mode$ is N, $level(AV)$ = network, where function $level(AV)$ represents the level of base metric AV; if $Mode$ is A, $level(AV)$ = adjacent; if $Mode$ is L, $level(AV)$ = local; if $Mode$ is P, $level(AV)$ = physical. The default initial level of AV is local.

C refers to confidentiality. If the attacker illegally reads the data, the confidentiality is affected. We define the characteristic IR to represent whether the read permission of the file is modified. The rules for evaluating the level of C are defined as follows. C has three levels: high, low, and none. If the user privilege is root, $level(C)$ = high. If IR is true and the file is sensitive, $level(C)$ = high. If IR is true and the file is non-sensitive, $level(C)$ = low. Otherwise, $level(C)$ = none. The default initial level of C is none.

Attribute Analysis. After modeling the base metrics, each characteristic is depicted by several attributes which can be monitored during the attack process. Considering that these attributes are related to the system that AutoCVSS is implemented on, we will provide the attributes for base metrics in Sect. 4. In this subsection, we take an attribute of an exploitability metric AV related to IP information for example to show the process of attribute analysis before generating the monitoring program.

First of all, when the attribute t of AV is captured, the IP address in t is obtained. By comparing the IP obtained from t with the IP of server, we can get the attack mode, and then obtain the temporary level of AV. Then a separate judgment is made to obtain the temporary level of AV, since the physical attack requires the access to physical devices. Finally, the temporary level of AV returns. It should be noted that the temporary level of AV does

Table 1. Base metrics modeling involves characteristics and corresponding rules. *level(bm)* represents the level of base metric *bm*.

Base metric	Characteristics	Meaning of characteristics	Rules
AV	$Mode$	$Mode$ denotes the attack mode that the attacker could choose. The value of $Mode$ involves network attack (N), adjacent attack (A), local attack (L), and physical attack (P)	If $Mode$ is N, $level(AV)$ = network. If $Mode$ is A, $level(AV)$ = adjacent. If $Mode$ is L, $level(AV)$ = local. If $Mode$ is P, $level(AV)$ = physical
AC	$Cond, Action$	$Cond$ denotes the conditions under which the attack occurs. $Action$ denotes the actions performed by the attack	The number of conditions and actions that occur during the attack is counted. If $\#Cond = 0$ or 1, and $\#Action \leq 3$, $level(AC)$ = low. If $\#Cond = 0$ or 1, and $3 < \#Action \leq 5$, $level(AC)$ = medium. If $\#Cond > 1$ and $\#Action > 5$, $level(AC)$ = high. The default initial level of AC is low
PR	Fp, Up	Fp denotes the file privilege, and contains three file permissions: read, write, and execution. Up denotes the user privilege, and contains three user-level permissions: root, user, and guest	If Up is root, or Fp is the privileges of sensitive files for reading and writing, $level(PR)$ = high. If Up is not root, or Fp is the privileges of non-sensitive files for reading and writing, $level(PR)$ = low. Otherwise, $level(PR)$ = none. The default initial level of PR is none
AU	Os, Sw	Os denotes the operating system authentication, and reflects the attacker needs to authenticate the operating system. Sw denotes the software authentication, and reflects the attacker needs to authenticate the software	The number of operating system authentications and software authentications is counted. If $\#Os \geq 2$ or $\#Sw \geq 2$, $level(AU)$ = multiple. If $\#Os = 1$ or $\#Sw = 1$, $level(AU)$ = single. Otherwise, $level(AU)$ = none. The default initial level of AC is none
UI	sh	sh denotes the interactive interface with the operating system. If the exploit/PoC successfully creates an interactive interface or opens an interactive interface, it indicates that the exploit/PoC needs interaction	If sh is required, $level(UI)$ = required. Otherwise, $level(UI)$ = none. The default initial level of UI is none
S	Vc, Im	Vc denotes the vulnerable component, and its privilege belongs to the authorization scope $s1$. Im denotes the affected component, and its privilege belongs to the authorization scope $s2$. The authorization scope is the collection of privileges defined by a computing authority	If $s2 - (s1 \cap s2) \neq \varnothing$, and the privilege of Vc and Im does not belong to $(s1 \cap s2)$, $level(S)$ = changed. Otherwise, $level(S)$ = unchanged. The default initial level of S is unchanged
C and I	IR, IW	IR indicates whether the read permission of the file is modified. IW indicates whether the write permission of the file is modified	If the user privilege is root, $level(C)$ = high. If IR is true and the file is sensitive, $level(C)$ = high. If IR is true and the file is non-sensitive, $level(C)$ = low. Otherwise, $level(C)$ = none. The default initial level of C is none. The rules of I is basically similar to those of C, but I concerns whether there is illegal writing
A	Nu, Mu, Du, Cu	Nu denotes the network utilization, Mu denotes the memory utilization, Du denotes the disk utilization, and Cu denotes the CPU utilization	If the user privilege is root, $level(A)$ = high. If Nu (or Mu, or Du, or Cu) $\geq 80\%$, $level(A)$ = high. If $60\% \leq Nu$ (or Mu, or Du, or Cu) $< 80\%$, $level(A)$ = low. Otherwise, $level(C)$ = none. The default initial level of A is none

not mean the final level of AV which will be obtained from the hierarchical evaluation in the vulnerability severity assessment phase (Sect. 3.3).

Monitoring Program Generator. Based on the metrics model and the attribute analysis, the monitoring program can be generated by the probes of attributes. It is used to monitor the attributes during the attack process. These attributes can reflect not only the features of the attack, but also the impact of the system or software caused by the attack. The generated monitoring program is as one input of both attribute instrumentation and attribute monitor in the vulnerability severity assessment phase.

3.3 Vulnerability Severity Assessment

In the vulnerability severity assessment phase, the probes of attributes involved in the monitoring program are used to instrument the exploits/PoCs, capture the attributes, and monitor the state of vulnerable software and its environment. Then the vulnerability severity is obtained by hierarchical evaluation. The process involves three modules: attribute instrumentation and capture, attribute monitor, and hierarchical evaluation.

Attribute Instrumentation and Capture. The exploits/PoCs are instrumented with the attributes involved in the monitoring program. These attributes are related to the exploitability metrics AV, AC, PR, UI, AU, S and impact metrics C, I. The exploitability metrics mainly reflect the features of attack behavior, and the impact metrics monitor the impact of the system caused by the exploits/PoCs. The attributes that reflect impact metrics C and I are closely related to the exploitability metric PR, therefore the impact of C and I can be obtained based on the attributes of PR. The instrumentation does not affect the execution of the exploits/PoCs, and can be used to obtain the values of attributes accurately. In this paper, the instrumentation mainly focuses on system calls.

With the aid of instrumentation tool, the probes for attributes that are monitored in the monitoring program instrument the running exploits/PoCs. If the exploits/PoCs call the attributes monitored, the information on these attributes can be intercepted. The dynamic instrumentation approach to attribute capture can reflect the features of attack behavior and the impact of the system more objectively and accurately. Finally, the captured attributes are input to the hierarchical evaluation.

Attribute Monitor. Monitoring attributes is mainly related to the characteristics of impact metric A. The purpose is to monitor the impact of the system and vulnerable software caused by exploits/PoCs. A mainly reflects the availability of the system or vulnerable software throughout the attack process. Attributes related to A need to monitor the running status of the system or vulnerable software in real time. Finally, the monitored attributes are input to the hierarchical evaluation. It should be noticed that monitoring the attributes is significantly different from instrumenting and capturing the attributes. Capturing the attributes occurs only when the instrumented attributes are encountered, while monitoring the attributes needs to continue throughout the attack process.

Hierarchical Evaluation. There are two inputs to the hierarchical evaluation: the captured attributes from the attribute instrumentation and capture module, and the monitored attributes from the attribute monitoring module. The output is the set *Result* which involves two parts: the vulnerability severity score and the assessment process involving the captured attributes and the final level of each base metric. The process of hierarchical evaluation has three steps.

Step 1: Deal with attributes related to exploitability metrics AV, AC, AU, PR, S, and UI. Each captured attribute is processed by the attribute analysis corresponding to the exploitability metric. The temporary level of the exploitability metric is generated and compared with the level of the exploitability metric previously stored in the *Result*. If the temporary level of the exploitability metrics is greater than the level stored in *Result*, store the temporary level and other related information of the exploitability metric into *Result*, then go to Step 3. In addition, if the attributes contain read or write permission on the file, the attributes are selected and then go to Step 2.

Step 2: Deal with attributes related to impact metrics C, I, and A. The relevant path name of the file is extracted from the attribute selected in Step 1. It is compared with the path of the system sensitive files to get the levels of impact metrics C and I. If the attribute contains the read (write) permission, it is related to C (I). If the level of the impact metric is greater than the level of the impact metric previously stored in *Result*, the level and other information of impact metric override the previous information in *Result*. In addition, the evaluation method for impact metric A is similar to that for C and I. The only difference is that the level of A can be read directly from monitored attributes.

Step 3: Generate the vulnerability severity. The values of each base metric (i.e., exploitability metric and impact metric) are extracted from *Result*, and are used to generate the vulnerability severity. Finally, the vulnerability severity score and the information about assessment process are stored into *Result*.

4 Experiments and Results

In the experiments, we select the attributes to depict the characteristics related to each base metric according to the established model, and monitor the programs by using the dynamic instrumentation tool Pin [14]. We use the API given by Pin to instrument the exploits/PoCs and monitor the attributes for Linux. Since the experiments are based on the Linux and the tool Pin requires a binary executable file, the exploits/PoCs we choose are limited to those which are written by C or C++ and can run on Linux.

We divide the base metrics into three types according to the nature of their attributes. The first type contains base metrics AV, AC, AU, PR, UI, C, and I whose attributes are mainly related to system calls, the paths of sensitive files, and so on. These metrics can be evaluated by capturing related system calls and their parameters. The attributes related to this type of base metrics are shown in Table 2. The second type involves the base metric A which needs to monitor the status of system continuously. The specific attributes of A is shown in Table 3. The third type involves the base metric S, which change can be determined by the change of authority domain. It can be obtained during the attack process directly. Therefore, we do not provide the specific attributes for S.

In practice, human experts who assess the vulnerability severity can get the exploits/PoCs from the vulnerability discoverers for the first time to carry out the vulnerability assessment. In our experiments, we collect vulnerabilities and their corresponding exploits/PoCs from the public website EDB [2] to reproduce the attacks for the vulnerabilities. Figure 2 shows the number of exploits (written by C or C++) for Linux kernel, Apache service, and FTP service published by EDB from 1999 to 2016. We select vulnerabilities from Linux kernel, FTP service, and Apache service because they have more exploits and most of these software are open source. From Fig. 2, we can see that in recent years, most of the exploits are for Linux kernel and few exploits are for Apache service and FTP service. In the NVD, almost all vulnerabilities provide CVSS v2, and many of them do not provide CVSS v3 at the time of writing. We select the version(s) of CVSS for each vulnerability as the NVD does in our experiments.

Our experiments involve 98 vulnerabilities from the above three products (i.e., 74 Linux kernel vulnerabilities, 8 FTP service vulnerabilities, and 16 Apache service vulnerabilities) whose exploits provided in the EDB can be used to successfully reproduce the attacks. We adopt AutoCVSS to assess their severity. The result is that only two vulnerability severity scores assessed by AutoCVSS are obviously different from those in the NVD for CVSS v2, as shown in Fig. 3. One

Table 2. Attributes for the first type of base metrics

Base metric	Attributes
AV	$socket, connect, hub\_nport\_nconnect\_nchange, usb\_nprobe\_ninterface$
AC	$setregid, umount, mkdir, umount2, socketcall,$ $open, link, symlink, setresuid, setreuid, setuid, setfsuid,$ $setgroups, setgid, setfsgid, setfsgid, setresgid, chmod, fchmod, chown,$ $fchown, lchow$
AU	$execle, execl$
PR	$chmod, fchmod, chown, fchown, lchown, setresuid, setreuid, setuid,$ $setfsuid, setgid, setfsgid, setfsgid, setresgid, setregid$
UI	$clone, execute, fork$
C and I	$/bin, /boot, /dev, /etc, /lib, /proc, /root, /srv, /sys$

Table 3. Attributes for base metric A

Attribute	Operations
CPU utilization	Access the file */proc/stat* to extract the relevant data of CPU
Disk utilization	Use the shell command to the disk and extract the relevant data
Network bandwidth utilization	Use the shell command to obtain the network bandwidth usage and extract the relevant data
Memory utilization	Access the file */proc/meminfo* to extract the relevant data of memory

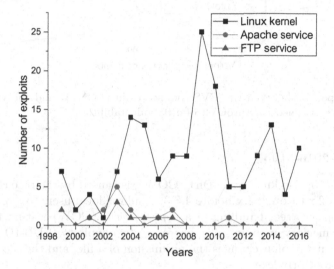

Fig. 2. The number of exploits (written by C or C++) for Linux kernel, Apache service, and FTP service published by EDB from 1999 to 2016

deviation is caused by the inaccurate level of AU. Specifically, the authentication may be occurred before the exploit. For example, the attacker may log into the system before exploiting the vulnerability. Therefore, the authentication information which the exploit does not contain cannot be captured. Another deviation is caused by the incomplete attributes we consider during the implementation, which will be improved in our future work.

In what follows, we select two vulnerabilities (CVE-2016-5195 for Linux kernel and CVE-2011-3192 for Apache HTTP Server) with three exploits from EDB (EDB-ID 40611 and 40847 for CVE-2016-5195, and EDB-ID 18221 for CVE-2011-3192) to illustrate the specific process of AutoCVSS.

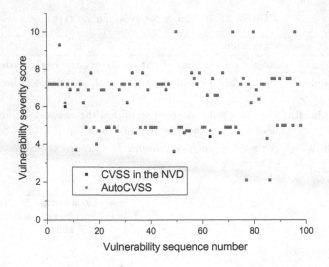

Fig. 3. Comparison between the CVSS v2 scores in the NVD and the vulnerability severity scores obtained by AutoCVSS for 98 vulnerabilities

4.1   CVE-2016-5195

CVE-2016-5195, also known as "Dirty COW", is caused by the race condition in Linux kernel 2.x through 4.x before 4.8.3. It allows local users to gain privileges by leveraging incorrect handling of a *copy-on-write* (COW) feature to write to a read-only memory mapping [3]. There are two exploits (EDB-ID 40611 and 40847). The first exploit changes the permission of a file, and the second exploit can get the root privilege.

As shown in Fig. 4, the exploit EDB-ID 40611 creates two threads: *madvise* and *procselfmemThread*. Thread *madvise* is responsible for the memory page allocation, and thread *procselfmemThread* mainly tries to write the data to memory. The exploitation process is as follows. For the first time, the write operation could cause page fault, then Linux deals with this page fault. For the second time, Linux deals with the write permission error by removing the write permission requirements and calling *madvise* to overwrite the previous cow pages. For the third time, Linux finds the page fault, but this page has no FOLL_nWRITE permission requirements, then the memory page mapped can be directly accessed, leading to permission issues.

The exploit EDB-ID 40847 is to gain the root privilege. The exploitation process mainly has three steps. First, *"bin/bas"* information is written to the file *tmp/.pwn*. Second, the permission of *pwn* file is modified, so that this file has the executable permission. Third, the shell in */etc/passwd* is modified to point to *"root:x:0:0:root:/root:/tmp/.pwn"*, that is, point to *tmp/.pwn* executable file. At last, the shell can be run under the authority of root.

In both attack processes, AutoCVSS does not catch system call *connect*, which indicates that it is a local attack. The non-sensitive file *pwn* is created,

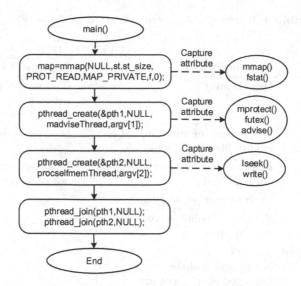

Fig. 4. The attack flow of CVE-2016-5195 (EDB-ID 40611) and the main attributes captured by AutoCVSS

and its permission is modified, thus the level of AC and PR is low. There is no interaction with Linux, no system authentication and software authentication, and the authorization scope is unchanged, which indicates the level of UI is none, the level of AU is none, and the level of S is unchanged. For the first exploit, only the permissions and contents of a non-sensitive file are changed, and the system can run properly without impact. Therefore, the level of C and I is low and the level of A is none. While for the second exploit, the root privilege is obtained after the attack, thus the level of C, I, and A is high. As the impact caused by the second exploit is more serious, the vulnerability severity assessed by the second exploit is selected as the severity of this vulnerability. As NVD provides the vulnerability with both CVSS v2 score and CVSS v3 score, we list base metrics for both CVSS v2 and CVSS v3 in Table 4. The result obtained by AutoCVSS is 7.2 for CVSS v2 and 7.8 for CVSS v3, which are the same as the results in the NVD.

4.2   CVE-2011-3192

CVE-2011-3192 is a vulnerability in the Apache HTTP Server 1.3.x, 2.0.x through 2.0.64, and 2.2.x through 2.2.19. It allows an attacker to cause a denial of service attack via a Range header that expresses multiple overlapping ranges [3].

The attack flow in function $thread\_nstart()$ is as follows. The request packet is send to Apache HTTP Server continuously by function $write()$. The HTTP header information in the request packet contains the range option, which defines how to request fragmented resource files. If a large number of overlapping range specification commands are set in the range option, Apache HTTP Server will

Table 4. Levels of base metrics obtained by AutoCVSS

Base metric	CVE-2016-5195		CVE-2011-3192	
	Level	Assessment basis	Level	Assessment basis
AV	Local	Default level	Network	IP is not on the same network segment as the IP of server
AC	Low	Write some information, modify file permissions	Low	Send a message
AU	None	Relevant attributes are not captured	None	Relevant attributes are not captured
PR	Low	Need to user permission	-	-
UI	None	Relevant attributes are not captured	-	-
S	Unchanged	The vulnerable component and the impacted component are the same	-	-
C	High	Get root privilege	None	Capture $read()$, but there is no file path matched in $read()$
I	High	Get root privilege	None	Capture $write()$, but there is no file path matched in $write()$
A	High	Get root privilege	High	Complete memory is exhausted

consume a lot of memory and CPU resources to construct the response data, causing the operating system to run out of resources.

In this process, AutoCVSS can intercept the main system calls *socket*, *connect*, and *write*. Since *connect* can be successfully connected, it indicates that a remote connection is made. In the server system, AutoCVSS monitors the network utilization, disk utilization, and CPU utilization, which basically remain unchanged. But the memory utilization continues to increase, basically more than 80%. From this perspective, we can see that when the memory is low, it would cause the system to deny service. At last, the vulnerability severity score obtained by AutoCVSS is 7.8, which is the same as the CVSS v2 in the NVD. Table 4 shows the level of each base metric for AutoCVSS.

5 Related Work

AutoCVSS is used to assess the vulnerability severity based on CVSS and attack process. In what follows, we review the prior works from two aspects: CVSS and attack process.

Prior Work Related to CVSS. CVSS is proposed by NIAC to solve the inconsistency and incompatibility problems caused by various security assessment systems. There are many studies about CVSS. Some studies [15, 20] pointed out that the factors considered by CVSS were not comprehensive enough and the scores obtained could not truly reflect the vulnerability severity. Younis et al. [20] proposed to use the attack surface to increase the accuracy of assessment. For the assessment problems of CVSS, some approaches were presented to improve the CVSS [7, 9, 16]. In addition, there are also some approaches to the prediction or assessment of vulnerability [4, 5, 10, 13]. For example, Khazaei e al. [13] proposed an automated approach to assess vulnerabilities. Their vulnerability features were generated from the vulnerability description information. However, the above studies about CVSS are basically static approaches. They do not involve the attack process which has more valuable information for vulnerability severity assessment.

Prior Work Related to Attack Process. Many researches used the attack graph to evaluate or predict the level of network security. Huang et al. [12] extracted the characteristics from the attack graph. These characteristics were combined with CVSS to statically evaluate the network security. However, our characteristics are based on attack process and our approach to vulnerability severity assessment is dynamic, which can more accurately obtain the attack data. Hu et al. [11] provided more information about the future of network attack behaviors by dynamic Bayesian attack graph. The information is limited to network attack behaviors, and the evaluation method does not apply to the severity assessment of vulnerabilities without network attack. Besides, some attack models [6, 8] were also used to predict the attack behaviors.

The previous studies show that there is few concern about the combination of CVSS and the attack process to dynamically assess the vulnerability severity. Our goal is to use the attack process to make the assessment process of CVSS automatically and objectively, and the experimental results show the effectiveness of AutoCVSS.

6   Conclusion

We present AutoCVSS, an approach for automatic assessment of vulnerability severity based on attack process. It leverages the characteristics and rules we define to model the CVSS base metrics, and assesses the vulnerability severity automatically and objectively by capturing the attributes related to the characteristics during the attack process. Our results show that the vulnerability severity scores automatically obtained by AutoCVSS are basically in accordance with those assessed manually by security experts in the NVD, which verifies the effectiveness of AutoCVSS. For future research, we will improve the characteristics and rules of AutoCVSS for more comprehensive vulnerability severity assessment and strive to assess the vulnerability severity through multiple exploits/PoCs more effectively.

Acknowledgments. This paper is supported by the National Key Research & Development (R&D) Plan of China under grant No. 2017YFB0802205, the National Science Foundation of China under grant No. 61672249, and the Shenzhen Fundamental Research Program under grant No. JCYJ20170413114215614.

References

1. Common Vulnerability Scoring System. https://www.first.org/cvss/
2. Exploit database. https://www.exploit-db.com/
3. National Vulnerability Database. https://nvd.nist.gov/
4. Allodi, L., Banescu, S., Femmer, H., Beckers, K.: Identifying relevant information cues for vulnerability assessment using CVSS. In: Proceedings of the 8th ACM Conference on Data and Application Security and Privacy (CODASPY), pp. 119–126. ACM (2018)
5. Allodi, L., Biagioni, S., Crispo, B., Labunets, K., Massacci, F., Santos, W.: Estimating the assessment difficulty of CVSS environmental metrics: an experiment. In: Dang, T.K., Wagner, R., Küng, J., Thoai, N., Takizawa, M., Neuhold, E.J. (eds.) FDSE 2017. LNCS, vol. 10646, pp. 23–39. Springer, Cham (2017). https://doi.org/10.1007/978-3-319-70004-5_2
6. Almasizadeh, J., Azgomi, M.A.: A stochastic model of attack process for the evaluation of security metrics. Comput. Netw. **57**(10), 2159–2180 (2013)
7. Cheng, P., Wang, L., Jajodia, S., Singhal, A.: Aggregating CVSS base scores for semantics-rich network security metrics. In: Proceedings of the 31st Symposium on Reliable Distributed Systems (SRDS), pp. 31–40. IEEE (2012)
8. Del Valle, S., Hethcote, H., Hyman, J.M., Castillo-Chavez, C.: Effects of behavioral changes in a smallpox attack model. Math. Biosci. **195**(2), 228–251 (2005)
9. Gallon, L.: On the impact of environmental metrics on CVSS scores. In: Proceedings of the 2nd International Conference on Social Computing (SocialCom), pp. 987–992. IEEE (2010)
10. Ghani, H., Luna, J., Khelil, A., Alkadri, N., Suri, N.: Predictive vulnerability scoring in the context of insufficient information availability. In: Proceedings of 2013 International Conference on Risks and Security of Internet and Systems (CRiSIS), pp. 1–8. IEEE (2013)
11. Hu, H., Zhang, H., Liu, Y., Wang, Y.: Quantitative method for network security situation based on attack prediction. Secur. Commun. Netw. **2017**, 1–19 (2017)
12. Huang, H., Zhao, F., Ye, M.: Estimate the influential level of vulnerability instance based on hybrid ranking for dynamic network attacking scenarios. In: Proceedings of the 10th International Conference on Information Sciences Signal Processing and their Applications (ISSPA), pp. 586–589. IEEE (2010)
13. Khazaei, A., Ghasemzadeh, M., Derhami, V.: An automatic method for CVSS score prediction using vulnerabilities description. J. Intell. Fuzzy Syst. **30**(1), 89–96 (2016)
14. Luk, C., et al.: Pin: building customized program analysis tools with dynamic instrumentation. In: Proceedings of Conference on Programming Language Design and Implementation, pp. 190–200. ACM (2005)
15. Luo, J., Lo, K., Qu, H.: A software vulnerability rating approach based on the vulnerability database. J. Appl. Math. **2014**, 932397:1–932397:9 (2014)
16. Ross, D.M., Wollaber, A.B., Trepagnier, P.C.: Latent feature vulnerability ranking of CVSS vectors. In: Proceedings of the Summer Simulation Multi-Conference, pp. 19:1–19:12. Society for Computer Simulation International (2017)

17. Spanos, G., Sioziou, A., Angelis, L.: WIVSS: a new methodology for scoring information systems vulnerabilities. In: Proceedings of the 17th Panhellenic Conference on Informatics, pp. 83–90. ACM (2013)
18. Tripathi, A., Singh, U.K.: Estimating risk levels for vulnerability categories using CVSS. Int. J. Internet Technol. Secured Trans. **4**(4), 272–289 (2012)
19. Younis, A.A., Malaiya, Y.K.: Comparing and evaluating CVSS base metrics and Microsoft rating system. In: Proceedings of the IEEE International Conference on Software Quality, Reliability and Security (QRS), pp. 252–261. IEEE (2015)
20. Younis, A.A., Malaiya, Y.K., Ray, I.: Using attack surface entry points and reachability analysis to assess the risk of software vulnerability exploitability. In: Proceedings of the 15th International Symposium on High-Assurance Systems Engineering (HASE), pp. 1–8. IEEE (2014)
21. Younis, A.A., Malaiya, Y.K., Ray, I.: Assessing vulnerability exploitability risk using software properties. Software Qual. J. **24**(1), 159–202 (2016)
22. Younis, A., Malaiya, Y.K., Ray, I.: Evaluating CVSS base score using vulnerability rewards programs. In: Hoepman, J.-H., Katzenbeisser, S. (eds.) SEC 2016. IAICT, vol. 471, pp. 62–75. Springer, Cham (2016). https://doi.org/10.1007/978-3-319-33630-5_5

Retraction Note to: U-Control Chart Based Differential Evolution Clustering for Determining the Number of Cluster in k-Means

Jesús Silva, Omar Bonerge Pineda Lezama, Noel Varela,
Jesús García Guiliany, Ernesto Steffens Sanabria,
Madelin Sánchez Otero, and Vladimir Álvarez Rojas

Retraction Note to:
Chapter "U-Control Chart Based Differential Evolution
Clustering for Determining the Number of Cluster
in k-Means" in: R. Miani et al. (Eds.): *Green, Pervasive,*
***and Cloud Computing*, LNCS 11484,**
https://doi.org/10.1007/978-3-030-19223-5_3

The Editors retracted this paper because an almost identical paper was under consideration at other publishers at the same time with a different author group and later published (1). Representatives of Universidad de la Costa and Universidad Peruana de Ciencias Aplicadas confirmed this study was not carried out at their institutions.

None of the authors responded to correspondence from the Publisher about this retraction wording.

1. Ilham, A., Wahono R. S., Supriyanto, C., Wijaya, A.: U-control Chart Based Differential Evolution Clustering for Determining the Number of Cluster in k-Means. International Journal of Intelligent Engineering and Systems, 12(4), 306–316 (2019). https://doi.org/10.22266/ijies2019.0831.28

The retracted version of this chapter can be found at
https://doi.org/10.1007/978-3-030-19223-5_3

Author Index

ted in the United States
ker & Taylor Publisher Services